FLIGHT
WITHOUT
WINGS

FLIGHT
WITHOUT
WINGS

THE ARABIAN HORSE
AND THE SHOW WORLD

PATTI SCHOFLER

THE LYONS PRESS
Guilford, Connecticut

An imprint of The Globe Pequot Press

The Lyons Press is an imprint of The Globe Pequot Press.

10 9 8 7 6 5 4 3 2 1

Printed in the United States of America

ISBN-13: 978-1-59228-800-7
ISBN-10: 1-59228-800-6

Library of Congress Cataloging-in-Publication Data is available on file.

To Marshall and Star

Contents

Foreword by Pete Cameron *ix*

Acknowledgments *xi*

Introduction *xiii*

CHAPTER ONE
The Arabian *1*

CHAPTER TWO
The Versatile Breed and
Its Infinite Possibilities *27*

CHAPTER THREE
Introducing Performance Disciplines *37*

CHAPTER FOUR
Saddle Seat *43*

CHAPTER FIVE
Hunter Pleasure/Show Hack *59*

CHAPTER SIX
Western Pleasure *77*

CHAPTER SEVEN
Introducing Sport Horse Disciplines *93*

CHAPTER EIGHT
Sport Horse In-Hand/Under Saddle/
Show Hack *97*

CHAPTER NINE
Dressage *117*

CHAPTER TEN
Hunters and Jumpers *139*

CHAPTER ELEVEN

Introducing Working Western Disciplines *153*

CHAPTER TWELVE

Trail *157*

CHAPTER THIRTEEN

Reining *173*

CHAPTER FOURTEEN

Working Cow Horse *195*

CHAPTER FIFTEEN

Halter and Breeding *209*

CHAPTER SIXTEEN

Specialty Classes *227*

CHAPTER SEVENTEEN

The Show Scene *253*

Index *273*

FOREWORD

AS A JUDGE FOR NEARLY FIVE DECADES, WITH ALMOST 900 horse shows under my belt, I have a reputation for speaking my own mind—and not in a timid manners. So when I was asked to write this foreword, you can believe it when I say I approached it skeptically. I had been asked other times to read such books and write a foreword, but each time I turned down the invitation.

However, this book is different. I feel it is the ideal tool for success, providing an in-depth picture of the Arabian horse and his show world in a solid, friendly, intelligent, and readable way. For that reason, it will pilot the beginning horse owner through the show world, providing both the big picture and the details. It also will serve Arabian owners and fans of the breed who wonder what reining is like, or whether their horse's future be in the Working Cow division, or as a show hack or in dressage.

Further, the book will guide future horse people and horse show spectators who want to understand what they are watching when they attend Arabian shows. And it will introduce the breed to those intrigued by the Arabian horse.

The answers are in this book, which passes on insights in a way that you don't have to be a professional to understand. Yet, professionals will find this useful as a concise manual for teaching and training. In fact, this book would be great reading for those interested in becoming judges.

The more I read, the better I liked it. The writing is lively, clear, and yet filled with valuable information. I was born into the horse world and have judged 445 Arabian shows, and yet I learned from this book.

Clearly, Patti Schofler's great affection for and understanding of the horse and her ability to research and portray a vast variety of disciplines inspired top professionals in our business to come together as if in a forum in which to share their knowledge, experience, and viewpoints for you, the reader.

PETE CAMERON
St. Catharines, Ontario, Canada
member, Arabian Horse Association
Judges Hall of Fame, and the only
person to be named twice Judge of
the Year.

ACKNOWLEDGMENTS

WHILE WRITING, RESEARCHING, AND INTERVIEWING FOR this book, I was in perpetual surprise at the amazing generosity of the people connected with this breed. With ease and graciousness, they gave their time and expertise, openly and without hesitation, for no other reason than that they are so enamored of the Arabian horse.

I could not have started and completed this book without the aid and support of the Arabian Horse Association's Susan Bavaria. My thanks also to Molly Benstein and Karen Karvonen.

I am immensely grateful to the Arabian horsemen and horse-women who gave me so much of their time, of which they have none extra, and gave me so much of their knowledge, of which they have so much. Gary Dearth and Mike Damianos, thank you for your support of and enthusiasm for this book. All I had to do was ask and you came through. I am so appreciative for the access to the thoughts, history, and encouragement of Chris Culbreth, Wendy Potts, Lou Roper, Greg Gallun, Gene La Croix, Mary Trowbridge, Tony Boit, Greta Wrigley, Lorne Robertson, and Bazy Tankersley.

My thank you goes out as well to Kim Potts, Wendy Gruskiewicz, Cynthia Burkman, Gordon Potts, John O'Hara, Michelle Mahoney, Russ Vento, Jim Lowe, and Debbie Compilli. I offer my appreciation to Molly Stanley, Deborah Johnson, Wanda Funk, Bob Hart, Pa-tience Prine-Carr, Kristen Hardin, and Carolyn Mysliwiec.

I extend my heartfelt thank you to Suzanne Beauregard and Becky Duckles for reading my manuscript and making many helpful suggestions. To Victoria Smith, I hope you enjoyed creating your illustrations as much as I enjoy looking at them. Thank you.

And my gratitude goes to Colleen Swift, Michele Gagne, and Debbie Wiegmann for supplying me with indispensable research material.

I offer my sincere thank you to Janet Brown Foy, Bitsy Shields, and Hilda Gurney for their expertise. And to my editor, Steve Price, who always signs his letters, e-mails, and manuscript corrections with "cheers," I do so much appreciate the very demanding, patient, and nudging person that you are.

Thanking one's husband is not unusual. What is exceptional is how my husband cleaned stalls, ran errands, and indulged in some strange dinners without a single gripe or guilt-imposing look, so that I could focus on my writing—even though all along I told him he would get second billing to Star. Well, thank you, Marshall Patterson. You're number one.

INTRODUCTION

"The Horse: Friendship without envy, beauty without vanity,
nobility without conceit, a willing partner and yet no slave."

—Ronald Duncan

THE OPPORTUNITY TO WRITE THIS BOOK CAME AT A TIME when I watched my beautiful, loving Arabian slip into old age, burdened by Cushing's disease. As I write this I see that I am losing his powerful, strong body, developed from years of dressage work and hilly trail rides. He has less energy and less pizzazz. He is not always comfortable. I feel sad because I think about not having him to look at and I really can't do anything about it. I think how gorgeous he was.

And then I look at his face and focus on his eyes. And, just as he has done for me for over twenty-four years and Arabians have done for others for thousands of years, he draws me into his soul, and I see just how beautiful he still is.

Because of Star (Staraba Rocket) I had watched probably every type of event and class that an Arabian can do. And as you read this book, you will see that is many. I would watch Eventing, English Pleasure, or reining and think, Star could do that. And he would look so handsome doing it.

And if he was performing in those classes, Star would probably look just as he did when he was moving up the levels in dressage. People always told me that when Star competed he looked as if he was thinking, "I don't know why we're out here, but if she wants to do it, it's fine with me." And it was. We tried a cow class, we jumped, we did Halter, Show Hack, Hunter Pleasure, and Third Level Dressage.

And it was always such a great outing when I could spend all that time with Star.

When Star was young, an acquaintance attempted to belittle Arabians by saying to me "beauty is as beauty does." Today I know she is right: my Arabian is a beauty who kept me out of harm's way when without him, a horse would have trampled me. My Arabian is a beauty because he will not move a foot when a small child brushes his legs. My Arabian is the same horse who bursts with energy in a Show Hack class, but who moves like a whisper when a terrified complete novice sits on his back for a walk around the arena. And what is our world without beauty for beauty's sake?

Because my Arabian is no exception, my hope for this book is that it will lead you to the honor of having a relationship with an Arabian horse.

Chapter One

THE ARABIAN

By reason of his elegance, he resembles an image painted in a palace, though he is as majestic as the palace itself.

—Emir Abd-el-Kader 1830s

The mare will carry her master
Through fire and water.
She will stand over her disabled lord
Til help arrives . . . .
She will kneel for him to mount and bear him bravely home.
. . . These are not always fables.
The horse, treated as she should be
Generation after generation,
Develops a rare intelligence and shows as noble an affection as
   the dog . . .

—Theodore A. Dodge, 1893

The grey mare, the renowned, in the world there is none
   like her:
Not with the Persian kings, the Chosroes, the Irani.
Spare is her head and lean, her ears pricked close together;
Her forelock is a net, her forehead a lamplighted
Illumining the tribe; her neck curved like a palm branch
Her wither clean and sharp . . . Her forelegs are twin lances,
Her hoofs fly forward faster ever than flies the whirlwind,
Her tail-bone held aloft, yet the hairs sweep the gravel.
Her height twice eight, sixteen, taller than all the horses.
Every name of worth a gallant band of fighter,
Like locusts on the plain. And he tightened his mare's girthing

1

*And they gathered near and near and the dust of their hard
    riders
Rose like a cloud of heaven, and presently they saw him,
And he could see their eyes, and the flashing of their spear
    points.
And I saw my death by the spear as the best of doubtful issues
    . . . So go I to destruction . . .
And I turned my mare and sprang like a lion in the seizing,
And I pressed her flank with my heel and sent her flying
    forward,
And I charged home on their ranks nor thought of wound nor
    danger,
And I smote them with my sword till the air shone with
    smiting.*

—Abu Zeyd, "The Stealing of the Mare,"
told over 900 years ago, translated by
Lady Anne Blunt, put into verse by
Sir Wilfred Scawen Blunt

THE ARABIAN HORSE IS WITHIN HIMSELF A MESH OF CON-
trasting characteristics that by their combination make an ideal show
horse. He is at once a lively, fiery spirit, proud and regal in his carriage, his presence and charisma, and yet also a gentle, docile soul.
His intelligence, willingness to please, and comfort with the human
species allow him to, on command, exude tremendous vitality, and
yet at another moment to welcome a child to safely lead him and ride
him. A fairy-tale horse, he is bred for his exquisite beauty, quality,
and refinement, and yet his genes are coveted for their link to soundness, stamina, and endurance. He is rock-hard tough in spirit, flesh,
bone, and ligament.

Whether he is a drop-dead gorgeous reiner or a floating, elegant,
power-driven English horse, or quiet master of ease Western Pleasure
champion, the qualities that make an Arabian unique and treasured
as a show horse have a practical origin in his ancient history.

Dating back 3,500 years, the Arabian is the oldest, the purest, and the first man-manipulated breed. Perhaps no other breed has been so engaged in the romance and history of the world. He has made his presence loudly heard not just in the Middle and Near East, in Egypt and North Africa, but also in England, Poland, Spain, Hungary, Russia, and the United States, both in his pure state and as a contributor to the improvement of some breeds and the creation of others. Today virtually every light horse breed, from Appaloosa to Welsh, has Arabian blood coursing through its veins.

According to the prophet Mohammed, when God wished to create the horse he summoned the South Wind, saying, "I shall create from thy substance a new being which shall be good fortune unto my followers and humiliation to my enemies. Condense thyself!"

The wind did so and the angel Gabriel caught a handful and God created the Arabian horse from it and said, "I have created thee and named thee faras (horse). I have bestowed my blessings upon thee above all other beasts of burden and made thee their master. Success and happiness are bound in thy forelock; bounty reposes on your back and riches are with you wherever you may be. And I have endowed thee to fly without wings; you are for pursuit and for flight."

To Ishmael, the son of Abraham, God gave the gift of a wild Arabian mare. The angel Gabriel said to Ishmael: "This noble creature of the dark skin and painted eyes is the gift of the Living God to serve you as a companion in the wilderness and reward you."

The breed is said to descend from five foundation mares called "Al-Khamsa," or "The Five," or "related to" the five. Some wrote that all were owned by King Solomon around 1600 B.C. Many other versions read that the mares belonged to the prophet Mohammed. Early Western travelers to the extended Arabian Peninsula (today much of the Middle East) frequently reported that the term "al khamsa" was used to designate the best or favorite "breeds" (strains or families) of the unique and ancient breed of horses of the native Bedouin.

In one variation of the "Al Khamsa" story, a tribe of Bedouin, after a long journey in the desert, released their mares to quench their thirst at a distant watering hole. As a test of their loyalty, their masters called back the mares before they reached the water. Five returned faithfully without drinking. These became the five favored mares of the Bedouin, and each was given a strain name which would be carried by their descendants.

3,500 YEARS AGO

The reality of man's first encounters with the Arabian horse runs the gamut of theories. The ancestral Arabian most likely was a wild horse native to northern Syria and southern Turkey and the northern edge of the Fertile Crescent, a well-watered grassland connected to Mesopotamia (modern Iraq), along the Euphrates river, west to a coastal strip and down to Egypt.

This prototype of the Arabian and his descendants did make his way to the Arabian Peninsula in pre-Islamic times and was referred to as the "Kehilan-Ajuz," or old breed—the foundation. Additional horses were added to the collection, some no doubt from looting in Syria.

This gift from Allah continued to be bred for his loyalty, trainability, and athleticism, for his strength, intelligence, and courage to survive in the bitterly harsh world of the desert. If he was to survive, the horse's life, from birth to death, was an endless demand for top performance.

By our standards his plight was cruel. Care was negligible. Nomadic tribes survived by moving, and those who could not move were left behind. Should a mare fall ill after giving birth, she might be left to die in the desert. Pitiful weather and sparse food were the norm. Only the fit lived to see another day.

C. Guarmani wrote in 1864, "Indeed, the Arabian is the most important war horse in the world; he can bear privation and hardships better than any other horse, for his unflagging courage stimulates his physical abilities."

The Bedouin often hobbled their horses because the tribe could not stable them. A fierce sandstorm might mean a mare would wander off, losing her way. So often, the highly valued mare was sheltered in the family tent, allowing children to sleep by her feet; this is said to be the reason for the Arabian's gentle and affectionate character and why the horse's closeness to humans is legendary and inheritable.

Often today, owners and trainers choose Arabians as their breed because they are so tuned into people with their "live in your tent" personality. You may hear: "Like no other breed, they appreciate people and actually like you. They care that you are there. It's rewarding," or "I like walking into the barn and have them respond to me."

A man named G. Jacob wrote in 1897: "The greatest merit of the Arabian horse is its intelligence which has developed to a great extent through its interaction with man. Tales of the horses waking their sleeping master with their hooves as danger approaches . . . should not simply be regarded as an idealization of nature."

Tribal life created in the Arabian his uncanny instinct, patience, and gentleness with vulnerable children and those unfamiliar with horses. The horse that had a loyal disposition and desire to please his owner survived and bred on.

War Mares

Mares of the desert were honored above all others. Only mares were ridden on raids and into battle. Was it because, unlike stallions, they did not trumpet their arrival at a camp or battle and thus the raiders arrived unnoticed?

The work required of the war mare under the most severe conditions created a tough breed. One visitor to the desert in the early 1900s wrote about the mare *Abeyah, who carried his traveling partner, tack, guns, ammunition, and Turkish gold, "to a total of

300 pounds without showing fatigue, even though the temperature registered 135 degrees."

The war mares, however, were not ridden on a daily basis. When the tribe moved, the mares were led from the camels. Breeding stock could be bought and sold, but for the most part, the war mares were priceless. They changed hands only as the most privileged gift. Daughters of the war mares were usually acquired by theft or in trade for colossal riches.

The seventh century poet Yazid sang praises of the war mares: "And in truth she has ever been to me a precious possession, born and brought up in our tents: of all possessions that which has been born and bred with one's people is the most precious. And I will keep her as my own so long as there is a presser for the olive, and so long as a man, barefoot or shod, wanders on the face of the earth."

Prophet Mohammed received the mare with the words, "Blessed be ye, O Daughter of the Wind." He said never to "utter curse remarks on the subject of the camel or the wind: the former is a boon to man, the latter an emanation from the soul of Allah."

In the eyes of today's Arabian show mare we might recognize *Wadduda 30, a war mare befitting of legend. Her name means "love and affection," and she was the favorite war mare of the Supreme Ruler, Sheik Hasem Bey. In 1906, political cartoonist Homer Davenport described meeting *Waddada 30 in Aleppo, Syria. She was galloped down a stony street, "tearing down toward us all afire, and the bounding tassels around her knees looked like silk skirts. Such action over such rolling rocks? Her tail was high and her eyes fairly sparkled!"

On her neck she bore lance scars and on her pastern the mark from a bullet that she had carried on an 80-mile run. She was said to have raced from Iskanderoon to Aleppo, 106 miles in 11 hours, in pursuit of an enemy caravan. *Wadduda 30 was stunning, fiery, brave, enduring, and willing. And it is said she lived to 40.

Today, unlike among other breeds that prefer a gelding, then a stallion, and lastly a mare for riding, there is no evidence of gender prejudice when it comes to riding, driving, and competing Arabian mares.

How Do You Know He is an Arabian?

Desert life created physical attributes that made the horse both beautiful and useful, a pleasure to view, while heroically enduring and hardy. The very features that define the Arabian breed today are ones that brought buyers to the desert hundreds of year ago. These characteristics are referred to as "Arabian type" and, when combined with correct conformation, create the breed standard.

Five key elements distinguish the Arabian type and create a beautiful athlete.

HEAD: Short and refined; the artistically chiseled look of the head is enhanced by the "jibbah," or protrusion of the forehead that extends to just below the eyes. The Bedouin claim it holds blessings of Allah, and its size measures of the horse's intelligence. The jibbah creates a straight or, preferably, slight concave or dished profile below the eyes. The head sports a small muzzle and flaring, elastic nostrils that allow for maximum oxygen intake and thus greater stamina and endurance.

A deep jowl with wide branches also aids the breathing process. The breadth between the branches of the jaws gives room for the supple, large windpipe that gives him such phenomenal air exchange.

Large, expressive dark eyes are set wide apart for better peripheral vision than most breeds, making the horse less apprehensive. Long eyelashes protect the eyes from wind and sand. Ears are short and fine.

NECK: The long, arched neck, set on high and running well back into the withers, meets with a fine, clean, arched throatlatch (in

This painting by the late Gladys Brown Edwards serves as a model of the ideal Arabian in terms of type and conformation. REPRINTED WITH PERMISSION OF THE ARABIAN HORSE ASSOCIATION.

Arabic called the "midthbah," and literally meaning the place where the throat is cut), which in its design keeps the windpipe clear to carry air to the lungs. The neck affects the grace and elasticity of the horse's movement, how well he balances, rounds his back, and engages his hindquarters. The midthbah influences the horse's ability to give to the bit.

BACK: The short back is strong under saddle. Well sprung ribs and a deep chest cavity allow plenty of room for lung expansion.

CROUP: A fairly level, strong topline and croup contribute to a sweeping stride.

TAIL: The tail is carried naturally high, but relaxed and straight. It is said that this tail carriage was desired by the Bedouin because it helped the horse to cool himself.

As one might expect, a story goes with this feature. Dressed in a beautiful bejeweled robe that was a present from his father and worth a fortune, a sheik raced across the desert to escape an army of enemies in hot pursuit. Fearing that the stunning robe was slowing down his horse, he threw it off. When he and his horse finally reached the safety of his camp, he turned around to be sure that his enemy was out of sight—and there was his robe, wrapped around his horse's lofty tail.

SIZE: The average size is between 14.1 and 15.1 hands, although today a taller Arabian is not so unusual.

Overall, the ideal Arabian presents a balanced outline of three equal circles: the shoulder, the barrel, and the hindquarters. Generally he has a "dry" or "desert" look, whereby bone structure and veins are distinguishable on the head and leg tendons and ligaments because of thin skin and fine hair. Dense bone provides strong legs and hooves, protecting against lameness.

It is said that when a buyer came to a tribe, the seller put the potential purchase in a tent. The buyer stood outside the tent while the seller slowly raised the tent flap. Consider that the order in which the buyer saw the parts of the horse was in order of importance: first the feet (and so the adage going back to ancient Greece, "no feet, no horse"), legs, etc.

COLOR

Purebred Arabians come in basic colors: bay, black, chestnut, gray, and occasionally roan. Variety stems from the amount of white on the legs and face. In the search for splash and flash, breeders will create Half Arabians in order to benefit from the attributes of the Arabian in the lively colors of buckskin, palomino, Appaloosa, or pinto.

The ancient breeders of Arabians had strong feelings about color. As we see in the following quotes, prophets, poets, and warriors believed that the horse's coat color was an indicator of his character.

About bays it was said: "If you hear that a bay horse fell from the highest mountain and was safe, then believe it."

"Of all the horses in my armies, the one that has best borne the fatigues and privations of war is the true bay."

As white was symbolic of victory and success, the Arabs said of the white horse, "This is the mount of kings, because it brings good fortune and luck, and with it you are able to obtain what is necessary."

Chestnut horses were symbolic of bloodshed and war. The prophet Mohammed said, "If thou hast a dark chestnut, conduct him to combat, and if thou hast only a sorry chestnut, conduct him all the same to combat. The good fortune of horses is in their chestnut coloring, and the best (probably meaning the fastest) of all horses is the chestnut."

A proverb read, "If you hear that a chestnut has been seen to fly, believe it."

Of black horses it was said: "And I beheld, and lo a black horse: and he that sat on him had a pair of balances in his hand."

"Good fortune is in the pure clear black, with three leg markings and the right fore free; and he is the most precious of the blacks."

"Fly from him like the plague, he is the brother of the cow" was written of the piebald gray, as was "Never purchase a bald-faced horse with four white feet, for he carries his shroud with him."

ON TYPE AND STRAINS

As early as the fourteenth century, the Bedouin identified a horse's lineage through strains, via the tail female line of descent (also called the dam or family line, it is the bottom line of the pedigree chart). This pedigree, evidence of the horse's purity, was passed between owners through "hojjas," Arabic sworn oral statements. Even if a mare was captured in war, both sides of the "deal" were concerned that her descendants remain pure and correctly bred.

The five Arabian horse families, earlier described as "Al Khamsa," include Kehilan, Seglawi, Abeyan, Hamdani, and Hadban. On other lists, Muniqi and Dahman replace Abeyan and Hamdani.

Lady Wentworth of the English Crabbet Stud pointed out in her book *The Authentic Arabian Horse* that "the so-called five taproots are never the same five." Judith Forbis claims that over twenty-two strains were described in the desert and elsewhere, while Gladys Brown Edwards wrote in her book *The Arabian: War Horse to Show Horse* that at one time the desert claimed around 200 family strains.

Substrains developed in each main strain were named after a celebrated mare or sheik that formed a substantial branch within the main strain. These were a family of horses bred by a certain breeder, clan, or tribe. So you might have Seglawi-Jedran, the Seglawis of Jedran. The Maneghi-Hedruj horses of Ibn Sbeyel of the Gomussa tribe became Maneghi-Sbeyel.

The esteem of a strain was not based on conformation, but on pedigree and on the prodigy's skill at raiding, which required speed, courage, stamina, and hardiness. The theory that only three true strains lived in the desert (Kehilan, Seglawi, and Muniqi) and they could be given physical descriptions was devised by Carl Schmidt (1893–1966), later known as Carl Raswan, a prolific writer (*Drinkers of the Wind, The Black Tents of Arabia, Escape from Bagdad*), who for many years lived with and fought beside the Bedouin.[1]

A Kehilan (also spelled Kuhaylan or Koheilan or Kuhailan) is generally heavily muscled, wide-chested, with a masculine appearance. He has a rounded outline with a bold and powerful expression.

---

[1] Ranch manager for the W.K. Kellogg Ranch, today the campus of California State Polytechnic University, in Pomona, California, Schmidt adored the stallion *Raswan whom Kellogg had imported from the English Crabbet Stud. In defiance of the owner, Schmidt one day rode the horse off the ranch. Taking a break, he tied *Raswan to a fence. *Raswan broke loose to play with a team of mules, stepped into a harrow to which they were hitched, and cut his fetlock so deep he had to be put down. Schmidt was so devastated that he changed his name to Raswan.

His head is short, with a broad forehead and great width in the jowls. The most common colors are gray and chestnut.

A Seglawi (also spelled Saklawi, Seklavi, or Saklawiyah) is known for refinement, grace, and feminine elegance. This strain is recognized more for its speed than its endurance. Fine-boned, with longer faces and necks than the Kehilan, the Seglawi is more commonly bay.

A Muniqi (also spelled Muniqui or Maneghi) has a racier build, with straighter and more angular lines. He is taller, coarser, and faster, with a look similar to the Thoroughbred.

Abeyan is similar to the Seglawi, refined, often with a longer back than a typical Arabian. He is a smaller horse, commonly gray with more white marking than other strains.

Hamdani is often plain, with an athletic, somewhat masculine, large-boned build. His facial profile is more often straight. Common colors are gray and bay.

Hadban is a smaller version of the Hamdani, with an extremely gentle disposition.

The importance of the strains and their use has been argued over the years. A breeder might breed a Kehilan type horse that is very correct and athletic, but not particularly pretty, to a Seglawi type to add more beauty. Matching the names with horses of today and yesterday is an interesting exercise.

HALF ARABIAN AND ANGLO-ARABIAN

How do the Half Arabian and the Anglo-Arabian fit into the picture?

In the 1920s, the United States Army inducted Arabian horses into its breeding program to improve the durability and stamina of its horses. The officers were convinced of the Arabian's value when Arabians won three times the Cavalry Endurance Ride, in which horses traveled 300 miles in five days carrying 245 pounds. After World War II the cavalry became mechanized, and the Army sold its Half Arabian and Anglo-Arabian registries to the newly formed Arabian Horse Association.

Half Arabians are the designer crosses of performance classes. Usually bred for a certain job in the show world or to add color to the Arabian look, his ability is upgraded by the fortitude, athleticism, intelligence, refinement, and stamina of the Arabian, with the bonus of the breed's beauty, charm, and people-oriented attitude.

Fantine, a Half Arabian created from the cross of an Arabian mare and an Oldenburg stallion, exhibits the mix of Arabian elegance with Oldenburg substance. Both breeds contribute athleticism. PHOTO BY RAINBOW BEND EQUINE PHOTO.

For devotees of Western disciplines, the Arabian Quarter Horse cross is nirvana. Mixing the Arabian with the high stepping breeds of American Saddlebred, Hackney, or Dutch Harness Horse produces an animated, stylish horse for English Pleasure. Dressage, jumping, and eventing riders find answers with the Arabian warmblood cross and the Anglo-Arabian (any combination of registered Arabian Thoroughbred, or Anglo-Arabian, provided there is no more than 75 percent or less than 25 percent Arabian blood) that shares the registry with the Half Arabians.

For purposes of this book the word "Arabian" will stand for the purebred Arabian, Half Arabian, and Anglo-Arabian.

COUNTRY OF ORIGIN TAKES THE LIMELIGHT

For the past fifty years, the country from which the horse traces his bloodlines has been given more emphasis and credence than strains. Breeders, trainers, and show exhibitors may favor an imported line, known, for example, as "pure Polish" or "straight Egyptian" or "Crabbet-bred," or an American-bred horse with lineage to one of these.

Exportation from the desert stretches back well over 400 years, as nobility, military, and adventurers from many parts of the globe came calling on the nomadic people of Northern Africa, the Arabian Peninsula, Turkey, Syria, and nearby areas in search of breeding horses that were known for their toughness and beauty.

In the late 1700s, French emperor Napoleon obtained his famous Arabian stallion Marengo from Egypt as war booty and rode him on the rugged retreat from Russia. That same century the first Arabian arrived in the United States. George Washington rode an Arabian during the Revolutionary War.

Three Arabians served as the foundation stallions in the creation of the Thoroughbred. In 1690, Captain Byerley captured in battle his namesake, the Byerley Turk, and rode him as a war mount until retiring him to breed to native ponies in England. Thomas Darley, British Counsel in Aleppo, Syria, in 1704 sent his Arabian stallion to England. Darley offspring went on to found the famous Eclipse line of Thoroughbreds. And finally, a present to France's Louis XV by the Sultan of Morocco, the Godolphin Arabian went on to suffer the misfortunate life of a cart horse until he was rescued and shipped to England and the Earl of Godolphin. His story was immortalized by Marguerite Henry in the book *King of the Wind*.

The early Thoroughbred offspring of these three Arabian stallions were exported to many continents. In the late 1700s the Thoroughbred became an official breed, and its General Stud Book listed 100 "oriental" stallions.

In 1873 a Turkish sultan gave General Ulysses S. Grant two Arabian stallions, *Leopard and *Linden Tree.

About that same time Syria, Egypt, and Arabia played host to an English couple who would form the single most influential stud farm in the history of the breed, Crabbet Park. From these desert importations, Lady Anne, her husband Sir Wilfred Blunt, and later their daughter Lady Judith Wentworth bred mares and stallions that became the foundation of significant breeding programs in the United States, Poland, Russia, and Spain.

The stories of the family, their desert adventures, and their horses are beautifully chronicled and illustrated in Lady Wentworth's book, *The Authentic Arabian Horse.*

The influence of Crabbet-bred horses was significant in the United States, especially the importation of *Raffles. In 1932 the 13.3 hand stallion arrived in America "sterile"—or so it was thought. The son of the famous Polish stallion Skowronek, who was considered by some to be the greatest Arabian stallion in history, *Raffles was a gift from Lady Wentworth to Roger Selby. With care and attention by Selby and trainer Jimmy Dean, the little gray stallion turned out to be a gem. He was prepotent enough to affect four and five generations with large dark eyes, a quintessential Arabian type, a strong square trot, and extreme intelligence.

Other Crabbet breeders in the United States have included W.K. Kellogg of the breakfast cereal company, the Hearst family of newspaper fame, the Gainey ranch, Alice Payne, and John Rogers, bringing to the fore such famous stallions as *Raseyn, Indraff, Abu Farwa, and *Serafix. Today most notable is the breeder Bazy Tankersley, whose Al-Marah Arabians has influenced the Arabian breed since 1945 and produced more than 2,500 purebred Arabians who perform in the show ring and in distance riding.

The Crabbet stud was greatly influenced by the prized horses of Egypt. Today, in the United States the Egyptian Arabian stands as a unique type under the guardianship of the Pyramid Society, which defines a "straight Egyptian" horse as one which traces every pedigree line to a horse born in the Arabian desert. It must also trace every line to a horse from the stud farms of Abbas Pasha I (1813–1854) or Ali Pasha Sheriff (died 1897) and used for breeding by the Royal Agricultural Society/Egyptian Agricultural Organization (EAO).

Remarkable in its classic refinement, astonishing beauty, and the look of the desert, the Egyptian type is clear in such renowned stallions as *Sakr, *Morafic, Nabiel, *Ansata Ibn Halima, and Nazeer. Significant American breeders, importers, and devotees of Egyptian horses stretch back to 1895 and forward with W. R. Brown, Henry Babson, Douglas Marshall, Tom McNair, and Richard Pritzlaff. Perhaps most honored today is the breeder Judith Forbis, the first woman jockey in the Middle East and a breeder of Egyptian Arabians since the 1950s. Her treasured books are valued sources for information on Egyptian horses.

In 1906, America saw a boost in Arabian blood when Hearst newspaper political cartoonist Homer Davenport traveled to the desert. He carried with him a permit issued by the Supreme Sultan of the Ottoman Empire and obtained through his friend President Theodore Roosevelt that allowed Davenport to import authentic Arabian mares and stallions. He brought home ten mares and fillies and seventeen colts and stallions, which became the foundation of a senior bloodline in American Arabian horse breeding during the first half of the twentieth century.[2]

TURNING TO EASTERN EUROPE

The Arabian breeding program in Poland dates back to the 1700s, when Polish princes owned the stud farms. As foreign armies invaded

---

[2] More information on Davenport horses can be found in either *My Quest of the Arabian Horse* by Davenport or in the annotated and more available book *The Annotated Quest*.

with horses of Arabian blood, the princes too turned to the desert to improve their stock. The Russian Revolution of 1917 contributed to the demise of Polish aristocracy and their individual Arabian herds. Bolsheviks had slaughtered horses at the state stud Janow Podlaski. World War I (1914–1920) reduced the breeding stock. By 1926, Janow had dropped from 400 to 45 broodmares. That war marked the end of the nobility's stud farms and led to state-operated facilities.

During World War II, the Arabian Polish breeding program was decimated by invading Nazi Germans and by Russians who appropriated Arabians from the Polish to stock their own breeding programs or to feed their starving citizens. The book *And Miles To Go* by Linell Smith draws a fascinating picture of the World War trials of the stallion *Witez II. Due to a brave, calm, and loving spirit, the dark bay stallion survived to become a leading sire in the United States.

By 1938, the year of *Witez's birth, the Polish state stud was on the mend, with 237 horses steeped in precious bloodlines. In keeping with his valuable ancestry, the young colt was named "Witez," which means chieftain and knight, prince and hero. During his first year, the Ministry of Agriculture rated him as the top colt at the stud.

In August, 1939, Germany and Russia signed a non-aggression pact, which essentially gave Hitler freedom to invade Poland. In September, the Nazis began moving east across the country. Janow evacuated the horses, sending them and their handlers 30 kilometers a day eastward toward Brest Litovsk, a town near the Russian border.

Witez and his young groom Stasik Kowalski walked with the other yearlings along a road filled with human refugees escaping the invading Germans. Flies and heat were deadly. People and horses were exhausted. Hundreds of Nazi aircraft droned through the sky. Soon heavy bombing blasted the road. To shield the frightened horses from the explosions, the yearling group was moved deep into the forest and took up travel only at night. On the third night they stopped at a farm for rest and food. A Polish military unit and their loud machinery caused the youngsters to break through the fencing and scatter in every direction.

Stasik found *Witez in the forest, alone and terrified. Rather than continue with the others toward the Russians who were advancing from the other direction, Stasik chose to take *Witez home, even at the risk of facing bombing and the German army. They tramped through marshes and forests, living without food for Stasik or grain for *Witez. Along their way, a Polish Army unit supplied some nourishment, but only momentary rest. The German army was in pursuit. Shots sent Stasik and the colt racing through the forest. A rifle bullet grazed Stasik. He remained conscious long enough to get *Witez away from the conflict.

A woodcutter found the two and hid them while Stasik rested and tended his wound. When they were ready to depart, a Polish partisan group opened fire on a German patrol to distract the enemy from *Witez and Stasik.

In November, two months after they had left home, *Witez and Stasik reached Janow, both thin and weary and worn. *Witez's hooves were chipped and broken. His ribs and hipbones protruded. His coat was rough.

While they were gone, Poland had been divided up by the Germans and the Russians. Heading home, Soviet troops stopped at Janow and took 400 horses, including mature breeding stock and about 100 young ones. Among them were *Witez's parents Ofir and Federacja.

Under the German direction of Janow, *Witez became the head stallion. He was started under saddle and learned to hunt and jump. He was being prepared for racing when Germany declared war on Russia and everything changed. Stasik joined the partisans, first as a spy, then as a fighter. In March 1943, *Witez and nine other Janow horses were taken to Hostoun, Czechoslovakia, and the "super horse" stud farm where the Nazis had gathered 1,500 of Europe's best horses. He lived in style, but left behind at Janow many sad people who cared for him.

Two young veterinarians, Dr. Erich Müller and Dr. Willi Dressler, feared that the advancing Russians might slaughter the horses for meat. With the Twelfth Corps of the American Third Army and General George S. Patton Jr. near Hostoun, the two German vets, at great risk, surrendered to the Americans in an effort to save the horses. At the Second Calvary Group headquarters in an abandoned farmhouse in Austria, the two explained that the defense of Hostoun was minor. They wanted General Patton to take the horses. Via radio communication, Patton barked, "Get them."

On April 28, 1945, the Americans overtook Hostoun. They headed 200 stallions, broodmares, and young stock for Monsbach stud farm in Hessen, Germany, headquarters of the American Remount Service. Mares with foals traveled in trucks. The others were ridden. Dr. Müller rode *Witez.

In eight days, horses and riders covered 200 miles. They continually met sporadic small arms fire. Although no horses or riders were injured, several horses suffered from shattered nerves and, being unshod, from severe foot soreness. They say that *Witez never altered his stride in the shooting and actually thrived from the journey.

On May 7, Germany formally surrendered. The two vets are said to have celebrated with a bottle of champagne in *Witez's stall.

*Witez II was chosen by the U.S. Remount to sail to America. When the U.S. Remount Service shut down, Earle E. Hurlbutt bought *Witez II at auction for $8,100 in 1949. Owned by governments and nations, this newly private citizen spent the rest of his days at stud and as a show horse. He died in 1966 with Hurlbutt in California.

Poland fell behind the Iron Curtain, but its breeding program flourished. In 1961, U.S. breeders began importing stars that would change the show arena forever. Among those who imported significant contributors were the family of Dr. Eugene LaCroix, who brought home *Bask; Sheila Varian, who imported the three mares

*Naganka, *Bachantka, and *Ostroga, and Anne McCormick, who brought over the stallion *Naborr.

Between the World Wars, Poland had instituted the practice of racing her Arabians to test the breeding stock's stamina, athleticism, substance, power, and trainability, traits for which the Polish horses are known today. After the country's independence from the Soviet Union, the Arabian horse was named a "Polish National Treasure" by the government.

RUSSIAN ARABIANS

As early as the year 1533, Russians brought Arabian horses home from the desert. The Bolshevik Revolution of 1917 brought the nationalization of private studs and the creation of the state stud Tersk, which stands today. In the 1930s, the stud purchased twenty-two horses from the Crabbet stud, a French Arabian stallion Kann, and six mares to develop a thriving program. During World War II, the Russians "liberated" Polish horses from the Germans. A gift from Egypt of the stallion Aswan in 1963 completed the mix.

The 1970s American Arabian breeders arrived at Tersk to buy horses. They were headed by Howard Kale Jr., who imported *Muscat on his first trip, which led the way to the importation of stallions and mares that would make history. Movement characterized by soundness and tremendous action, temperaments defined by enthusiasm for and willingness to work are hallmarks of Russian Arabians. As in Poland, racing serves as a means to test breeding stock and a place to show horses to the public as both a breeding selection guide and a performance venue.

THE SPANISH ARABIAN

The Spanish Arabian has seen his share of wartime sorrow as well. His history is long, though today the numbers are small. The first

Arabian listed in the Spanish Arabian Registry Stud Book was imported by Queen Isabella II in 1847. Subsequently, horses were imported from the desert, Poland, and France, mostly by the Yeguada Militar (the military stud).

In the early 1900s, private breeders began importing horses. Among them was Don Cristabal Colon, the fifteenth Duque de Veragua and a direct descendent of Christopher Columbus. As the foundation of his breeding program, the duque imported horses from Lady Wentworth at the Crabbet stud.

In 1936, at the start of the Spanish Civil War, the duque, his brother, and most of his employees were brutally assassinated by Republican troops, and the palace and papers, including his stud books, were destroyed. Seventeen Arabian stallions and thirty-three mares died or disappeared. Fortunately and unbeknownst to the troops, a broodmare band with foals and young stock was grazing across the river that ran through the estate. A month later, Nationalist General Francisco Franco's troops drove out the Republican troops and trucked the mares and youngsters to the Yeguada Militar.

The thirteen colts and forty-six mares and fillies were branded with a "V," and the foals were given names beginning with the name "Vera." However, questions arose about the legitimacy of the foals and young stock, and the World Arabian Horse Organization and the Arabian Horse Registry of America did not accept horses of this breeding line until 1972.

Though it has been slow, the Spanish Arabian is making a return and contributing to the breed his good mind and solid beauty.

AMERICA BECOMES THE MECCA

At the 1893 Chicago World's Fair, Turkey chose to exhibit forty-five Arabian horses in a "wild eastern" exhibition. Among the imported Arabians shown were the mare Nejdme and the stallion Obeyran. Both subsequently became foundation horses No. 1 and No. 2 in

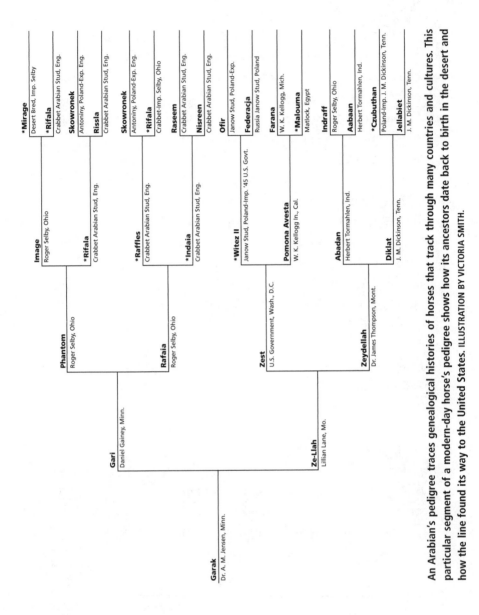

An Arabian's pedigree traces genealogical histories of horses that track through many countries and cultures. This particular segment of a modern-day horse's pedigree shows how its ancestors date back to birth in the desert and how the line found its way to the United States. ILLUSTRATION BY VICTORIA SMITH.

the Arabian Stud Book of America, the world's first all-Arabian registry. Formed in 1908, the registry later changed its name to the Arabian Horse Registry of America. In 2003, the Arabian Horse

Registry merged with the Half Arabian Registry and the breed association, International Arabian Horse Association, to become the Arabian Horse Association.

Today America is the center of Arabian breeding. As a clear indicator of the United States Arabian's status, American-bred Arabians have been exported to Egypt, Kuwait, Qatar, and Saudia Arabia as these countries realize the significance of the Arabian horse to their culture.

American-made horses deserving mention include famed show stallions Khemosabi++++, Ferzon, Indraff, Bay-Abi, Bay El Bey, Abu Farwa, Xenophonn, Fadjur, and great mares Bint Sahara, Susecion, TW Fortenya, Saki, Autumn Fire, and Moska. These horses were produced by breeders who have dedicated their lives to the breed and just knock our socks off with their knowledge, horsemanship, and vision: Bazy Tankersley, Sheila Varian, Judith Forbis, Alice Payne, Tish Hewitt, Kay Patterson, Dr. Bill Munson, Ed Tweed, J. M. Dickenson, Edna Draper, Frank McCoy, the Tone family, and Dr. Eugene LaCroix and sons Gene and Ray, to name just a few.

Strain names once revealed the history of the individual Arabian horse and his family. Then the country from which his ancestors hailed became the yardstick. Today we see a move into the show arena to test and evaluate. This venue becomes the Arabian's war theater, a place where she raids like the war mares of old, with all the outstanding character that made her the pride of the Bedouin and the desire of princes and heads of state.

WHAT'S IN A NAME?

The Arabian horse's name often tells more than just what to call that individual.

Some names are preceded by an asterisk (*). This sign indicates that the horse was imported either to the United States or Canada.

Arabic words in a name often link the horse to his parentage:

Abu: father of
Bint: daughter of
Ibn: son of

An Arabian name may also leave clues as to the horse's breeder. A breeder may add the initials of her farm at the beginning or the end of the horse's name. Here are some examples:

Gai Argosy (Gainey Farm), Desperado V (Varian Arabians), AM Dreamazon (Al-Marah Arabians), WN Ultimate Star (Wayne Newton Arabians).

A name may reflect the farm and the stallion on which it hangs its star. *Ansata Ibn Halima, whose name translates to "The Son of the Gentle One," was imported (note the asterisk) from Egypt and was the namesake for the Ansata Arabian Stud. The name of his offspring start with "Ansata." "Zee" is often attached to the name of working Western horses in honor of their sire Xenophonn. Horses whose names begin with "Kh" are likely related to the stallion Khemosabi ++++.

Attached to the end of some names might be various combinations of pluses and slashes, symbolic of points awarded from show ring successes. Following are the awards and their symbols:

Legion of Honor: +
Legion of Supreme Honor: +/
Legion of Merit: ++
Legion of Supreme Merit: +++
Legion of Excellence: +//
Legion of Masters: ++++

Until discontinued in 1940, certificates of registration and stud books indicated, when possible, the strain of the horse. A pedigree today may indicate the studbook in which the ancestral horse is registered, usually shown by the following initials:

AAS – Austrian Arabian Studbook
AHSB – Arabian Horse Society of United Kingdom
ASBB – Babolna State Stud (Hungary)

CAHR – Canadian Arabian Horse Registry
EAO – Egyptian Agricultural Organization
FRSB – French Arabian Studbook
GSB – General Studbook (England)
IOHB – Inchass Original Herd Book (Egypt)
NSB – Netherlands Studbook
PASB – Polish Arabian Studbook
RAS – Royal Egyptian Society
RASB – Russian Arabian Studbook
SAHR – Swedish Arabian Studbook
SBWM – Studbook for Wurttemburg Marbach
   (Germany)
SSB – Spanish Arabian Studbook

In Arabian horse breeding today, you will hear the argument that the most significant part of the pedigree is the tail female line (also called the dam or family line, the bottom line of the pedigree), reflecting the Bedouin reverence for the mare. Strains are said to inherit through the tail female line, never via the sire line. The tail female line descends through the dam, her dam (the granddam), etc., to the taproot mare, which is always a desertbred mare and the bottom name on the most distant generation. In the eyes of many, the female tail line must be strong because it is the anchor of the pedigree.

Significant to the pedigree are the initials D.B., which stand for "desertbred," and therefore bred by one of the desert tribes of Arabia or the Middle East.

CHAPTER TWO

THE VERSATILE BREED AND ITS INFINITE POSSIBILITIES

*"The Arabian horse will continue to exercise its magic over
enthusiasts worldwide. This enchantment is born of beauty of
bodily form and movement. It is nurtured by the sweet
temperament of the breed . . . And it is brought to full stature
by the Arabian's ability to tackle anything it is asked to do.
From carrying a rider over 100 miles to posing statue-like in
a show ring, or simply standing, eyes half-closed, listening in
silent sympathy while its owner confides to it the tragedies and
triumphs of the day."*

—Australian photographer Pat Slater

WATCHING THE WARM-UP ARENA OR TRAVELING THE BARN
aisles and passageways of an Arabian horse show feels akin to walking the streets of New York or any other great multicultural city of
the world. Here the variety makes a very spicy life.

On your right, a woman in a black tailcoat, white breeches, and
tall boots canters by on her English show hack horse. From behind
you hear the clink of Western rowel spurs as a cowboy ambles past
with his reining horse, heading to the warm-up arena, where a man
in khaki pants and tennis shoes runs alongside his trotting sport
horse stallion. The horse and rider to your left are cloaked in the bejeweled and embroidered cloth of a Bedouin costume. They pass a
high-stepping park horse that crosses in front of a ground covering,
thrusting hunter.

All the horses are Arabians.

As a breed, the Arabian horse defines the word "versatility," as if he is able to morph himself from one job into another. He has the physical design and resulting athleticism to perform in a vast number of disciplines and work in a variety of outlines, speeds, and degrees of collection. His exceptional trainability drawn from his intelligence and willingness also leads him down many roads.

Each Arabian discipline requires unique physical attributes. English Pleasure calls for great strength. Working Western requires handiness and agility. Dressage demands regularity and elasticity of gaits. Each one calls for a common thread that is a characteristic to Arabian horses, and that is heart. Heart makes a gifted horse breathtaking and an average horse a winner. Outside the arena, Arabians don't own the sport of endurance simply because of physical ability. It takes tremendous heart to travel 100 miles in 11 hours. And it takes tremendous heart to carry on through the physical and mental challenges facing a competitive show horse. There are aches and pains. There is mental stress. But these Arabians are the descendants of warriors, and though they no longer carry a rider with a rifle or lance, that gift of willingness, giving, and joie de vivre has not been breed out of them. Heart is the element that makes any show horse great, and Arabians are born with an abundance.

To satisfy these talents, Arabian shows offer an incomparable list of ways in which to compete.

When people in the United States began showing Arabians in the late 1940s, the individual horse did it all, until the late 1970s. In one afternoon he was a halter horse, a Western horse, and an English horse. Today, the breed has not lost its vast variety, but instead, horses have been bred for specific divisions. Furthermore, horsemanship and training have become more specific to each discipline to such a degree that it takes an exceptional individual to excel and win in multiple disciplines at the competitive level. With the right training, a great saddle seat horse can be taught to be a Western Pleasure great. More likely, however, the horse will be shown in the manner which best suits his individual athletic ability, conformation, and temperament.

Arabian horse shows and the registration of Arabian horses today are governed by the Arabian Horse Association (AHA) in Aurora, Colorado. Founded in 1950, AHA has grown into a membership organization dedicated to promoting the Arabian and Half Arabian/Anglo-Arabian horse. It consists of eighteen regions within the United States and Canada, 270 affiliate clubs within these regions, and 40,000 members. Responsibility includes the recognition of 450 all-Arabian, Class A shows yearly, plus regional and national championships.

Arabian shows are organized on a type of pyramid. On the ground floor is the schooling show, which is usually held by a club at a local stable without recognition by show associations. Classes are often limited to the pleasure divisions, and the show usually runs one day. While the results do not count toward regional or national points or awards, the low-key show prepares new riders and/or inexperienced horses for their future and can be a lot of fun for friends and family.

An Arabian circuit is a series of shows, often unsanctioned and defined by a geographic location, that are tied together by year-end awards earned at the series shows, often presented at an annual banquet. It caters to the amateur, the junior, the first-timer, and the experienced exhibitor trying out a new horse or a new discipline.

Each circuit has its own character. Some are open to other breeds. Some give prize money. In common, they are designed as confidence builders and a place to have more fun than stress. Examples are the Eastern Amateur Arabian Horse Show Circuit, the Zone One Arabian Circuit Shows, and the California Arabian Horse Shows Circuit.

The Arabian Community Show (ACS) is designed as a venue with an awards system worthy of a challenge, but without the high cost of showing at the Class A level. ACS shows are held in local communities for national, annual high point awards organized by AHA. To be eligible for awards, the horses must be registered with AHA, the Canadian Arabian Horse Registry, or Canadian Partbred Arabian Register, and riders must be members of AHA. No other membership is required. AHA lists these shows in its magazine calendar.

"The ACS is about fun, family, and friends. This is for people just getting into showing or who don't care to show at a rated Arabian show, but who like having a goal for which to compete," says Cynthia Richardson, chair of the AHA marketing development committee. "They are created for competition, but also as a place for people to learn, where judges can talk with exhibitors after the classes about why they placed the classes as they did."

The next level up on the pyramid is the Class A, B, or C-rated show. These are recognized by AHA and the U.S. Equestrian Federation (USEF) and are conducted under the rules of these organizations. The Class A show has stiffer competition, membership requirements, costs, and a large variety of classes. Depending on the area of the country, the show may run from one to five days and field as many as 500 horses. Points gathered at these shows qualify competitors for AHA-sponsored programs such as achievement awards and for participation in regional and national championships. Some disciplines such as dressage and reining also may be eligible for national recognition from their discipline's organization if the show is registered with that association. Show organizers are usually member organizations such as an AHA club, but may be a non-affiliated entity or individual.

Among the larger Class A shows are the Ohio Buckeye (Memorial Day weekend), the Arabian Horse Association of Florida/Ocala Arabian Horse Association Thanksgiving Show, and the Arabian Horse Association of Northern California Show (April).

Class A shows serve as qualifying shows for the esteemed regional championship shows, which are organized by each of the eighteen AHA regions. They may include classes that correspond with those held at the national championships and therefore afford competitors the chance to quality for national competition.

Of equal status with regional championships are three wider ranging shows: Pacific Slopes Championships, the East Coast Championships, and the East and West Canadian Breeders Championships. Depending on the size of the region, these shows can last from one to ten days.

The Egyptian Event is dedicated to spotlighting horses of Egyptian bloodlines. In one show, the Egyptian Arabian is showcased through the Performance Pyramid classes, futurities, and 25- and 50-mile endurance rides. Held in recent years at the Kentucky Horse Park in Lexington, this annual event is organized by the Pyramid Society, founded in 1969 and devoted to the Egyptian Arabian.

Standing at the pinnacle of the show pyramid are the prestigious national championships. Held yearly, they are the U.S. National Championship Show (October), in Louisville, KY, 2006, Albuquerque, NM, 2007, and Tulsa, OK, 2008–2010; Canadian National Championship Show (August) in Regina, Saskatchewan, Canada; the Youth National Championship Show (July) in Albuquerque, NM; and the Sport Horse National Championship Show (September), alternating every other year between Lexington, VA, and Boise, ID. At these shows owners, trainers, amateurs, juniors, and breeders alike keep their eye on the beautiful blanket of red roses draped over the shoulders of the winners. These national competitions are carried on with impressive grace, pomp, and pride.

Scottsdale Arabian Horse Show stands alone. Started in 1955 by the Arabian Horse Association of Arizona, this extravaganza is in actuality a Class A show, and yet it equals the prestige, panache, and depth of competition of the national championships. In fact, Scottsdale forms a third of the triumvirate known as the Arabian Triple Crown: U.S. Nationals, Canadian Nationals, and Scottsdale. Do well at one or all three of those and you have more than arrived.

The Scottsdale show mirrors the history of the Arabian show. It began like an old Mickey Rooney/Judy Garland movie, with the kids deciding to put on a show in the barn. Everyone in the club volunteered and volunteered their wives, husbands, mothers and brothers, grandmothers and grandfathers, who did everything from bathe horses to cook hot dogs. It was held at Anne McCormick's private ranch.

The show grew every year, but the big explosion came in the 1970s and early 1980s. In conjunction with the growing Scottsdale show, Lasma Arabians in Scottsdale and the family of Dr. Eugene LaCroix produced public auctions, the likes of which had never been seen. These lavish spectaculars were masterpieces of lights, music, decorations, and elaborate staging. Upon the parting of massive velvet curtains, well-trained horses groomed to perfection trotted onto the stage to strobe lights and rock 'n' roll, charging through the smoke of dry ice in the presence of high rollers and movie stars dressed in gowns and tuxedos. Invitations were at a premium.

At the Scottsdale Arabian Show, barns turn into neighborhoods welcoming spectators, Arabian horse lovers, and new and old friends. PHOTO BY PATTI SCHOFLER.

Horses line up for the judges' final inspection of a large Hunter Pleasure class at the Scottsdale Arabian Show. PHOTO BY PATTI SCHOFLER.

The horses were handled by a cadre of assistant trainers under the direct guidance of Gene and Ray LaCroix, as if it were a graduate school for horsemen.

Other breeders, farms, and trainers from the Arabian-populated Scottsdale area opened their barns to the auction's mystique. The breed's popularity enjoyed an all-time high, and so the Scottsdale show grew to become the largest, most prestigious Arabian horse show in the world. Each February, more than 2,000 horses compete for $500,000 in prize money in over 400 classes in eight arenas. Over 300 vendors make this place heaven for shoppers.

Decorations turn barns into towns: one decorated as a Texas saloon, another as a Bedouin tent. Still others set up welcoming living rooms behind grassy lawns. Horses led by cowboys, by hunt riders, by Bedouins, by men in suits, by grooms in golf carts steadily flow past. All around horses jump, spin, chase cows, and pull carts. They remind spectators of England, ancient Arabia, the Old West, or the fox hunt. Halter horses trot to their arena wearing gossamer thin halters. Visitors may encircle a bay mare standing in just her plain halter. She becomes more and more at home and happy, her eye growing softer and softer as more people pet her, admire her, and ask her owner a million questions.

The show is electric. Professionals come to see who the new horses are and watch the great and legendary ones win. Amateurs put their toe in the big water. At night, judges dress in tuxedos and gowns. Spectators and exhibitors alike get a kick out of the decorations, the outfits, and the spectacle.

GREAT VARIETY AND BREED CAMARADERIE

Arabians also compete at shows open to all breeds from local to national levels, particularly in dressage, three-day eventing, carriage driving, cutting, and reining. However, those who compete regularly at open shows often find their way to an Arabian show because of its great variety and breed camaraderie.

Look at the class list at most Arabian shows, and you'll see that you can do just about anything about which you might dream. For purebred Arabians, the AHA national championships include: Mare Breeding, Stallion Breeding, Gelding In-Hand, Sport Horse Mare, Sport Horse Stallion, Sport Horse Gelding, Park, English Pleasure, Country English Pleasure, Pleasure Driving, Country Pleasure Driving, Informal Combination, Pleasure Carriage Driving, Mounted Native Costume, Ladies Side Saddle, Western Pleasure, Trail, Reining, Cutting, Working Cow Horse, Working Hunter, Jumper, Hunter Pleasure, English Show Hack, Sport Horse Under Saddle, Sport Horse Show Hack, Dressage Training Level through Grand Prix Level, Walk-Trot Pleasure, Dressage Walk-Trot, Walk-Trot Equitation, Showmanship, Saddle Seat Equitation, Reining Seat Equitation, Hunter Seat Equitation Not To Jump, Hunter Equitation Over Obstacles, and Western Horsemanship.

Most of the same classes are offered for Half Arabian/Anglo-Arabian competitors. Furthermore, these sections may be divided into classes for everyone (open), amateurs, amateur owners, juniors, junior owners, and junior horses.

"There is nothing an Arabian can't do and do well, especially competing among themselves," says Gary Dearth, AHA officer, 2004 Horseman of the Year, and several times national champion and reserve champion. "Some people have more than one Arabian and often show in multiple divisions. Our shows are more interesting and fun than those of other breeds, certainly for a horseman."

"It's important for amateurs and their horses to get experience in the arena, and with our shows you can do that. At one show you can participate with your horse multiple times," says Gordon Potts, multi-national-championship-winning trainer and Arabian judge. "Other shows have only one class for each division, if they have multiple divisions, and you wait forever to show. It's boring. Our shows are never boring."

The following chapters will introduce you to the many choices: from pleasure to sport horse to working Western to specialty classes. From there you will find out how to put yourself in the picture of the Arabian show arena.

CHAPTER THREE

INTRODUCING PERFORMANCE DISCIPLINES

"The aim of this noble and useful art is solely to make horses supple, relaxed, flexible, compliant and obedient . . . without all of which a horse—no matter what his use—will be neither comfortable in his movements nor pleasurable to ride."

—François Robichon de la Gueriniere,
Ecole de Cavalrie (1729)

IN THE FLUID RHYTHM AND FLOATING GRACE OF CARNIVAL carousels, Arabians of performance disciplines journey around the show arena, smoothly shifting from trot to walk to canter, staging a performance which will highlight their skill and beauty. Like the carousel horses, their saddles and bridles, their outlines, and their riders' costumes vary according to their calling, be they saddle seat, hunter pleasure, show hack, or Western pleasure horses. Nonetheless, all performance disciplines share a method as to how the classes are conducted and how exhibitors approach their classes.

Riders and their Arabians compete in pleasure and performance classes before one to five judges, who rank them based on their execution of the various forms of the walk, trot, and canter in both directions of the arena. When a discipline has attached to its name the word "pleasure" (Country English, English, Hunter), primarily the judge expects the horse to appear as a pleasure to ride and show an agreeable attitude. Other performance classes are conducted similarly, but emphasize different elements. For example, in a Park class, a brilliant performance takes precedence. In Show Hack class, flawless training is the essence. Specialty classes such as Sidesaddle and Mounted Native Costume consider costuming as a criterion.

When a judge studies the horses in her class, she is thinking about attitude, manners, performance, conformation, quality, brilliant performance, presence, and suitability. In her mind, she appoints quite specific meanings to each word.

ATTITUDE: Attitude is the horse's mental approach to his job. How willing is he to perform? Does he have a relaxed, pleasant approach to the class requirements? He reflects his attitude through soft eyes, alert ears, quiet mouth and tail, and an overall soft, content appearance.

MANNERS: A horse may have a forward or pleasurable attitude, but he may pull on the reins. He may move along great until the rider puts her leg on for the canter, and then he wrings his tail. Essentially, manners are the behavior with which the horse performs. A mannerly horse is safe, obedient, and responsive and willingly complies with the rider's wishes.

PERFORMANCE: How does the horse perform the gaits in the manner particular to that class? Is his frame correct during those gaits? Are the gaits balanced and cadenced with the expected amount of collection and extension? Are the transitions smooth and clear? Does he move straight? Does he take and stay on the correct lead in the canter, lope, or hand gallop?

CONFORMATION: Does the conformation fit the discipline in which he is performing? In other words, form is to follow function.

QUALITY: We all think we know a good horse when we see him, but do we know that what we like is defined by the degree of excellence, condition, presence, carriage, athleticism, balance, and strength required to perform effortlessly and with finesse?

BRILLIANT PERFORMANCE: The horse who meets this criteria does the job, fulfilling all the requirements, but does so with drama and excellence, quite distinctive from the average entrant.

PRESENCE: "Look at me" says it all.

SUITABILITY: Suitability refers either to the horse in relation to the rider or to the discipline in which he is performing. Do the horse and rider work together as a team and present a harmonious picture? Is the rider over-mounted? Does the horse suit the image of the discipline in his conformation, temperament, and way of going?

A useful exercise when watching a class is to assign these qualities to the performing horses.

In performance classes at recognized shows, horses enter the arena counterclockwise at either the walk or trot. The ring steward signals instructions to the announcer on which gaits the judge wants the riders to perform. The riders usually walk, trot, and canter in one direction and then perform the gaits in the new direction. They then form a line, usually standing side by side in front of the ring steward. While the horses are in the lineup, the judge may ask that the horses back up. Within a few moments the announcer reveals the winning placings.

ARENA STRATEGY

Performing in that arena as if you own it takes talent and experience. The good exhibitors seem to always be in view. Their horses stand out in their brilliance, positioning in the arena, and confidence. The skilled performers draw the judge's attention during their horse's moments of brilliance in a place where he is clearly separated from the other horses. What could be better than a dark horse trotting perfectly along a white fence with no other horse within 30 feet? They make it easy for the judge to pin a ribbon on them.

Unless your horse boards at a crowded barn with very few arenas, you may not have experienced the ambiance of the ring before. Consider the distraction of spectators chattering and moving about. Consider a herd of horses moving in the same direction as yours. Some speed past you. Others move sluggishly, but in a bunch, making your job of passing them difficult. Some act up, bucking or spinning. If your horse needs correction, you really cannot school him without drawing negative attention from the judge.

Riding a ring successfully requires imagination and visualization. The good rider envisions where she is, where she will go next, and at the same time imagines the best way to show off her horse. All in one ride, she thinks about the footing, how her horse is going, how deep to ride the upcoming corner, when to pass another horse, when to be on the rail and when to drift off, and when to come up the middle of the ring.

"You stay in the zone and in tune with the horse, and yet you go through that ring and stick your head out like a turtle and see where you're going next," says Mary Trowbridge, three-time Arabian Horsewoman of the Year, Arabian judge, and specialist in English disciplines. "Like driving on the freeway, you don't get up on the bumper of another car. To get around him, you don't wait until the last minute and then jerk the wheel around. Or you don't drive up and hit the next guy."

Speed and forward momentum are the thrill, the skill, and the downfall in English classes. A rider might feel the need to keep up with others in the class and as a result her horse moves out of balance. "Sometimes it becomes a trotting race," points out Wendy Potts, an Arabian trainer with several national championships in Hunter Pleasure and Show Hack. "Each horse has a different speed at which he is balanced and looks best."

"I would video my horse at different speeds and see what makes my horse look best," says Arabian judge and trainer Wendy Gruskiewicz. "Then I would stick to the correct tempo and rhythm, and I don't get caught up with other horses. The trick is finding that sweet spot so that your horse moves effortlessly."

Riding in a class with twenty horses requires a different strategy from riding in one with only four. If you stay on the rail in a big class, the judge might see not enough of your work. On the other hand, riding 40 feet off the rail all the time in a small class becomes offensive to the judge, as though you are telling her how to do her job.

Riding with the pack may challenge your horse's ability to focus on you, the rider. Horses react to each other, and if one horse makes a mistake, speeds up, or bucks, possibly the others will as well.

The very skilled competitors get their horses in front of the judge and seem to be in the open every time the judge looks their way. It's not luck; it's skill. Even in the large Hunter Pleasure classes, they seem to always ride in a spot outside the inevitable two or three packs that form, dissolve, and reform in a class. As if they are driving a car in traffic, the riders look in front and back. Some slow down and let the pack move ahead. This strategy beats speeding ahead and putting the horse out of balance.

Others make good use of the arena corners. For example, if you want to drop behind someone so the judge can better see your horse, you might ride deep into the corner to give yourself a greater riding distance. If you want to get ahead, cut the corner shorter.

"With this dynamic, you can place yourself almost anywhere in the arena without having to circle or cross or be obvious," advises Gary Dearth. "You can keep yourself out of trouble and be seen without appearing to do much."

When the judge calls for the horses to line up at the end of the class, some riders take their time. "If I have a hint of a chance to win, I won't come to the lineup until the last minute. I keep circling around to show off my horse, but not so long that I make the judge angry," says trainer Jim Lowe.

This method may also help to keep your horse guessing. Wendy Potts affords this advice: "Any horse with half a brain will figure out the system. So I always try to make whatever we do my idea, not his. I make him wait. If he wants to do something, I never do it. I will blow a great class to not let him do what he wants to do. Better, you might try this at a schooling show. Change things so he doesn't know what to expect. For example, when the announcer asks for the lineup, reverse and then line up. Then he will have to wait for you to tell him what you will be doing."

Overall, you can have a great ride, and this may be its own reward. But if you wish to take home a ribbon or a trophy, your great ride will not matter if the judge does not see you.

CHAPTER FOUR

SADDLE SEAT

*"If you teach your horse to go with a light hand on the
bit, and yet to hold his head high and to arch his neck,
you will be making him do just what the animal himself
glories and delights in."*

—Xenophon

MY FRIEND'S FIRST HORSE WAS A YEARLING ARABIAN COLT.
As he grew up to become a riding horse, she grew a fantasy about what
she and Novio would become together. It only took her one visit to
an Arabian show to create a dream: one day she would don the day
coat with the long tails, jodhpurs, and homburg of a Saddle Seat rider
and ride her stunning gray through San Francisco's Golden Gate Park.

Novio would float airy and light in a high-stepping, elegant trot
down park paths, his neck arched, his thick, long mane drawn back
by the breeze created from the power of his movement. How graceful she would look as Novio bounded into a canter, moving with the
suppleness of a cat and the spring of a lion. Then she would think
"walk," and Novio would walk while still maintaining the proud and
pleased look of an English Pleasure horse.

Novio never went to that park. Instead he went on the trail and
became an endurance horse. Nonetheless, saddle seat horses are the
stuff that fantasies are made of. The way they go is reminiscent of a
time when people competed with their neighbors by riding through
the park on their fanciest horses. And which horse is fancier or more
graceful than an Arabian, unmistakable by his lofty tail carriage and
beauty and presence?

By nature these horses move forward with authority and elegance, in an uphill carriage, with a high placed, arched neck. The strength, energy, and substantial engagement of their hindquarters creates high-stepping front legs and elevated front ends, giving them the unique mixture of grace and deliberate power.

These horses move as they do in part because of conformation, in part natural gaits, and in part training, but not to be considered lightly is the contribution of a zealous spirit and the desire to work hard. They share with one another an incredible vigor, vibrancy, and ambition. The best ones are sensitive and powerful, yet move with ease and relaxation.

So it was and so it is with legendary Arabians and Half Arabians that take people's breath away: FF Summer Storm, Hucklebey Berry+/, A Temptation, Red Tape+//, Gai Argosy+//, Allience+//, Aploz+//, Apollopalooza, Zodiac Matador+, Huckleberry Bey++, and MHR Nobility.

Arabian Saddle Seat divides into three quite distinctive categories: Country English Pleasure, English Pleasure, and Park.

COUNTRY ENGLISH PLEASURE

The Country horse is singled out by his attitude. He goes forward comfortably and calmly in a free, floating stride with grace and style, his alert ears reflecting a willing, but not overly ambitious, attitude. No less athletic or bright in his way of going than his other English counterparts, he has a quieter demeanor.

"Country English Pleasure is like English Pleasure going to boarding school," describes Jim Lowe, Arabian trainer and judge.

"It's not how high they trot, but how they trot high," says judge, trainer, and national champion Michael Damianos. "They go unassuming and unforced, with light contact, without resistance."

One of the challenges of Country English Pleasure is to maintain this lovely and fluid picture throughout the class. While he has consid-

Aploz+// shows the mannerly elegance of a Country Pleasure horse. He is shown by Gary Dearth. PHOTO BY MIKE FERRARA.

erable motion, his work looks effortless and his attitude is willing. Foremost, his manners are impeccable. He is quiet in the bridle. He walks flat footed as if he could walk for hours. And yet he must work with vigor at the trot and canter.

"My mantra when I'm riding a Country horse is that I could do this all day long, at whatever gait," says Mary Trowbridge. "The horse is enjoying what he's doing, with an 'ears up' attitude, and you are set in cruise control."

"Winding up is not the challenge; it's coming back down that is the challenge," points out Gary Dearth. "He can't make mistakes and he can't look like he is on the verge of making mistakes."

While the Country horse has the upright conformation of an English horse, he does not have quite the high action of the English Pleasure and Park participants. High action includes but is not exclusive to the elevation of the horse's knees. It also describes the horse's overall animation, impulsion (energy and strength), balance, degree of collection, and attitude.

English Pleasure

Here the ambition steps up a notch, and here Arabians excel. Good English Pleasure horses are by nature smart and ambitious. They

HF Mister Chips+ began his career as an English Pleasure horse. As he developed greater power, brilliance, and presence, he became a Park horse competitor with his rider Chris Culbreth. PHOTO BY HOWARD SCHATZBERG.

are so motivated and eager to go forward that for some walking becomes difficult. He looks ready. "He has a sense of energy that starts in the hind limbs, goes through his spine to his neck, to his mouth, through the reins to the rider's hands, and he looks like he's ready to hear 'cluck, cluck' and trot off or pick up the canter. He's ready to work because he's ambitious," describes Michael Damianos.

PARK

The Park horse is the kid in the class whose hand is always up first. He pushes the edge of the envelope whenever he enters the ring. He is the overachiever distinguished by his ambition and animation. He is the horse that everyone wanted to take to the park to show off for the neighbors.

He has "dirt-moving elevation and dig and drive in his hind legs," describes Mary Trowbridge. "A great Park horse wants to go to the ultimate. But you are teaching him to wait. You are saying to the horse, 'Here is how you do it correctly, do it soft, do at a low speed.' Then you teach him to be ultimately responsive, and

When Saddle Seat trainers and judges recall great Park horses, Red Tape, ridden by Mary Trowbridge, is usually on the list. PHOTO BY ROB HESS.

when you do say to go for it, he will exhibit his own dynamic and energy and exhilaration."

"In a Park horse you see a natural vitality, bounce, and spring, the ability to be loose and move freely," says Chris Culbreth, Arabian judge and national champion trainer. "He is happy going forward hard and strong, big and animated."

Not many horses compete in Park because few have the mental and physical gifts to perform well in the expected manner. Park horses must be very strong, very fit, and be very well cared for to perform at the expected level.

How Do We Judge?

Going from Country to English to Park, we essentially move from more to more to more. Class specifications from the U.S. Equestrian Federation (USEF) Rule Book detail the difference.

COUNTRY ENGLISH PLEASURE: "A quiet, responsive mouth is paramount. All gaits must be performed with willingness and obvious ease, cadence, balance and smoothness." Judging in order of importance: **attitude**, **manners**, performance, quality, conformation.

ENGLISH PLEASURE: "It is imperative that the horse display a pleasurable attitude. To this end, all gaits must be performed with willingness and obvious ease, cadence, balance and smoothness." Judging in order of importance: **manners, performance**, attitude, quality, conformation.

PARK: "The horse is to give a brilliant performance, with style, presence, finish, balance and cadence. Judging in order of importance: **brilliant performance, presence**, quality, manners, conformation.

Notice that "attitude" is not listed for the Park horse and that "presence" is not listed for either the Country English or English Pleasure horse. Also note that the description for Park horse does not mention the word "pleasure" in its name. This does not mean that riding a Park horse is not a terrific event. In fact, the term "adrenaline rush" is often associated with the ride.

COMPARISON OF COUNTRY ENGLISH,
ENGLISH PLEASURE, AND PARK
Designed by Michael Damianos

COUNTRY	ENGLISH	PARK
Free-flowing stride	Brisk, animated stride	Brisk, animated stride
Comfortable, calm, with grace and style	Goes forward with authority, grace, and elegance	Goes forward with authority, grace, and elegance
Bright and alert, remains attentive and responsive	Bright, confident, and responsive	Brilliant, confident, reactive
Attitude is bright, confident, responsive, and obedient	Attitude: good temperament, willing and inherent ambition	Performs gaits in spectacular fashion
Unassuming and unforced	Spirit of a show horse	Physical talent to perform tasks explosively

COUNTRY	ENGLISH	PARK
Desire to please, quiet nature, and easy	Power	Confidence that borders on arrogance
Discipline and finesse	Charisma, strength and finesse	Spirit of an overachiever

Conformation

The ideal Saddle Seat Arabian meets the following conformation and gait guidelines. All three disciplines require the same basic conformation. Horses that excel in one or the other vary more in the extent of their ability to collect and elevate, the extreme and intensity in which they move, and their mental traits.

Any English performance horse must be a beautiful Arabian with a lovely head and a bright, alert expression in his Arabian-type face, showing interest in his surroundings. Well-set ears on a horse that uses them in an expressive, forward-looking manner is a bonus.

As for his overall balance, longitudinally (back to front) the horse should be built uphill with his withers higher than his croup.

The shape and suppleness of the neck is more important than the length. It should be upright and well-arched, with a long, open, well-defined throatlatch that blends smoothly into the neck, allowing the horse to more easily carry his head high with a flexible poll. The base of the neck should be set high on the chest.

A sloping shoulder creates a loose, round moving front end, with legs that move forward and upward. An extremely steep scapula, the bone that runs from the withers to the point of the shoulder, produces short strides, often a rough ride, and possible soundness issues because of the resulting pounding nature of the gait. Look for a long, steep humerus, the bone that runs from the point of the shoulder to the elbow. The elbow should stand away from the body to provide more front leg freedom. In good movers, the front limb will show more elevation because of greater flexion in the elbow joint, according to Dr. Hilary Clayton in her book *The Dynamic Horse: A Biomechanical Guide to Equine Movement and Performance.*

Classical, sound leg construction is critical. The extreme nature of the Saddle Seat horse's movement, with its great range of motion, can create stress on less than well-designed legs. Feet should be big and round with wide heels. Here the phrase "No feet, no horse" is quite relevant.

A relatively short back, in balance with the rest of the horse's body and with well-defined withers, aids collection.

Most trainers start their evaluation of a Saddle Seat prospect by looking for strong, deeply muscled, round hindquarters, which are the source of the power to drive forward and collect. A long croup with some slope aids the range of motion. The hind leg should angle under the horse with a good size, low set hock. A long line from the point of the hip to the point of buttocks is desirable. The line from the hip socket to the stifle joint should be longer than the line from the stifle joint to the hock.

Size is irrelevant to the outcome of these classes. In fact, some trainers contend smaller Arabians are handier, lower to the ground, and therefore more athletic than larger one. A 14.2-hand Arabian, The Noblest, won National Champion English Pleasure with a 6'3" rider.

"Though a big trot, long neck, and good tail carriage matter, the physical construction of the horse is the most important element," says Jim Lowe.

The Gaits
An Arabian Saddle Seat horse generally moves loose and free-moving, with big, fluid, ground-covering strides. The motion of the hind legs nearly matches that of the front legs. Michael Damianos reminds

viewers, "If you are taking a protractor and watching just the front legs, you are missing the point of all Saddle Seat classes."

As in all disciplines, the strides should be even and equal in speed, length, and degree of collection.

WALK: The walk is a four-beat gait with at least one foot on the ground at all times. It is flat-footed, with the heel striking the ground first, followed by the toe. The Country walk is ground-covering and relaxed. The English Pleasure walk is brisk, with good reach. The Park walk is cadenced, animated, brisk, and brilliant.

TROT: Though judges are instructed to consider each gait equally, the trot is the dominant gait of the classes. The front legs should first bend at the knee, then the fetlock in a round, curling, flexible motion referred to as "folding." For a competitive trot, the front leg should move at or over level, meaning the forearm extends upward, knee flexed, until it is at least parallel to the ground. The hind leg also should show good height.

In the collected gaits, the hind legs do not step further underneath themselves. "What actually changes is that the hind limbs do not push out so far behind the horse. Therefore, it is important to observe limb position and angulation" when the hoof contacts the ground, according to Dr. Clayton.

The Country trot is elastic and free, relaxed and easy-going. High action is to be penalized. In English Pleasure, the trot is performed at medium speed in moderate collection, mannerly, cadenced, balanced, and free-moving. The Park trot is described in the USEF Rule Book as bold, brilliant, animated, natural, and cadenced. While appearing effortless, the forelegs' airy motion combines with the powerful, well-raised, driving hind legs.

STRONG TROT: This power gait is faster and strong than the normal trot. The power comes out of collection. The horse is not strung out. He reaches forward and lengthens his stride.

CANTER: This gait is active, smooth and unhurried, straight, and on the inside lead. English Pleasure canter is a step more collected than the Country canter. The Park canter is light and airy with more elevation than its counterparts. Judges look for a gait that is mannerly, cadenced, balanced, and free-moving.

HAND GALLOP: An extension of the canter, this gait has a longer, not just faster, stride. Extreme speed is penalized.

SHOEING

The Arabian division specifically requires that shoes measure a maximum dimension of ⅜ inch thick by 1⅛ inches wide. The maximum toe length is 4½ inches for purebreds and 5 inches for Half Arabians and Anglo-Arabians.

Exempt from these rules are horses competing in Dressage, Hunter, Jumper, Eventing, Combined Pleasure Driving (Carriage Driving), Sport Horse, and Working Western. While most horses in other disciplines are shod in an average manner, horses in the English division are often shod with pads and a longer toe, but within the legal limits.

The longer toe encourages the horse to break over more slowly and increases the motion of the front legs. "Our shoeing rules don't give latitude to change movement. These horses trot high because of God-given talent," says Gary Dearth.

Pads are often used to protect the bottom of the foot. "The higher they trot, the harder they drop the foot," explains Dearth. "The pad keeps the foot more comfortable."

Temperament

The way the English horses carry themselves equals conformation plus what is inside them and what they have been taught. Mary Trowbridge looks for horses that are bright, thoughtful, and want to learn. Trainability is most important to Jim Lowe.

"An English horse that is hot or nervous and high strung is very hard to train," contends Gary Dearth. "Though they have desire, they have trouble turning it off. I look for a lot of desire and a horse that likes to go forward. You want one that is ambitious: that way the more trained and stronger they become, the more they do."

The Saddle Seat horse must focus on his job, and he must stay relaxed in order to move in a soft and round, but engaged manner. "The best movers are the loosest. It has nothing to do with tension," says Chris Culbreth.

These horses have ambition, presence, and a "look at me" attitude. They move around the arena as if they own it.

Riding the Class

The attraction of riding Saddle Seat is locked up in the essence of the gaits: forward, animated, and intense. The challenge rests with the necessity to keep these sensitive and powerful horses, moving with speed and intensity, in balance, at ease, and relaxed. The rider must be simultaneously allowing and controlling, patient and yet clear with her aids. For the horse to perform at his best, she must keep him out of trouble without getting in his way. She must put him in a place where he is in balance and feels confident that he can perform with ultimate effort and show himself as the most flamboyant horse in the ring.

"It's the wonderful feeling of walking on a living tightrope," Mary Trowbridge describes. "While you have all this power and intensity, the least little movement by the rider or inappropriate increase in pressure on the bridle brings about a huge change in the horse.

"Balance is everything: how the horse balances on his hind end, how he elevates his front end, how he reaches to the bridle, then comes off it. He continues to go forward, get to it, and come off it. The rider balances in the stirrups and saddle, so as not to fall behind the horse's movement. She takes care not to put too much pressure on the bit, so as not to disrupt the horse's ability to reach under himself."

The degree of challenge increases the more powerful and high-moving the horse is, from Country to English to Park. Like with a race car, the faster you are driving around the track, the more precise you have to be to keep the car on the path.

In any arena class, the ultimate responsibility for how the horse shows himself falls with the rider. In a Saddle Seat class, that responsibility becomes weightier because the rider must make decisions and react quickly without disturbing the horse's ability to respond in a fluid and balanced manner. Showing an English horse is fast-moving, multitask riding. Because there is little time for thoughtful evaluation, seat-of-the-pants instinct is sometimes the best tool.

Gene LaCroix, legendary Arabian trainer and breeder, describes the best Saddle Seat riders. "The ones that make the great horses are on the inside of their horses. They are not on the outside of those horses; they are riding the inside of them. Someone on the outside of the horse is on top of that horse, staying balanced on that horse. When you are on the inside, you are with the horse, influencing his gait, balance, and carriage. You are not worried about staying on top. You are part of that horse. You ride every stride. You know what he's doing through this body, from front to back, through his neck and through his face. It's easy to ride a good English horse once you understand the horse, the discipline, and the feel. You must have natural balance or you can't feel the horse all through your body. When the feeling is right, you're not on the outside; you're on the inside."

Mistakes come quickly in these classes. Some of those mistakes include:

1. Speed over form and balance.
2. Little or no difference between strong trot and normal trot.
3. Extreme motion in front and dragging motion behind.
4. Riding with the pack in the arena.
5. Ignoring the importance of transitions between gaits.
6. Darting in and out of traffic and sacrificing cadence.
7. Fitting a horse into an English frame when he is better

suited for another job.

8. Allowing the horse to become strung out, not collected.
9. Overriding and going for it too much.
10. Showing an unfit horse, especially for a show at the end of the year, or a national competition.

Appointments

In all disciplines, appointments refer to the horse's tack and the rider/handler's clothes.

Tack

BRIDLES: A Park horse shows only in a single curb, curb and snaffle, or Pelham bit. An English and Country English Pleasure horse has the option of the above or a single snaffle. A double bridle, however, is what most exhibitors choose.

SADDLE: The USEF Rule Book calls for an "English-type saddle. No forward seat saddles allowed. Girths either leather, web, string or suitable material." Many English competitors ride in a Saddle Seat saddle (commonly referred to as a "cutback") because the design of the pommel gives greater front end freedom of movement. Furthermore, the saddle with its flat seat places the rider further behind the wither than, say, a Hunt Seat saddle. The flaps are wide and straight, with no knee rolls.

Clothes

While your outfit is not the subject of evaluation, you might dress as you would for a job interview or a business meeting. A clean, neat, co-ordinated appearance demonstrates respect for the judge and the show. An elegant horse with such great style deserves an equally elegant rider.

The USEF Rule book suggests a conservative colored (black, blue, grey, beige, or brown) Saddle Seat suit with matching jacket and jodhpurs. Fashions change, and one year brighter colors with plaid or prints, or vests festooned with glitter, appear, while the next year dusty blue and chocolate brown suits with matching vests (an optional item) are the preferred choices. The base color should look good with your horse and yourself.

The day coat and pants should fit differently when you ride than when you walk around the show grounds. When you sit in riding position, the coat should drape well, with the shoulders and waist feeling comfortable. With your arms bent, the shirt cuffs should not show below the sleeve. The bottom of the coat should reach down to just above the bend in your knee, and the vent should allow the jacket to part around the saddle cantle. Pants should fit loosely in the seat and legs. The pant legs cover the boots. For riding, elastic jodhpur straps attach to buttons or clips just inside the bottom of the pant legs, then pass under the boot heel to prevent the pants from riding up your leg. Off the horse, the pants will be much too long and loose.

Three hat styles appear in the ring: the derby, similar to an English bowler; the snap brim, a fedora type reminiscent of the 1930s and '40s with the brim turned down in the front and up in the back; and the homburg, a narrower brim, usually turned up on the sides. While women seem to prefer derbies and homburgs, men tend to the informal snap brim and to the homburg for a formal look. Hat color should match the suit.

Ankle-high jodhpur boots come in black, brown, and patent leather. Gloves should blend with your suit for a stylish look and to make your hands less obvious. Leather fits well and gives you a more consistent hold on the reins. Spurs, if needed, should be English type.

A starched, plain shirt and tie, of average size, enhance the business look of the suit. A bow tie with a wing collar shirt is acceptable for formal wear in evening classes at large shows. For Park horse classes after 6 P.M. or championship classes, riders don a tuxedo-type jacket, formal jodhpurs, and top hat. A dark saddle suit and derby also work well.

---

*BASK++
(Witraz x Balalajka)
(1956–1979)

When Poland-born *Bask++ entered the American show ring, a new standard for the Arabian Saddle Seat horse was born. In the skillful showing and marketing hands of the LaCroix family, this different and exquisite bay horse became one of the most prominent Arabians in the second half of the twentieth century and into the twenty-first century because of who he was as an individual and because of the influence he had as a sire.

*Bask++ was the first Arabian National Champion Halter Stallion (1964) to win a national championship under saddle, which he did in the Park class (1965). He sired 1,050 registered purebred foals and 196 U.S. and Canadian National winners.

In 1962 Dr. Eugene LaCroix, then a breeder of Crabbet-bred horses, traveled to Poland with his teenage son, Gene, to purchase horses. When presented with the spectacular bay stallion, lean from just two months off the racetrack, "you could see he was different. By his conformation, but mostly it was his spirit and athleticism," recalls Gene LaCroix, who became one of the most influential Saddle Seat trainers and breeders in the breed.

"When he was relaxed in his stall, he could look like the most beautiful Thoroughbred you ever saw. You wouldn't know his mental characteristics were right for Saddle Seat. He was the most kind, relaxed horse. Kids could walk in his stall. When he came out, he picked himself up, grew two hands and you couldn't find a more upright horse," says LaCroix. "He loved to work. When he headed for the gate at a show, he would build and build, getting blown up and full of himself."

The *Arabian Horse World* magazine described his movement as light and precise, like a ballet dancer's. Bright and trainable, in the show ring, he knew he was the best, and he put fire and brilliance into this work. "He could hold his form with a lot of speed," says LaCroix. "He was an exciting horse that brought the crowd to their feet."

The key in his conformation that changed the English horse was the length of his front legs compared to his hind legs, which at the time were shorter on most Arabians. He had a particularly short cannon bone behind and very low hocks. His back was strong and his neck long and beautifully shaped. These elements gave him uphill, vertical carriage, making it easy for him to collect and express power and animation.

He passed on to his descendants his vital spirit, a beautiful and harmonious body style, and a high-stepping, athletic way of going.

One such horse was FF Summer Storm (*Bask x Zarahba), a mare of exceptional beauty, who, though she died in 1989, is remembered today as the consummate Arabian English Pleasure horse.

Gene LaCroix rode her to the 1980 U.S. National English Pleasure championship. "She was extreme. She framed and carried herself so wonderfully. She had *Bask's long, beautiful neck and a beautiful head, but also long front legs. She delivered her motion effortlessly with a very open stride. She had a normal trot and a definite transition to strong trot—truly two trots. I don't think the judges have seen that since."

Others recall her as dynamic and yet performing with ease in all that she did. Moving brightly and with great power, she seemed to have two times more to give of her talent. She moved as if all her joints were oiled, equally supple and articulating both front and back ends. She had great style, and she was gorgeous.

CHAPTER FIVE

HUNTER PLEASURE/ SHOW HACK

"The horse moved like a dancer, which is not surprising. A horse is a beautiful animal, but it is perhaps most remarkable because it moves as if it always hears music."

—Mark Helprin, *A Winter's Tale*

IMPORTED FROM ENGLAND, HUNTER PLEASURE AND SHOW Hack are relative newcomers to the U.S. Arabian show scene that have increased the breadth of versatility of the multidimensional breed. Riding horses with characteristic or "typical" Arabian way of going, Hunter Pleasure competitors flood the show ring in huge numbers. At the other end of the spectrum, the smaller numbers of English Show Hack horses arrive with specialized movement and precision training.

At their inception, both classes began under the misconception that they were homes for horses that missed the boat in other disciplines.

Hunter Pleasure was offered as a class for Country English Pleasure horses that did not have enough motion to be competitive and Western Pleasure horses that did not go slow. Imitative of the English hunter scene, horses initially had to jump two rounds. Some could jump quite well, and they also were winning in classes over fences.

Show Hack originated in England in the 1940s as a preparatory class for horses not ready to compete in dressage. Known as the "ridden" class, it became popular in Canada, was picked up on the West Coast, and filtered through the rest of the country. At one time

Show Hack was perceived as another place for Hunter Pleasure competitors to ride at a show, or for dressage riders who were desirous of a spot in the main arena. In those days a debate raged as to whether this class was judged too much like a group dressage class or as a hunter class. Others said it was neither.

Today both classes have leaped out of their toddler stages and matured into distinctive domains requiring a specific type of horse and training to succeed in their specialized arenas. Today a Western Pleasure horse would not be competitive in Hunter Pleasure, and most Hunter Pleasure horses do not fit into Show Hack.

HUNTER PLEASURE

Hunter Pleasure has roots in the hunt field and its strong traditions. When these horses are in a hand gallop, the arena transforms into a cross-country chase enhanced by the Arabian's distinct look. Not only does this horse move in a forward, relaxed, swinging, fluid gait and manner, with his ears up, as if he is joyfully looking for a fence, but he looks like an athlete that could easily and happily jump that illusory fence.

At almost any Arabian show, Hunter Pleasure classes are the largest, sometimes attracting over twenty competitors per class at a local Class A show. The reasons for its remarkable popularity are manifold.

For one, Hunter Pleasure horses are generally more affordable than Saddle Seat Arabians, especially Park horses, whose prices are high because there are not very many of them. More Arabians move in the manner desirable for a Hunter Pleasure horse. Therefore, supply and demand determine the lower price.

Yet more relevant, the Hunter Pleasure horse is most inviting to amateurs because of his trainable frame when compared to that of the more extreme English or Western Pleasure horse. The Hunter Pleasure horse is characteristically quieter and calmer, with a temperament and gaits that do not require as much finesse and tuning. He does not

Safire Star+// served many times as a National Hunter Pleasure Champion in the amateur division with his owner Katie Russell. PHOTO BY MIKE FERRARA.

need the close and continual watchful eye of a professional. An amateur who works on her own or only part-time with a trainer may do quite well with this horse.

A Hunter Pleasure class, however, is hardly a pushover. Like any competitive venue, it calls for the right horse with correct training that performs a specialized job.

Conformation

A good Hunter Pleasure Arabian tends to have a more rectangular than square shape to his body and is more level than uphill in overall balance. While his neck is characteristically arched, it sets neither high nor low out of the shoulder, adding to his horizontal look. He has considerable substance. "You don't want a tiny-legged horse that's so refined that he looks like he couldn't withstand work," says trainer Cynthia Burkman, a multinational winner in Hunter Pleasure and Show Hack.

While exhibiting Arabian type, this horse is rounder, fancier, and usually prettier than the hunters that compete over fences on the open, all-breed hunter/jumper circuit dominated by Thoroughbreds and warmblood breeds.

The significance of size relates more to the horse's stride than to his height. Cynthia Burkman's 2004 National Purebred Hunter Pleasure champion WF Reining Heir is over 16 hands. NDL Pericles+// (see sidebar) is 14.2 hands.

Temperament

Entering the arena with a relaxed attitude, he is a laid-back, free-moving, happy-go-lucky guy who must at the same time be bold, confident, forward thinking, and willing to drive off his hindquarters. The extreme size of these classes makes it necessary that this guy be level-headed, especially when he is faced with so many horses charging around the arena in the faster gaits.

Movement

Hunter Pleasure strides are long, stretchy, and ground-covering, creating forward, fluid, and swinging movement. Envision a horse galloping across an English field on a cool foggy day anxious to get home to warm bran mash.

The walk is frequently ignored in training, but its success is critical in this class. It should show as four beats and be straight, regular, and flat-footed, but also unconstrained and relaxed, with good reach and ground cover. Burkman allows her horse to stretch out his neck a bit so that he walks out in a longer stride.

Two beats—straight, regular, mannerly, cadenced, and balanced—characterize the trot, which is performed at a medium speed in a free-moving, ground-covering stride. His free-moving shoulder allows the Hunter Pleasure horse to swing up and out with his front legs. With a strong, driving hind end, his back legs reach forward and underneath him rather than with the up-and-down hock flexion of a Saddle Seat horse.

How desirable is a "fancy" trot, with how much knee action? One school seeks to emulate the open Hunter/Jumper circuit with a flatter stride. Others look for some roll of the knee and extension in the trot. In favor of the latter, Burkman says, "We don't want our Arabs in a Hunt class moving flat with their noses out. It's not pretty."

Wendy Potts agrees. "You don't want extreme knee that snaps up and out because then the movement won't look effortless and ground covering. But our Hunter Pleasure horses have more roll than hunters. They move more like the Grand Prix jumpers."

The canter should be three beats, even, smooth, unhurried, and straight on both leads. A big, forward, and bounding stride wins the day. Up and down and choppy does not.

The hand gallop is a long, free, ground-covering stride shown while the horse remains controlled, mannerly, and straight on both leads.

Overall Balance, Carriage, and Frame

The USEF Rule Book requires that "the neck should be carried lower, and the head should be carried in a more relaxed manner with less bend at the poll and the horse should be in a generally longer frame than that of an English Pleasure, Country English Pleasure or Show Hack Horse. High headed horses and horses behind the vertical must be penalized."

While he is engaged in his hindquarters, stepping underneath himself and moving forward in a regular rhythm, the Hunter Pleasure horse carries himself in a horizontal frame with his head in a balanced, relaxed, vertical position, soft and flexed in the poll and maintaining contact with the bit. He is neither behind the vertical nor behind the bit.

The position of the horse's head and neck depends on his conformation. "Compare the height of the head and neck to the body structure," explains Burkman. "Some go higher, some lower." Care should be taken not to destroy his fluid movement and the use of his hindquarters in attempting to create a headset.

In the Arena

In this class, a judge looks for the tradition of the hunt field enhanced by Arabian type. His criteria, in order of importance, are manners, performance, suitability as a hunter, quality, and conformation. Classes for junior horses five years old and under are judged first on quality, then performance, suitability, manners, and conformation.

Trainer and National Championship winner Wendy Potts recalls a ride that so perfectly fit the criteria. She was on Half Arabian Buried Treasure, and she won the Canadian National Championship in 1999. "I couldn't ask for it to be different. Whatever I asked him, he did. And he wasn't always a completely honest horse. He could act out and then he wouldn't win. When he was great, he was unbeatable. That ride he was soft and responsive. If I asked him to go on, he'd move right up. If I needed him to come back, he came right back, which could at other times be like stopping a freight train. It was a powerful feeling."

Problems in this class usually appear as:

1. The horse is behind the bit, held with tight reins, and looking down at the ground.
2. The horse moves too flat.
3. The horse moves with his nose stretched out and is not round enough in the bridle.
4. The horse is long and low and ridden with flapping loose reins without contact.
5. The horse loses his relaxed, easygoing way and becomes tense in the large classes.

Though the rider is not judged in this class, how a person rides affects the overall picture and how well the horse goes. In the correct hunt seat position, the rider sits with a closed hip angle, bent in the waist, and slightly forward to better stay with the rhythm of the horse. Heels are down and toes are slightly out so that calves have contact with the horse.

The rider may have problems because:

1. Her stirrups are too long.
2. She grips with her knees and holds her toes forward with the weight on the outside of the foot. This position prevents her lower legs from contacting the horse's sides.
3. She sits too much at the vertical by not closing her hip angle. "If you went to a fence like that and the horse stopped, you would go right over his head," says Wendy Potts.

Preparation at Home

Controlling the horse's speed in a crowd and maintaining forward, ground-covering movement in a relaxed, fluid, effortless manner are the challenges of this class, which can be met at home by teaching the horse to work off his hindquarters and to soften in the bridle.

"People think that to get him long and low, they put on draw reins," explains Arabian trainer and judge Wendy Gruskiewicz. "Not so. This tends to cause him to dump all his weight on his front end or to stop pushing from the rear end and go behind the vertical. He then trots and hand gallops much too fast and in shorter strides."

Longing the horse with side reins attached from a surcingle or saddle to the rings of a snaffle bit will begin to develop the muscles necessary for a rounded topline and for engaged hindquarters. The first few times out, the side reins should be attached fairly loosely to encourage the horse to stretch forward and down in a relaxed manner. As time goes on and the horse increases his strength, gradually shorten the length of the side reins and change their point of attachment so that the horse works in a comfortable, round hunter frame, with a slightly arched neck, flexion at the poll, head on the vertical, hind legs reaching underneath, and always in a rhythmic, cadenced gait. The horse should always move and reach forward both in his gaits and his body.

Under saddle, ask the horse to change speeds and extend and collect in all gaits, always moving forward to the bit and softening. This skill will give you the tools to put your horse where you want him in the arena. The transitions are as important as the gait or pace itself. They will develop his ability to carry himself in a forward, ground-covering stride, in a medium frame, engaging the hindquarters and not falling on the forehand.

Dressage figures will help achieve this goal as well. They include bending, circling, half circles, figure eights, serpentines, counter canter, direction changes, and leg yields.

Tack, Clothes, Grooming

In the spirit of the chase, Hunter Pleasure encourages a conservative presentation of horse and rider. The traditional, workman look makes the horse, not the outfit, shine. Any style changes are subtle. For example, a lemon yellow or tangerine shirt adds color and a little fun while staying traditional. A minority of exhibitors fill their need for more pizzazz with decorative clothes and saddle pads, but do not mistake this voice as a shout. Most contend that this is not the class in which to make a statement or set yourself apart because of the clear intent expressed in the USEF Rule Book.

SADDLE: The USEF Rule Book recommends a forward seat type and prohibits a cutback saddle. The girth may be leather, web string, or suitable material.

BRIDLE: Acceptable bits include snaffle, Pelham, full bridle, or Kimberwicke. Only hunter-type brow bands and cavessons are allowed; saddle seat-style colored brow bands and cavesson, figure eight, drop, and flash nosebands are not. Martingales and tie-downs are not permitted.

CLOTHES: Conservative is the watchword. Informal attire of suitable material for hunting is required. It consists of a conservatively colored coat of any tweed or Melton, breeches or jodhpurs, and boots. A dark-colored hunting cap, derby, or protective headgear is mandatory. Spurs and crops are optional.

To help the horse shine through the crowd, grooming must be impeccable.

MANES AND TAILS: While the USEF Rule Book states that braiding the mane and tail is optional, rarely are manes left unbraided at recognized shows. Probably half the horses have their manes pulled and braided in the traditional hunter style; the others keep their long manes tied up in a French braid. The choice depends on the shape and length of the horse's neck and which style makes it look longer and cleaner. If the horse is showing in another division which requires a long, natural mane, the French braid is the only option. (See the sidebar on mane and tail braiding in chapter 8.)

ENGLISH SHOW HACK

Show Hack is a demanding, beautiful class, spotlighting a supple and elastic horse who easily shifts in balance from a shortened, active outline to a lengthened, power-driven, ground-eating silhouette, and then back to the shorter, more vertical carriage. Absent of tightness, evasion, or resistance, in harmony with his rider, the Show Hack horse executes with elegance, animation, and vitality ten paces or versions of the basic three gaits.

This clean, fine-limbed horse in a class that asks him to be at once flexible and powerful, active and obedient, light and engaged, demonstrates the union of high-level training with an excellent quality horse.

Wendy Gruskiewicz reminisces about her most memorable ride on her horse Gwalzzat, who had been Park horse, English Pleasure horse, Hunter, Show Hack Top Ten horse at the U.S. Nationals, and Prix St. George dressage competitor.

"When I'm showing, I usually don't know what's going on outside the arena, who is standing at the rail, who is watching, or who is in the class. I just pay attention to my horse and the ground in front of me. But I remember walking into the ring feeling incredibly elegant, as if the world could stop for a few minutes. I could actually look at people in the stands and smile at them and enjoy the moment because everything was so perfect, so right and so pretty, and we were very much in tune with each other. He seemed to know what to do even before I asked him. I don't even remember cueing him. He was an extension of my mind."

Overall Balance and Look

"People don't always agree with the style of the horse that wins this class," says Cynthia Burkman. People do agree, however, that it is demanding. "We want it to be pretty, effortless, exciting, and correctly executed. And the Show Hack horse should look like an Arabian, not a Thoroughbred. It's a whole picture where you say 'man, that's beautiful.'"

Many of these horses come from the Country English Pleasure arena. They often do well because their animated stride and uphill frame allow them to put the "show" into Show Hack. The downside for this kind of horse is his tendency to stay in one position with his head, neck, and shoulders. The Show Hack horse must change his entire frame, not just his legs, and demonstrate longitudinal flexibility when moving from collection to extension to collection. He must have the elasticity to stretch his topline into a longer frame and extend his gait, and to contract into a shorter frame for collected paces. The Country English horse may also be hindered by his neck, which is carried fairly high and tight in the bridle, and again, not the Show Hack frame.

NDL Pericles+// demonstrates the athletic ability to collect in this Show Hack performance with Wendy Potts on board. PHOTO BY JEFF JANSON.

Some Hunter Pleasure horses do well at Class A shows, but more and more the judges find the hunter movement and frame lacking sufficient animation and presence.

Medium and upper level dressage horses, beginning at Third Level, find a home in Show Hack because of their experience with extension and collection. However, because the class demands more animated gaits than many Arabian dressage horses show, fewer dressage competitors enter the English Show Hack classes.

Conformation

Superior quality is so important in this class that in the days when time restraints did not prohibit it, horses were unsaddled for conformation inspection.

The Show Hack horse is usually substantial. Many are taller than 15.1 hands. He should have a short back and low hocks well placed under him to facilitate collection. Add to that a sloping, free shoulder easily lifted, and a pretty, long, elegant neck with a clean throatlatch that allows him to round his neck and his back.

An elastic loin is necessary to coil and allow the croup to drop and the hind legs to step under and push off with power. A strong loin allows the horse to carry weight on his hindquarters, which is necessary for collected gaits.

Temperament

While this horse must have a quite agreeable temperament, it differs from that of the happy-go-lucky Hunter Pleasure horse. On one hand, he needs sparkle, brilliance, and the desire to show off. On the other hand, he must be quite trainable and tolerant of the great demands put on him from the variety of paces asked in this class. And he must be capable of a high degree of concentration.

For example, in a class of fifteen horses, the judge calls for the collected canter. Your horse is the only one carrying out the necessary collection. The other fourteen horses are cruising along in the normal canter and are likely streaming past your horse, who is concentrating to keep his collection and his lead. You want your horse animated in his collection, but not so animated that he becomes frazzled when these other horses charge past him.

Likely once a good Show Hack Arabian learns the variety of paces, he will like the class because it is an opportunity to show off.

Gaits

The gaits require the animation of a Country English horse and the balance and engagement of a middle or upper-level dressage horse.

In the Arena

The judge will ask in his order of preference for normal (working), extended, and collected paces at the walk, trot, and canter and for the hand gallop. The criteria in order of importance are manners, performance, quality, and conformation.

This chart outlines required gaits, their paces, and their problems.

WALK

is a four-beat, straight, regular, and flat-footed gait.

Normal: Regular, unconstrained, moving energetically and calmly forward.
Problems: Tension, behind the vertical.

Collected: Strides are higher and shorter than the normal walk.
Problems:

1. Lateral-gaited, pacing (incorrect walk rhythm).
2. The rider slows the walk, sometimes to nearly a crawl instead of collecting it. At a collected walk, the horse marches along quite actively. He moves in a shorter stride, not a slower tempo.

Extended: The frame and stride lengthen while the rider keeps a light rein contact. As a result, the horse covers more ground.
Problems:

1. Rushing, in which the horse takes more and shorter strides within a given area instead of longer, ground-covering strides.
2. The horse does not stretch his frame.

TROT

is a two-beat, free-moving, straight gait in which the rider maintains light contact with the horse's mouth at all times.

Normal: With the rider posting, the gait is characterized by its balance, cadence, clarity, and lightness.
Problem: Regularity of the stride.

Collected: Like an accordion, both the front end and the hind end come in, and the horse becomes shorter from front to back. He coils his loins, lowers his haunches by bending his joints more, lifts his shoulder, and the stride becomes shorter. The horse becomes taller. The gait is not as ground-covering as the normal trot, but is more active. The rider sits the trot.

Problem: Rider slows the horse, either because she considers the slower trot correct or because she has difficulty sitting a collected trot in which the horse is using his body fully.

Extended: The horse lengthens his stride and frame, with maximum reach from the shoulders and impulsion from the hindquarters. While remaining light in the hands of the posting rider, he remains cadenced and rhythmic.

Problems:

1. Confusion over the difference between extension and speed. The great Show Hack horses may look slower at this pace because of the hesitation or suspension in the gait. The suspension and added expression can be seen in the more pronounced articulation of the hind leg and the increased time the horse spends in the air rather than on the ground.

2. This pace is not the same as the strong trot in English Pleasure, which shows increased speed and tends to flatten out the gait when it gains ground.

CANTER

Normal: Light, matched strides moving forward without hesitancy.

Problems: Tension, speed.

Collected: The collected canter is characterized by engagement, carrying power of the hindquarters, and lightness and suppleness of the forehand. "The neck is more raised and arched than in normal canter as the head approaches the vertical line, never moving behind it." USEF Rule Book.

Problem: The collected canter should be bounding. If the rider keeps it too slow, the horse's legs do not have time to bound underneath him. Collection is derived from impulsion; impulsion is derived from the power of the hindquarters.

Extended: Remaining light in the rider's hands and cadenced, the horse lengthens his frame and stride, with greater impulsion from behind.

Problem: Running is extension without impulsion.

Hand Gallop: While the hand gallop is a long, free, ground-covering stride, like an extended canter, it is looser and more horizontal than the canter.

Problem: As in other classes that ask for the hand gallop, control, manners, straightness, and maintaining the correct lead become issues. Judges will penalize extreme speed.

Work at Home

The essence of this class is the horse's training, athleticism, and accomplishment. The horse who travels in and between gaits with fluidity, balance, expression, elegance, and beauty, in harmony with the rider, wins the class.

Because the judge will reward true extensions and true collection, preparation at home should focus on sharpening the differences among the normal, collected, and extended strides. Equally important are precise and clean transitions between gaits and paces. Your goal should be to create transitions that are at the same time powerful and soft, a difficult but rewarding combination.

Your horse should feel as if, should you ask for a little more, he could easily give it to you. This feeling and the accompanying beautiful look will happen when the horse honestly and willingly responds to your requests, not when he anticipates the gait or pace you need. When he clearly understands your cues, he will respond quickly, with vitality and without tension. Swishing the tail, bracing against the bit, hollowing the back, and opening the mouth are signs of disagreement.

Seat and legs influence extension, collection, and transitions. Therefore, the rider needs to work on the correctness of her seat, developing an effective leg position on the horse's sides and a balanced seat position in the saddle, especially if true collection makes it difficult for her to sit.

Several good dressage videos clearly demonstrate these paces and how they are ridden.

Tack, Clothes, Grooming

As with Hunter Pleasure, Show Hack is a traditional class. Some participants look for ways to stand out while still looking proper by choosing a fancier saddle pad or a coat with gold piping on the collar. Some judges who find these decorations annoying contend that the way to stand out in a ring is to have a good horse.

SADDLE: Though the USEF Rule Book states that any type of English saddle is acceptable, most riders show in a dressage saddle because it positions the rider in the center of the horse and allows her to facilitate collection. A hunt seat saddle puts the rider too far forward to move the hindquarters and free the shoulder for collection. A flat saddle seat saddle might put the leg too far forward and away from the horse's sides.

BRIDLES: The bridle must be a light, show type with a single snaffle, double (full), Pelham, or Kimberwicke bit. Most horses are shown in a double bridle because of its finished look and the rider's conviction that it helps to achieve the frame and collection required to win. Some judges prefer the shorter, dressage type curb bit to the long English Pleasure curb.

CLOTHES: The USEF Rule Book states that "acceptable hack attire is required," which means conservatively colored coats, breeches (many riders wear white), boots (usually hunt boots), and a conservatively colored hunting cap, derby, or protective headgear. Formal attire is worn after 6 P.M. and in championship classes, although some riders appear in white breeches, top hat, and shadbelly tailcoats before the accepted hour or in open classes.

Spurs, whip, or crop are optional, but often thought of as part of the outfit.

MANES AND TAILS: see Sport Horse sidebar in chapter 8.

NDL PERICLES+//

A horse that shows often enough to win thirty National Championships and eleven reserve National Championships must be remarkably strong, sound, and athletic. Mostly though, he must love his job.

NDL Pericles+// (Barbary+++ x *Poznan) is clearly a wonder boy. With many wins in highly competitive Hunter Pleasure and highly demanding Show Hack, he also has won in English Side Saddle and Country English Pleasure. And he has won regional championships in Mounted Native Costume and Western Pleasure. He was also shown in Driving and Halter and did not do too shabbily in those disciplines.

Over his show career he earned over $212,000 in the AHA Breeders Sweepstakes program.

Trainer Wendy Potts showed him to many of his successes and today looks after his retirement needs. She calls Perry an Energizer bunny. "He could keep going and going. He could show year after year and never get sour. He got very excited when he saw the in-gate open and would actually paw to go into the arena. He won so much of the time that he thought he should win all of the time. He would stand in the Top Ten lineup waiting for them to call out the champion, staring at the people holding the ribbons and trophy, and he really thought he should always win. It was very difficult to contain him and keep him from going to the winner's circle."

Another remarkable aspect of this horse is his huge, rolling stride. "He is only 14.3 if he's lucky, but he passed everyone trotting a normal stride. It was long, ground-covering, and effortless. As a hunter he was breathtaking. In Show Hack, when the announcer called for the different gaits, he would wait for you to ask him, but he knew what he was supposed to do. Once it was clear to him what you wanted and you could contain his energy, he would do exactly what you wanted."

Cynthia Burkman, who was Pericles' trainer from 1989 to 1995, had her most memorable ride on him. "He was the perfect show horse. He never messed up. At Nationals, you have to hand gallop in a small arena. No other horse could hand gallop and turn and cut those corners like him. He never switched leads. He just went. He was cadenced, balanced, and always very steady, with ears up. He had a smooth, flowing way of going. He was a great hunter, but in any class he was great."

She credits the correctness of his conformation and his heart that allowed him to perform in a variety of frames. "He was truly versatile. Few can excel in both Hunter Pleasure and Show Hack."

In 2004, Perry rode into the main arena at the National Championship for the last time. He stood quietly as the farrier removed two shoes, a groom removed his saddle and a garland of red roses was placed around his neck. Potts and owner Jill Zamboni-Contreras escorted him from the ring. Reports flew over the Internet about how he retired at age twenty so beautiful and so full of life.

CHAPTER SIX

WESTERN PLEASURE

"The air of heaven is that which blows between a horse's ears."

—Arabian proverb

AS A WESTERN PLEASURE ARABIAN MOVES, HE FASHIONS AN image of balanced arcs drawn from the arch of his neck, the roundness of his topline, the elegant bow of his tail, lifting hind legs, curved front legs. His fluid, relaxed way of going allows the rider to imagine long rides over open range. Her horse never loses his rhythm or his outline as he glides from gait to gait. Should the rider ask for more speed, the horse abides. The rider thinks what direction and the horse goes there. If she asks him to slow down, he does. He is in harmony with his rider and enjoys it that way.

This harmony and grace of a Western Pleasure pair elicit the impression that any horse and rider can accomplish this picture of relaxation and flow. So it was with greats like Mi-Tiffany, Quavado, Mikhail+++//, and Baskidandy.

Yet looks are deceiving. To maintain this round, slow way of going and purity of movement is physically and mentally demanding. It calls for a strong, well-muscled horse that is at once forward thinking, quiet, and capable of considerable concentration.

CONFORMATION

To accomplish the outline of the Western Pleasure competitor, the horse should have classic, positive conformation features, including a laid-back shoulder and a long, tapering hip. He is built more horizontal from poll to tail than the more vertical English Pleasure horse. His neck reaches out on a plane more level with his withers. "You don't want a Western prospect that wants to break in the withers and bend in the neck and come up in the bridle," Arabian trainer, judge, and breeder Gary Dearth explains.

MENTAL CHARACTERISTICS

In a sport characterized by finesse, the Western Pleasure horse has a quiet, happy attitude. Though Arabians are generally ambitious horses, a Western Pleasure horse is by nature more dialed down. The Western Pleasure prospect turned out in a pasture filled with horses may likely go along with the herd, rather than lead. He may stand and watch what the more active members are up to.

Following are stories of two national champions, one charming, one heart-wrenching, but both reflective of Arabian willingness and heart wrapped up in the quiet, tolerant package of a Western Pleasure temperament.

Story One

The trainer and his horse shall go nameless because to this day the rider's former employer does not know this story.

The setting is the Canadian National Championship in Edmonton, Alberta. At the show venue, the stalls are connected to the coliseum by a bridge that traverses a main thoroughfare. After crossing the bridge, the competitor and the horse circle the coliseum to the side opposite the bridge, where they find the warm-up area and the entrance to the show arena. People on foot could cut across by walking down steps that lead more directly to the warm-up ring.

Our unnamed trainer was late returning to the barn after having a long lunch with his girlfriend. In a very short time, the horse's owner was to show the horse in his first National Championship, for which our trainer had prepared him. The owner and the head trainer had already left the barn and were heading for the warm-up area, where our trainer was expected to school the horse before the owner rode in the class.

At this late hour, the distance to the opposite side of the coliseum looked to the trainer like a hundred prairie miles. But much to the trainer's advantage, the horse had many miles under saddle on Colorado ranch land.

"I jumped on, rode him over the bridge and rode him down the steps. The horse didn't care. When the owner and my boss came from the other side of the building, there I was, on that little patch of dirt, warming up. That horse was so relaxed and up for anything. He went in the show ring with the owner, and he won his first National Championship."

Story Two

SJ Mikhail+++// was the quintessential Western Pleasure horse, who moved in three effortlessly smooth and pure gaits. Though he was gifted and beautiful, it was his laid-back, tolerant attitude that not only helped him become U.S. Reserve National Champion and a champion at Scottsdale, but was also the reason he lived through a catastrophic freak lunging accident in which he shattered a hind pastern bone.

After Mikhail endured an excruciating 7½ hour trailer ride with the destroyed hind leg, the veterinarians at Colorado State University insisted he be euthanized. He would never survive surgery. His owner refused, and surgery was performed for eight hours on a leg that proved worse than expected. Three surgeons inserted rods in the cannon bone to support a pin cast, which he would wear for eight weeks. The horse had to not only tolerate this and many more casts, but he had to survive complete confinement for one year and three months.

Mikhail made it in a large part because of his attitude. He never got depressed. He greeted visitors every day with his ears up. He took care of himself and never became overwrought. One friend

As a show horse SJ Mikhail+++// was the master of quiet ease, a trait that saved his life after a freak accident. Here is his shown by Gary Dearth. PHOTO BY MIKE FERRARA.

who visited him regularly said this horse was so athletic that he could have laid down on a pile of feathers and not disturbed them. That talent was important because of the potential to break his weakened leg while in the pin cast. He got up and down like a cat, one joint at a time, calm and composed.

Today Mikhail has survived and continues as a breeding stallion because of his ability to cope with his life as it presents itself every day.

GAITS

Perhaps more so than other breeds that practice Western Pleasure, Arabian judging demands that the Western Pleasure horse have pure gaits in a classical definition. It is also paramount that these strides be comfortable and free-flowing. Some breeds do not require this purity and fluidity.

"There is a myth that a Western horse can't trot, but a good mover is a good mover," explains Gary Dearth. "A Western horse doesn't necessarily trot high, but he must be very fluid, flexible, and forward. Some of my best Western horses when turned free are very loose and have motion. They want to go forward, but because they have less ambition than an English horse and are built more horizontal, they perform in their own style."

The USEF Rule Book calls for gaits that cover a "reasonable amount of ground with little effort. Ideally the horse should have a balanced, sweeping motion that requires no more than light contact by the rider."

WALK: It is four beats, flat-footed, and ground-covering.

JOG-TROT: This two-beat gait is free, square, slow, and easy.

LOPE: A true three beats, this gait is characterized as smooth, slow, easy, and straight.

HAND GALLOP: This gait must show a clear difference between it and the lope.

This horse produces his slow and easy movement by balanced, impulsive collection, not by what some call "slow and low." While the Western Pleasure horse is not collected in the aggressive forward manner of an English Pleasure horse, he carries himself forward with strength and energy by shifting enough weight to his hindquarters, driving from behind, arching his back and neck, lifting the base of his neck, and raising his shoulders within the slow, fluid, relaxed nature of his own discipline. He needs this considerable collection and forward-going energy to maintain the slow speed.

The challenge of moving this way is to not allow the energy in the horse's body to escape out the front, but to instead recycle it back to the hindquarters. When an English Pleasure horse collects, he benefits from the powerful energy derived from his hard-driving forward motion. The Western horse, however, must maintain that collection in a slow jog or lope without the benefit of momentum.

OUTLINE

The round outline of a Western Pleasure Arabian is unique to the breed. The natural arch of the Arabian neck and his lifted back create the picture. Ideally the poll is slightly above the withers with his nose on or a bit in front of the vertical line of his head, but never behind the vertical, so the horse is looking down at the ground. If he is balanced, his carriage is not pointing downhill from hindquarters to poll. He is horizontal. This carriage is different than, for example, the Quarter Horse Western Pleasure horse.

"Our horses learn a position that's easy for them, and they like it. You can give a good Western Pleasure horse a year off, get on him, and, once you get the edge off, he goes right to that position," says Gordon Potts, a winner of many National Western Pleasure titles.

"Quavado (a horse that Potts rode to national championships) taught me what a Western horse was supposed to be. He always naturally carried himself, even in a snaffle bit. From the first day I rode him to the last time I rode him, he was always the same. It was almost as if I didn't have to carry reins," describes Potts.

That correct silhouette results in light contact and a drape or loop in the rein. Part of that frame is a type of head carriage, often referred to as a head set, but, "it's more than where the head is. It's the whole picture," says Potts. "Correct frame varies from horse to horse. It's where the individual horse is comfortable, natural, and relaxed."

JUDGING WESTERN PLEASURE

When the horse is not moving in true collection, but is pulling himself along by his front legs, the strongest indicator, and the one that most disturbs Arabian judges, is the destruction of the quality and purity of the gaits.

"He can be the slowest horse in the ring, but if his gaits aren't true, he is not a true Western horse," says Chris Culbreth, Arabian judge and trainer. "The quality of movement is paramount. A good Western Pleasure horse should demonstrate a high degree of collection and be soft in the mouth, while performing a true and proper stride in all gaits. The gait has to be engaged and fluid."

If the horse is restrained or jerked or pulled off the bit, he has not learned to carry himself and work throughout his entire body, moving forward with active impulsion. Likely the gait will become faulty: in the jog, the horse's hind legs will jog while his front legs walk; in the lope, he will move with four beats per stride, not the correct three beats.

The connection between the rider's hands and the horse's mouth reflect how well the horse is in self-carriage. Light contact is a relative term. One horse's light contact is another's chokehold. The USEF Rule Book reads "light contact should be measured by a horse's response to the rider's hands, seat, and legs, and not merely by the tension in the reins."

If the rider has a huge drape or loop in the reins, and he takes up the reins one inch, the horse should react one inch. This is light contact. If the rider has the same drape and takes up the reins a foot before the horse notices his request, perhaps that was not light contact for that horse.

"I judge first on the quality of the movement. If a horse is moving badly I don't care how much drape in the reins he shows," says Culbreth. "The worst is a horse that shows drape in the reins, but when he gets to the other side of the ring, he's picked on by his rider. If he's jerked on, that is neither light contact, nor quality performance. A horse creates his own softness; the rider doesn't create it by intimidation."

"Appropriate contact depends on the degree of collection and level of training," says Dearth. "A balanced and schooled horse is ridden with seat and legs and voice. He does not have to be reminded with the reins. Then you have a soft, loose rein contact without fussing with him.

"As a judge, I'd rather see someone that has rein contact with the horse's mouth but has a balanced horse, instead of someone who jerks

NW Beaudacious+, ridden by Chris Culbreth, jogs with a draped rein in a two-beat gait, the sign of a good Western Pleasure horse. PHOTO BY JEFF JANSON.

the horse when she thinks I'm not looking and tries to give the illusion that this horse is off the bridle. The rider shouldn't have to yank him off the bridle to help him around the ring. He should do it himself."

At the other end of the spectrum is the horse that drops his neck too low and his head behind the vertical line. "You won't see a horse loping across the pasture with his poll below his wither, looking at the ground. In the show arena, it's a bad style," says Dearth.

When he learns to carry himself on a light contact or loose rein, the horse is not rushing forward. The cycle of energy moves through him unencumbered. When he has lost the impulsion needed for self-carriage, when he is held or restrained into a frame or position or artificially backed off the bridle, the gaits usually suffer.

"Some horses are such good movers that it's hard for the rider to mess them up. But as a judge, you can see in their face and body that they are being held. Other horses that may not move so well naturally learn through collection and by yielding in their bodies to move better in the frame. If they don't move well, it's an uphill climb," says Potts.

Other problems for which a judge might penalize a horse include:

1. a gaping mouth
2. head tossing
3. breaking out of a gait
4. obvious schooling
5. at the walk: nervous, jogging, inattentive, disinterested
6. at jog and lope: hard or rough riding, too slow or too fast, pulling
7. at extended jog: inconsistent speed, pulling
8. improper or incomplete appointments

Specifically, judges make their decisions based on manners, performance, substance, quality, and conformation, in that order. In amateur and junior classes, they also look at the suitability of the horse to the rider.

PREPARATION AT HOME

The greatest challenge of Western Pleasure is to find and maintain the perfect balance and self-carriage for that horse. If you accomplish that with a horse built for the job that has the desired mental characteristics, everything else falls into place.

A horse that moves in self-carriage has learned a more efficient and effective way of carrying a rider. He no longer relies on the rider's hands for his balance. Instead of moving in a flat frame, he learns to bend longitudinally or round his back so that he can bring his hind end under him and lift his shoulders.

As a result of his training to move in self-carriage, the horse changes which muscle groups he uses and how he uses them. Thus he creates a new physiology. He develops a strong topline that allows him to carry the rider with power, balance, and grace. The physical demands to make these changes entail a slow process, much longer than what is needed for other pleasure disciplines.

"You can take a gifted English prospect that looks pretty shiny in ninety days and is ready to show competitively in six months. Not with Western. In six months you're barely getting started," says Gary Dearth.

Training and schooling usually begin and often end with a snaffle bit. He will learn to go in a curb bit and as he gets older he will show in a curb bit, but he will probably still be schooled in the snaffle. From the start, the horse is taught to go forward in response to the rider's legs and follow his nose when the rider requests with the reins that he turn. The rider does not worry about the position of his head. The horse needs only to go forward and learn to be soft and relaxed.

The rider might start the horse working in a loose martingale, not so much for leverage, but as a guiding tool. The rider takes great care not to support or restrict him with the reins so that he will learn to round his topline on his own, and, in time, to find that balance and position on his own.

Circling, changes of bend, teaching him to yield his hindquarters, move his shoulders, side pass, and perform two-track movements will help the horse find his position. He will learn to allow the rider to shape him, to place his body without resistance and bracing.

Only then does the rider teach him to flex his poll laterally (side to side) at a standstill and in response to the rider's cues, a foundation maneuver that leads to longitudinal flexion (over the horse's topline, from nose to tail).

Gordon Potts explains why these steps, taken in order, are important for the horse's future success. "Once you get a lateral flexion and you can move the horse's body, his ribs, his hips, and shoulder, you can develop collection. We try to make sure that there is nothing that inhibits forward motion, straightness, and impulsion to the bridle. The impulsion is forward energy that is not inhibited by the horse bracing in the body, or dropping a shoulder or a hip to a side. Neither his energy nor his body leak out the sides. Only then can a horse move the energy from his hind end to his front end, meet the bridle, and soften. Not from back to front. Only that way can he collect."

Tack and Clothes for Show

BRIDLES AND BITS: The USEF Rule Book allows any Western-type headstall without a noseband and any standard Western bit. It prohibits hackamore bits, cavesson type nosebands, martingales, and tie-downs. As with all disciplines, it is wise to consult the rule book before showing because rules change from year to year.

If the rider shows with Western snaffle reins or a hackamore bridle (junior horses are allowed to show in a hackamore), she holds the reins in two hands. If she rides with split or closed reins, she holds the reins in one hand, and only in that hand, throughout the class. When the ends of split reins fall on the side of the reining hand, one finger between the reins is permitted. When using a romal[3] or when the end of the split reins are held in the hands not used for the reins, one finger between the reins is not permitted. The rider may hold the romal or the end of split reins to keep them from swinging and to adjust the position of the reins, providing it is held at least 16 inches from the reining hand.

HACKAMORE

With roots in Moorish Spain and feet firmly planted in the lore of the ancient California vaquero, a simple rawhide noseband and a rein knot has had legendary use as a training tool over many centuries. Today it is an optional choice along with the standard snaffle bit for showing the young Arabian Western Pleasure horse.

---

[3] Romal reins are closed on the end. Attached to the center is a length of leather called a "romal" which is griped by the free hand at least 16 inches from the reining hand.

When the Moors of North Africa invaded Spain in AD 711, they introduced to European horsemanship the *al-hakma*, a simple noseband of braided material. Adopting the tool, the Spanish turned the word into *jaquima*, and their descendants, the conquistadors, in the 1500s carried the training device from Spain to the New World, where it again impacted horse training.

In the eighteenth century, when the vaqueros or cowboys of the landed Californios were chasing wild cattle on the open ranges of Spanish-ruled California, the training secrets of the jaquima converted the young and often rough stock horses into flashy, "turn at a touch" bridle horses festooned in silver and leather saddlery.

The California vaqueros' hackamore ensured that their young horses with mouths still maturing were soft and very familiar with the messages of the reins before they asked them to understand the spade bit.

The hackamore consists of the bosal, or rounded nosepiece, made commonly of braided rawhide and/or leather and sometimes horsehair with a non-metal, flexible core. The bosal is held on the horse's head with a headstall, which attaches to the bosal just below the empalme, or nose button, the place where the bosal is in contact with the bridge of the nose. The bosal ends meet under the horse's chin and join the heel knot. Reins are made from a mecate, traditionally a horsehair rope that attaches to the bosal also at the heel knot. Enough of the mecate is left over to act as a lead rope.

Unlike the snaffle bit that works off the bars of the horse's mouth, the hackamore works off the face. As the rider pulls the reins from side to side, the empalme applies pressure to the sensitive areas on each side of the nasal bone. The heel knot puts pressure on the muscle along the exterior of the lower jaw until the rider releases pressure on the mecate or the horse folds to the pressure.

As a show ring appointment, appropriate for young Arabians in futurities and junior horse Western Pleasure classes, the hackamore evokes the flashy, elegant look of the Old West. When given the choice to show in a snaffle or a hackamore, some trainers keep their horses in the hackamore because of a conviction that the old ways work, while others prefer the hackamore because the class calls for a pretty look. Still other trainers feel that the hackamore does not belong in the show ring.

Training and teaching begins and ends, however, with a snaffle. If an Arabian is worked and schooled in an arena in a hackamore for any length of time, he can come to resent its pressure. As Arabians are fairly thin-skinned, extended use of even the best hackamore may painfully rub their face. From the snaffle he learns that if he gives, pressure is released. Only then is he ready for the hackamore. A horse started in a snaffle may make the transition easier to the curb if he is broke to the hackamore. The hackamore works off the exterior lower jaw, as does a curb strap. Because of hackamore training, the horse may understand an additional piece of the puzzle for when he moves up to the curb bit.

On the other hand, some trainers feel that the hackamore is for the most part a decorative item and school junior horses in a snaffle bit 80 percent of the time.

The hackamore is not a piece of tack you put on the horse the day before a show. Learning to work in it takes time and preparation. The Western Pleasure horse needs to find a comfort zone for his face in the center of the hackamore. Correct use of it insures that the horse is neither scared away and backed off, nor leaning into the bosal. If the horse is intimidated, the rider should return to the snaffle and review the fundamentals until he is comfortable and secure, balanced and carrying himself.

Inferior-quality equipment made of braided, cheap material with a rough texture may injure the nerves in the horse's face. It may be soft on one side of the face and hard on the other; or maybe have a knot somewhere that you can't see but the horse can feel.

The bosal should fit flat over the bridge of the nose and round under the bars of the jaw. Look for a high number of plaits in the braiding. A good bosal should bend to apply pressure, not bump.

Even with top-quality equipment, the braiding of the rawhide bosal can rub away hair on the horse's face and build sores. Some riders wrap the bosal in electrical tape and rub Vaseline on the horse's face so the bosal will slide. Some clean it with a dry rag. Others rarely clean it. The dirtier, the smoother on the horse's face.

The right fit is also necessary for comfort. Too loose a fit will rub the face and leave sores on the nose and jaw; a too-tight fit crunches the nose and jaw. Too low interferes with the nasal cavity and restricts the airways.

Some prefer that the bosal top and bottom bend forward, so that when you wish to apply pressure, it applies pressure quicker and you have to correct your horse less. Others want the bosal curved backwards. Some hackamores are very soft; some are heavier and harder.

A rawhide bosal can be shaped to better fit the horse. Some will shape it in a coffee can—never with water, which will cause the edges to curl up and possibly tear up your horse's face.

As this is a specific tool, it is a good idea to turn to an experienced expert for proper and safe fit.

The hackamore of the vaquero is not to be confused with the hinged mechanical hackamore, which many Western trainers view as an intimidating gimmick that doesn't teach the horse anything. Similarly, the "hackamore bit" receives equally bad reviews.

SADDLES: The rules instruct judges to favor neither a working stock saddle nor Western stock saddle festooned with silver.

CLOTHES: Western outfits afford great fun with a Western hat, long-sleeved shirt with any type of collar, trousers or pants, or a one-piece, long-sleeved equitation suit with a collar. Chaps, shotgun chaps or chinks, and boot are required. Added touches may include a vest, jacket, coat and/or a sweater, some of which are quite handsome in brocade patterns. Glitter is making an appearance on shirts, jackets, and chaps.

KHEMOSABI++++
(Amerigo x Jurneeka)
(1967–2001)

There is no import asterisk by this horse's name: he was an all-American boy of all-American parents, foaled in the back yard. His pedigree reads like a summary of American Arabian breeding history. But that was not why so many hearts were broken when this stallion died just shy of 34.

Khemosabi++++ embodied all that made the breed proud. He was stunningly handsome: a deep, rich mahogany bay with four matched white socks and white blaze. His eyes invited friendship. Sound his entire career, he was the only stallion to win in one year both National Stallion Championships and both National Performance Championships. (He was U.S. National Champion Stallion in 1973, and U.S. and Canadian National Champion Western Pleasure Horse and Champion Stallion in 1976.) A testament to his persona, at the same National Championships he won the Halter championship, showing his fire and flare, responding to the crowd's support, and then settled down to a jog in order to win his Western Pleasure championship.

He was one of very few horses with four "+"s after his name, the Legion of Masters, and the highest AHA lifetime achievement award, and he was the only living horse entered in the Arabian Horse Trust Hall of Fame.

The outstanding list of his offspring with awards and championships still holds records. His offspring compete and win in Arabian and open reining, dressage, jumping, cutting, racing, and endurance. Even today, he ranks as a top sire of Arabian/Half Arabian Working Western horses. You can easily pick out a Khemo offspring: the rich dark coat and flashy white stockings show up on his get (offspring) and grandget.

The Khemo charisma was built on presence, pizzazz, and a welcoming, sweet disposition. When he entered the ring, you would think that the Beatles and Elvis had entered the building. Khemo's thirtieth birthday party at the Scottsdale Arabian Show brought nearly 4,000 people to their feet when he came into the arena snorting, showing off, trotting with power and flash, elegant and so handsome, dancing to his presentation music, the "William Tell Overture." In the last three years of his life, he saw 2,200 visitors. He still has a Web site, www.khemosabi.org.

CHAPTER SEVEN

INTRODUCING SPORT HORSE DISCIPLINES

". . . Her stride swallows the distance
Yet her canter becomes a soft cushion . . .
Her nostrils flare when she gathers the wind to her.
Her chest is power;
The grace and strength of her shoulders
Astonishes the eye.
Allah! Like a gazelle
Alert
She leaps from danger's path.
Her round jet-hewed hooves
Ravish the earth
Yet the desert takes delight
Wheresoever she treads . . .
Her shapeliness bears testimony to
Allah's enduring blessing . . .
She exemplifies that which is called beauty."

—Salim Abdulla Haj, 1860,
translated by Judith Forbis
and Hasan bin-Salah al-Ruwayi.

THE SPORT HORSE IS DEFINED BY HIS WORK, AND HE DRAWS his definition from a specific job list which includes the Olympic sports of dressage, show jumping, and three-day eventing. Broadening the description, we add USEF- and FEI-governed sports of combined driving and endurance. Spreading to a larger, but related group, we can expand the category to include working hunter and pleasure carriage driving. An even broader definition may include competitive trail and reining.[4]

Successful performance in these sports, particularly at the higher levels, requires a distinct type of horse. While the sport horse should look like an Arabian, his conformation, movement, and general impression should conform to the standards of a sport horse discipline. Form is dictated by function.

In a Sport Horse In-Hand class, a judge asks herself whether or not the horse's structure and way of going will allow him to perform well in a sport horse discipline with a good chance of maintaining soundness of body and mind. The score suggests his ability to do well under saddle and likeliness to succeed in a sport horse discipline that fits his individual conformation, temperament, and movement. The horse's performance in the group Sport Horse Under Saddle and Show Hack classes reflects how he did in hand and demonstrates his potential to specialize as a dressage horse, hunter, or jumper. As the horse specializes and moves up the sport horse ladder, the work becomes more difficult. Jumper fences are higher on more challenging courses, and dressage movements and test requirements grow harder.

Because of the significant popularity of sport horse classes, the Arabian Horse Association became the first breed association to hold a national championship just for sport horse disciplines. Today, the Sport Horse National Championships offer competition in Sport Horse In-Hand, Dressage, Working Hunter, Jumper, and Pleasure Carriage Driving. Most regional championships and many Class A shows hold sport horse classes, depending on the size of the show venue and their popularity in the area.

---

[4] Although reining is governed at the international level by the Fédération Equestre Internationale (FEI), it is not considered a "sport horse" discipline. The world of horses defines sport horse disciplines as "English" type. Reining is Western.

Competitors, however, can qualify for regional and national championships, as well as for Arabian achievement awards at shows open to all breeds in Dressage, Working Hunter, Jumper, and Hunter Hack classes. Notably, an increasing number of Arabians compete in these open shows in eventing and combined driving.

CHAPTER EIGHT

SPORT HORSE IN-HAND/UNDER SADDLE/SHOW HACK

"The horses see instead of me."

—Andrea Bocelli, blind opera singer
who breeds and rides Arabians

DOES YOUR TWO-YEAR-OLD ARABIAN HAVE THE RIGHT STUFF for dressage? Or is he a prospect for three-day eventing? Or endurance? As a breeder, are you on the right track for producing sport horses? As a hunter pleasure competitor, are you tempted by Working Hunter classes and wondering how your horse would place in a new field?

The Sport Horse division has your answers.

At these in-hand classes, no judge misses a beat, or, for that matter, a stride, a conformation plus, or a temperament snag. Exhibitors walk away with a clear message as to how the judge views the entrants as present and future sport horses. The relaxed atmosphere draws a mix of amateurs and professionals, serious and one-time breeders, riders from inside and outside the Sport Horse division, and owners who enjoy working with their horses in-hand. Furthermore, these classes are valuable venues for introducing young horses to the show world without exposing them to the pressures of the Performance or Halter divisions.

In their relation to in-hand classes, the Sport Horse Under Saddle and Sport Horse Show Hack classes are the proof that the way a horse walks, trots, and stands for in-hand evaluation correlates with his ability to do well under saddle.

CONDUCT OF THE IN-HAND CLASS

Judges for Sport Horse In-Hand classes hold either USEF dressage, dressage sport horse breeding, hunter, or hunter breeding licenses. They may or may not have a license for the Arabian division.

The playing field for Sport Horse (a shorthand term by which Sport Horse In-Hand classes have become known) is a triangular arena formed by ground poles, sometimes decorated with flowers. The judge and her scribe stand at the apex of the triangle where she evaluates each horse according to conformation, movement, and general impressions. She determines the individual's suitability as sport horse breeding and performance stock and prospective competitor. Groups gathered according to parentage are judged on the sire or dam's ability to produce quality breeding stock. On a score sheet filled in for her by her scribe, the judge describes her thoughts and their analogous scores.

Upon completion of the class and tallying of scores and placings, competitors receive their score sheets, in which each segment is scored from 1 to 10 (decimals are permissible). The numbers represent as follows:

10 – Excellent	5 – Passable
9 – Very good	4 – Fairly poor
8 – Good	3 – Poor
7 – Fairly good	2 – Very poor
6 – Satisfactory	1 – Not acceptable

The conformation score is a combination of scores assigned to the horse's head and neck, shoulder and saddle position, back, loin, hindquarters, and legs and feet. Scores for the walk and trot are multiplied by two, which makes the movement scores equal to the total for conformation. Therefore, the four segments of the score sheet break down as follows: 40 percent for movement; 40 percent for conformation; 10 percent for expression, manners, and willingness; and

The AHA Sport Horse In-Hand Individual Score Sheet outlines the judge's areas of consideration. REPRINTED WITH PERMISSION OF THE ARABIAN HORSE ASSOCIATION.

10 percent for overall breed characteristics, quality, balance and harmony, and suitability as a sport horse. With 100 possible points, the final score is reported as total points and a percentage derived by dividing 100 into the number of earned points. The horse with the highest percentage wins the class.

The conduct of the class is on its surface quite simple. The handler leads her horse up to the judge, who instructs her to move clockwise around the perimeter of the triangle, first at the walk, then at the trot. The handler walks her horse around the segment of the triangle designated for the walk work. Returning to the start position, she then trots her horse around the trot segment of the triangle. Back at the triangle apex, the handler positions her horse for conformation evaluation.[5]

Get of Sire and Progeny of Dam group classes are not necessarily shown on the triangle, but are scored on conformation, movement, and general impressions that include appraisal of reproductive likeness, uniformity, overall breed standards, masculinity or femininity, and

---

[5] Though the USEF Rule Book states that movement should be judged first, followed by conformation, some judges may ask for the reverse, because that is what they are accustomed to in all-breed shows.

apparent ability of sires and dams to produce or sire sport horse breeding and performance stock. Transmissible weaknesses or predisposition to unsoundness is penalized. Judges also like to see improvement in quality, movement, and conformation through the generations.

Though class conduct is fairly straightforward, success in this arena requires an understanding of the process and practice by handler and horse.

For many years a traditional venue in Europe for showing young horses, the triangle affords the judge ideal views from which to evaluate specific aspects of a horse's movement. Traveling clockwise around the perimeter, handler and horse present a rear view away from the judge, a side view down the long side of the triangle, and a front view coming toward the judge.

On the first leg, the rear view, the judge appraises the horse's straightness. She will also evaluate how the horse uses his hindquarters. Does he step wide behind? Or does he step under? Is he cowhocked? Are his hindquarters straight? The long side of the triangle offers the best view of the horse's length of stride, reach, suppleness, use of the back, overstep (the hind foot steps beyond the footprint of the front foot), and elasticity, as the judge looks for freedom, purity, and quality of the gaits. On the third side, coming toward the judge, she evaluates movement correctness, evidence of winging or paddling, and, again, straightness.

Hunter/jumper and dressage judges both value certain elements in the prospective sport horses. They, however, look for variations that depend on the job the horses will perform. For this reason, judges ask each exhibitor in which discipline the horse works, or, in the case of a young horse, what the future holds for him.

Conformation

Judges appreciate an attractive head, an eye with an alert, honest, and sympathetic expression, and correct teeth. A dressage judge might want to see good width between the branches of the jaw to allow the horse to better carry the bit and a mouth large enough for the two bits of a double bridle.

Legs must be straight, with proper angulation of the fetlock and hock joints for riding comfort and soundness. Joints should be good-sized and clean, with cannon bones correctly set onto knees and hocks. Hind legs are particularly important for dressage and jumper horses because they contribute to their power. The stifle should set under the hip, because if it sets even a couple of inches behind the hip, the horse will have a more difficult time bringing his hind legs under and carrying weight on them, and he will tend to push more on to his forehand. The hindquarters should form an equilateral triangle made from the angles of the croup to the point of the butt to the stifle. Both front legs should be the same size, with penalties given for club feet and corrective shoeing, particularly with breeding stock.

For dressage and show jumping, the judge might look for a higher set-on neck that is well arched and comes up out of the withers. For a hunter, the judge wants to see a lower, more horizontal outline, which will produce a long, ground-covering trot while still moving under behind, but not so low that the horse's balance is downhill and puts him on the forehand.

Judges look at both the slope and the length of the shoulder. Some consider slope the most important. Others feel that if you cannot have both, the shoulder can be long but a little straighter and still function well. The angle from the point of the shoulder to the point of the elbow gives an idea how free the shoulder will be when the horse moves. The length of the humerus, or arm bone, below the shoulder blade will determine the style of leg movement: scopey or short, horizontal or high. The elbow's range of motion also influences shoulder freedom. Therefore, some judges express concern if the elbow is too close to the body.

Critical to many judges is a strong, wide, flat loin, the bridge that carries the power from the hind end forward to the rider's hand and is the source of elasticity.

"You'd like form to follow function and there is an ideal you would like to follow, but it doesn't always work that way," says the late Bitsy Shields, a USEF "R" judge for hunter, jumper, hunt seat equitation, and hunter breeding. Though rarely, some horses win conformation classes and appear to make good hunter prospects, and yet they cannot jump well. Other horses do well jumping but are not conformed well. Some horses appear as if they would have tight shoulders, yet when they move off, they overcome their conformation flaws. There are horses whose mental keenness and heart overcome their conformation imperfections.

Movement

Gait purity and regularity of rhythm are paramount in all sport horse disciplines. A judge also appreciates a ground-covering stride, with front legs that reach from free shoulders, and with overstep created by the hind legs. The horse should freely and loosely use his back and neck. A great supple and balanced walk is described in some circles as a "Marilyn Monroe walk" or the walk of a lion. The trot should be elastic, reaching, and powerful.

Beyond these basic necessities, the style of the movement may differ according to the discipline. The way a dressage horse supports his balance with his hind legs suggests he has the capacity to carry weight. A propensity to flex his hindquarter and leg joints, lower the croup, and appear to "sit" with his hindquarters will facilitate his ability to create uphill carriage, balance, and motion, and to collect. Emphasis is on impulsion and spring. A hunter and an endurance horse show a similar but lower, more economical motion, with a great ground-covering stride and straighter knee action. Eventers and show jumpers move boldly and in uphill balance, showing great mobility, freedom, and ability to propel from behind, with enough strength in front to absorb the concussion when landing off jumps.

General Impressions

Ten percent of the overall score draws from the horse's expression, manners, and willingness. The judge looks for expressive eyes and alert ears that blend with a placid demeanor. She notices the way he takes in his surroundings and asks herself whether she would like this horse in her barn. The score moves up for the horse that walks in as if he owns the place, but yet is attentive to his handler and responds willingly to the handler's requests. The score descends for the horse that kicks at the handler, or rears and strikes.

Ten percent of the overall score is devoted to the horse's quality, balance and harmony, and suitability as a sport horse.

Quality is the "wow" factor in judging a horse as an athlete. He has a proud expression and shows interest in his environment. He looks strong and healthy. Generally, a sport horse needs a bit more substance and heavier bone than those that work in other disciplines, and perhaps even more so if a horse will jump cross-country. His body parts are balanced, harmonious, and matching. He stands quietly, and then actively moves off free and loose, with his hind legs under his body. He should not be skinny and short-necked, with big feet and heavy legs, looking bored with his job.

And most importantly, he must look like an Arabian, for all the practical and aesthetic reasons discussed under the earlier section of this book on type.

Training the Triangle

A horse that is shown beautifully around the triangle is dancing on a string, so in tune with the handler that their legs match stride for stride. The horse goes forward; the horse comes back, all from the handler's body language.

How well the handler works the triangle influences the result. She must stand her horse before the judge to his best advantage. She must allow the horse to show his best gaits.

The presentation, in theory, begins when the horse reaches the triangle. Since, however, the judge will likely see the horse's approach, even then the walk should be at its best. As the handler moves on to the walk triangle, both handler and horse walk big-strided. The horse stretches long and low and moves forward, staying aligned with his handler's shoulder.

On the first leg of the triangle, horse and handler move off together instantly, creating a forward, engaged trot, ideally with the horse on the bit, by which the horse flexes at the poll and, with supple and quiet acceptance, responds to the handler's cues with the reins or pressure points from the halter. When he moves "on the bit," he will not have any resistance in his body to block his ability to engage. The judge is not evaluating his promptness, but the horse's ability to engage.

Approaching the corner of the triangle, the horse shortens his stride, collects, and turns onto the long side parallel to the judge. There he extends his trot and really shows the judge his stuff by moving with long, bold strides, keeping shoulder

Shown by owner Kathryn Carlin, Jumpin' Jak Flash+++// trots away from the judge who looks for straightness and engagement. PHOTO BY TERESA TAL.

Jumpin' Jak Flash+++// and handler Kathryn Carlin move in sync as the horse shows the judge lengthened stride, self-carriage, and the power in the trot. PHOTO BY TERESA TAL.

to shoulder with the handler, who encourages the horse to maintain self-carriage and stretch. If the handler has a good thing going, he keeps the horse trotting past the end of the triangle, so as not to interrupt the tempo. Otherwise, the horse comes back into collection as he nears the corner, engages his hindquarters in the turn, then steps out as he straightens and remains "dead-on" straight as he approaches the judge.

Judges are happy to see even a few good strides. If the horse breaks into the canter, it is not an issue. If the horse canters most of the way, most judges will ask the handler to go again so she can see more trot steps. The judge will give the handler all the breaks she can to show the horse to its best advantage.

The judge, however, does not care to see the horse jerked down from the canter. Nor is she impressed with the handler who drags her horse behind her. Neither technique allows the horse to show his best gaits. The picture also tells the judge that the horse is not responsive or attentive to the handler. When the handler picks up her pace, the horse should join her.

For conformation evaluation, the handler stands the horse parallel to the apex, with the horse's right side at the apex, the left side to the judge. The horse should stand calmly, attentive and well-balanced over four legs in an "open position," which clearly exposes each leg to the judge, no matter what her vantage point.

The handler stands in front of the horse with loose reins or lead line. As the judge walks around the horse during the evaluation, the handler moves out of the judge's line of vision. The judge should not have to ask the handler to move out of the way, nor should the handler jump around like a rabbit. When the handler positions herself correctly, the judge hardly notices her.

The horse's neck should relax into his natural position. If it is too high, his back may look hollow, showing too much of an underline and not enough topline. Neither should the head stretch too low to the ground. He should stand with his hind legs under

Jumpin' Jak Flash+++// approaches the judge on the last leg of the triangle, showing front end straightness and correct front leg action. PHOTO BY TERESA TAL.

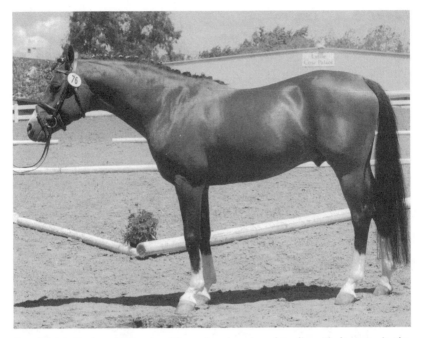

Jumpin' Jak Flash+++// stands with a relaxed neck and topline. His legs are in the "open position," which allows the judge to clearly see all four legs. PHOTO BY TERESA TAL.

himself, not parked out behind his hindquarters. Front legs should line up perpendicular to the ground.

Even in conformation evaluation, the handler with a well-mannered horse has an advantage. If the horse does not stand still, the judge has a difficult time getting a good look. She may not see all the horse's good points. In addition, a percentage of his score is based on his attitude, with which she may not be pleased.

"I don't mind if the horse looks up out of the ring," says Shields. "That shows a little brightness. But I don't want him wheeling around to see who's behind him. He needs to have his mind on the handler. And the handler needs to teach him to stand so as to diminish faults. This is show business, and you need to show yourself and your horse."

Preparation at Home

Horses that were not taught the program at home are the ones that do not move forward. They do not steer; they show short, hurried movement; they drag the handler around and run past or push into the handler. They run high-headed, rear, leap, or nearly knock over the judge. They do not know their job.

With proper training a horse can move at whichever speed or gait the handler chooses by responding to the handler's body language. The handler need not resort to using the reins or lead shank. He allows the horse freedom. A well-trained horse will even round himself "on the bit" in hand.

The U.S. Dressage Federation's training video, "Showing Your Sport Horse In-Hand," recommends a training regime that begins with a halter, leather lead or cotton rope, and chain over the nose at first (depending on your horse's knowledge, maturity, and focus). With more training and maturity, the chain can run under the chin or may be discarded.

Your grip on the line or reins should be shorter rather than longer to allow you to make small adjustments to the horse's head, though not so tight as to restrict the horse's head. Your right hand sits below the horse's chin or high on the neck, whichever is more workable for the handler.

To determine the horse's degree of responsiveness, run the whip quietly over his body and legs. This will desensitize him, so that the handler can make him responsive while staying relaxed. Then teach him to move back from an easy tap of the whip butt on the middle of the chest. Repeat patiently and consistently until he responds. Then rub him with the whip, as a way to avoid anxiety about the whip, which in sport horse classes is an aid, an extension of the hand—not a punishing instrument.

Next, teach the horse to lower his head on command. This response comes in handy if the horse reaches the triangle high-headed and inattentive, causing him to give the appearance of bad conformation and restricted movement. A jiggle of the reins or half-halts, taught in a casual, slow manner without jerking, gives the horse time to figure out what the handler's asking. Done well, the horse will lower and arch his neck, a great way to approach the judge on that last leg of the trot triangle.

Teaching the horse to move his shoulder and his hindquarters on request will not be asked for in competition, but these movements will establish a respectful relationship. Again, after rubbing the horse with the whip to desensitize, move his shoulder over with a tap from the whip butt on the shoulder and move his hindquarters over with a tap from the lash end on the hindquarters. Casual, calm, repeated requests with rewarding rubs of the whip keep the horse relaxed, thinking, and open to learning. Allow him to experiment and reward the right answer.

This work with your horse will give you tools to solve problems you may run into when standing before the judge. If your horse is nervous and acting up, moving his body and using half-halts will get his attention and remind him of how he is supposed to behave.

To teach that immediate depart that the judges like to see, put the reins in your left hand, the whip in your right, and tap the top of the croup, while at the same time using a clear voice command. A "cluck" works. Eventually use the whip on the side of the barrel, along with the voice command that the horse understands.

An assistant can help teach the horse to trot off by standing a safe distance behind with a longe whip. Rarely, though, is use of the longe whip necessary. Use the assistant's voice and whip only as reinforcement.

When trotting a horse forward, your raised left hand keeps the horse straight. This gesture is also an important tool in teaching the horse to make the right-hand turns on the triangle.

If the horse respects the handler's space and the handler has mastered a clear body language, turns are a snap. Start training at the walk and work slowly. When approaching the corner, give a soft half-halt with the reins, boldly lean into the horse's shoulder, and raise your left hand and whip to the height of the horse's outer eye. If the horse is inattentive, a slight tap on the neck with the whip butt end should suffice.

Some handlers nearly stop before turning, especially if the horse is tense. This maneuver works well to get the horse back on his hindquarters, providing that the slow-down is achieved from the handler's body, not the reins. Others shoot past the corners if a trot is going well. Try not to circle. Since you cannot control the swing of the hindquarters, you will likely lose momentum on the circle, rather than increase engagement.

"Have someone tell you if you need to get your horse more up and under, if in the trot the topline needs to be rounder, if the gait gets flat or if the hind legs trail out behind," says Janet Brown Foy, FEI "I" and USEF "S" dressage judge and USEF sport horse breeding judge. "Train the horse to work for you in-hand. Too many times handlers have the wrong idea, and they get the horses tense. We don't want to see the tail up in the air because then the back is tight. We want to see a good quality trot, with the horse using the legs and the topline."

"Handlers have to be fit if they want to show off their horses," says Shields. "Work with the horse, but don't overdo it. Keep him fresh and interested."

Grooming and Appointments

A well-turned-out sport horse is spotless, trimmed, and tidy, with excellent bloom on his coat. He is well groomed, but not oiled and greased. Mane braiding, while nice, is optional. Hunter judges are used to seeing tails braided; dressage judges are not.

"Whether braided or not doesn't bother me," says Peter Lert, "S" dressage and dressage breed judge. "But the horses need to have correct feet. I've seen horses with far too much toe on their feet and, as a result, contracted heels. These horses are not really presented as sport horses."

Horses under the age of two must be shown in a plain leather stable halter. Bridles are optional for two-year-olds, mandatory for horses three years old and older. A bridle should be a dressage or hunter type with a snaffle bit (with or without cheek pieces), reins, and headstall with throatlatch. A noseband is optional. A split or single chain may be used with or instead of reins (keep in mind that tack should be suitable to control the horse). Tack should be clean.

The handler should dress in neat, comfortable, inconspicuous clothes, so that the judge's attention is on the horse. Think wisely about your choice of shoes and remember that the bigger your stride, the bigger your horse's stride. You may carry a whip, maximum length six feet, including lash and without attachments.

SPORT HORSE UNDER SADDLE AND SHOW HACK

Sport Horse Under Saddle and Sport Horse Show Hack are conducted in a manner similar to other Arabian arena performance classes. The format and protocol of Sport Horse Under Saddle duplicates pleasure classes. Horses walk, trot, canter, and hand gallop both directions of the ring, stand quietly, and back readily. Show Hack resembles English Show Hack. Horses walk, trot, and canter in normal, collected, and extended paces, hand gallop both directions of the ring, and reinback.

Judges, who hail from the sport horse disciplines of hunter, jumper, and dressage, consider the horses' suitability as working sport horses. Generally they look for a horse that moves across the ground effortlessly and responds willingly and athletically. Dressage and hunter/ jumper judges essentially look for the same quality performance, but for different reasons.

The dressage judge emphasizes the suppleness of the topline, connection, contact, and balance in the normal, extended, and collected gaits, while looking for willing and prompt transitions performed with shoulder freedom and a tendency to balance uphill and toward the hind legs. This ability will demonstrate the horse's potential capability to collect and carry out the movements at the higher levels of dressage.

A hunter judge looks for an effortless, ground-covering way of going, accompanied by transitions that maintain the same rhythm from pace to pace. This movement facilitates the horse's ability to move down a line to a jump in a balanced, smooth manner. In a fairly level frame, he needs to smoothly extend and collect without much effort by the rider. In a jumping class, hunters and jumpers pick up their working pace on the circle before they begin the course. The judges expect them to maintain that pace around the course. When the rider needs to shorten or lengthen the strides to move up to a fence or come out of a turn, the canter must be smooth, willing, and in the same rhythm.

Clothes and Tack

Sport Horse Under Saddle riders dress in either dressage or hunt attire. A whip or crop is limited to four feet. Tack includes a forward seat or dressage saddle, and a hunter or dressage type bridle with a snaffle or Pelham bit. Kimberwickes and double bridles are not allowed.

Show Hack riders wear conservatively colored dark coats, breeches, and boots with hunt cap, derby, or other protective headgear. Formal attire, appropriate for after 6 P.M. and championship classes, consists of white breeches, top hat, and shadbelly coat. Saddles are either forward seat or dressage type. Bridles are dressage or hunter type, with single snaffle, double bridle, or Pelham bits. Again, Kimberwicke bits are not allowed. When using a double bridle, the length of the curb bit's lever arm may not exceed 10 cm (3.94"). The inside diameter of the bridoon bit ring may not exceed 8 cm (3.15").

In both classes, the use of "unconventional bits" such as Myler brand bits may be penalized at the judge's discretion.

Note that tack differences distinguish Sport Horse Show Hack from English Show Hack. Neither the saddle seat saddle nor the long shanks of the double bridle worn in English Show Hack are allowed.

BRAIDING MANES AND TAILS

Manes

While most Arabian classes call for a natural, loose mane, the formality and tradition of the sport horse classes suggest that braiding options be used. If the horse needs his long mane for other classes or the exhibitor prefers this fashion, she has two stunning options. They both work for sport horse in-hand and dressage, but are not appropriate for hunters and jumpers. The exhibitor may pull or shorten the horse's mane and braid the shorter hairs.

FOR THE LONG MANE

The French braid creates a neat, tight line of braid that climbs along the crest of the horse's neck and ends with a tail of braid running down his

The French braid lines the crest of the horse's neck, giving a clean look without the need to shorten a long mane. PHOTO BY PATTI SCHOFLER.

shoulder, tied with a ribbon or tape. This clean style shows off the horse's neck and can be fashioned quite quickly. The downside is that this plait is not as flexible as the neck muscles and may loosen and even unravel when the horse flexes and arches his neck. A mane that only grows to medium length may not stay in this braid for long. Turning this mane into a short version may work better.

The continental braid flexes nicely and makes an exotic picture. It turns the mane into the look of macramé and has the feel of Arabian costume. The downside is that this solid piece can flop around when the horse is cantering and may be a distraction.

The pulled mane braided into small button-like knots gives a finished look and can play down a less than well-conformed neck. For instance, a short or heavy neck will look longer with many small braids. Pulling out the mane[6] shortens and thins the mane for neater, shorter braids. If your horse really hates the pulling, and most do, check with your tack store for a razor designed for shortening the mane. Cutting the mane with scissors or clippers leaves an unattractive, squared off, unnatural look.

HUNTER STYLE: Hunter braids are always formed on the off, or right, side of the neck and number from seven to thirty or so, depending on the braider's ambition, the horse's neck length, and the thickness of the mane. Tradition calls for an even number of braids for mares and an odd number for stallions or geldings.

The braids are often sewn in with yarn, which is a time-consuming job, but one that does not break mane hairs and creates a neat broken color line along the crest of the neck. Because it draws attention to the neck line, it works best on a horse with a good neck.

DRESSAGE STYLE: Similar to the hunter style, dressage braids are fastened with thread, yarn, or rubber bands. They are often fatter and more

---

[6] To pull the mane, hold tightly about a half inch of the longest hairs of the mane from the underside between your thumb and forefinger of one hand, tease back the other hairs with your other hand or a small metal comb, and then pull the hair left between your thumb and forefinger with a quick down and out motion. Pull only a few hairs at a time. Your horse might not mind the pulling if it is done over several days. Pull after the horse has worked. The hairs release easier when the neck is warm.

Button braids, sewn into a knot with yarn, take skill and time, but give an elegant look. PHOTO BY PATTI SCHOFLER.

knob-like, with fewer of them than hunter style. Often they are covered with white tape (adhesive or electrical repair tape) on dark horses and black tape on light grays.

The forelock may be French braided, tucked under the brow band, unbraided, or left free.

Tails

Traditionally dressage tails are trimmed and hunter tails are braided.

Dressage: This tail is shaped. On the top 8 to 10 inches of the tail, down not farther than the point of the butt, the hairs on the sides of the dock are pulled or shaved. The skirt of the tail is grown full and long, then banged, or squared off, to a length between the fetlocks and the hocks.

Hunter: For a good braided look, the tail must have a nice shape. Especially with the arched tail of the Arabian, any deviation from the correct shape becomes all the more obvious when the hair is braided. So braiding a tail on a horse that usually holds it crooked, to one side, or too stiffly isn't the best idea, as judges look at tail carriage as a sign of a swinging back, relaxation, and suppleness.

Braiding is carried out over the length of the dock of the tail in several styles: French inside braid, French over method, finished with a sewn-in pinwheel, finished with a flat plait by a rubber band, and braided mud tail or stick.

The look is neat and down-to-business with a braided hunter's tail.
PHOTO BY PATTI SCHOFLER.

CHAPTER NINE

DRESSAGE

"In the practice of equestrian art a conversation on a higher level is established with the horse; a dialogue of courtesy and finesse."

—Nuno Oliveira, *Reflections on Equestrian Art*

THIRTY YEARS AGO, IN THE DAYS WHEN DRESSAGE PREMIERED in the class list at Arabian shows, a man jog-trotted into the dressage arena in a Western saddle, and he won his class.

Today that kind of quaint performance is history. Today Arabian dressage is the real deal.

Dressage has become a passion and a home for riders, owners, and breeders who once thought they had no place in the mainstream of the Arabian show community and were odd ducks at open shows. Now, in both their performance careers and breeding programs, these devotees have made a strong connection for their Arabians with sport horse temperament, conformation, and movement in both the open dressage world and the Arabian show scene. The quality of horses and riders make a respectable showing at open competitions, while the classes at Arabian shows are huge. Several Class A shows host well over 200 dressage test rides in one weekend. The Scottsdale show draws over 400.

Dressage's appeal is both its simplicity and its complexity. The word "dressage" simply translates from the French word "dresser," meaning "to train." And yet success at each dressage level requires the constant pursuit of knowledge. Its elegance and look of ease stem from a studious understanding of horsemanship and biomechanics.

Even such a successful rider as Olympic team gold and individual bronze medalist Klaus Balkenhol has said that he needs more than one lifetime to learn dressage.

The joy of the sport is in the details. A rider may feel that the end of her rainbow is experiencing a few strides that are so supple, so dynamic, so lofty, so different from those which came before. Or perhaps she simply thought "extended canter," and in that moment her horse responded with all his power and skill, with grace, fluidity, and expression, into an extended canter.

While watching the renowned Lipizzaner stallions of the Spanish Riding School of Vienna perform the complex movements of Grand Prix dressage, a friend overheard a man ask his partner how the horses know what to do. She answered, "They listen to the music!" While this may seem entertaining to people who ride horses, it is a testimony to the invisible communication between horse and rider expressed in the opening quote by Nuno Oliveira, one of the great dressage masters.

Dressage requires riding with feel, and yet it is a cerebral pursuit; a systematic, sequential, orderly gymnasticizing in pursuit of a stronger, healthier, more beautiful horse.

Ironically, so few humans and horses in the world can replicate the incredible beauty of an Olympic rider and her horse, and yet riders continue with great passion to add fiber by fiber to the fabric of their understanding and their horses' understanding.

Dressage history is matched only in longevity by the Arabian horse, dating back to 400 B.C. with the writings of the Greek general Xenophon. Over time the concepts and movements were developed as battle maneuvers, as pursuits for European aristocracy, and as ways to improve the quality of the gaits. For example, the flying change, a natural movement for the horse out in pasture, was initiated under saddle as a tool to train more jump into the canter.

Today dressage has three faces: basics for all riding disciplines; gymnastic training for its own pursuit; and a form of competition, which formalizes the daily gymnastic training.

TRAINING SCALE

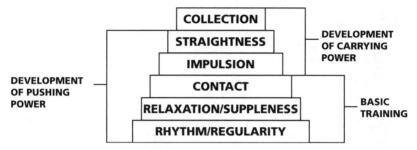

The training scale is the foundation of the dressage levels, from Training through Grand Prix. ILLUSTRATION BY PATTI SCHOFLER.

The fundamental concepts of dressage are explained by the training scale or training tree, a six-tiered pyramid of related components: rhythm and regularity,[7] relaxation/suppleness, contact, impulsion, straightness, and collection. The components have value as individual essentials and together as building blocks. This training scale was initially formulated in Germany, home of more Olympic dressage gold medals than any other country. Today it is the foundation of the USDF's certified instructors and "L" education for future judges programs.

The scale acts as a systematic guide for training a horse from Training Level through Grand Prix, and as an orderly checklist for the rider to review throughout daily work. In light of the training scale, Training Level, the very first level of recognized competition, is truly the first step toward the Grand Prix, the test performed at international events, including the Olympics. International level horses and riders are using the same training concepts as those working at the lower levels. They are refining, shaping, and improving the training scale components. For example, Training Level does not require

---

[7] Rhythm and regularity refer to the correct footfalls of the horse.

collection (the top of the training scale), but a Training Level horse is learning the qualities that contribute to and will ultimately allow the horse to achieve collection.

The training scale is useful in evaluating the competition level at which your horse is working. The scale also outlines the fundamental principles on which judges base their evaluations of dressage tests.

ABCs of Dressage Competition

How do dressage competitions work?

Worldwide, dressage tests are carried out in a standard arena 20 meters (66 feet) wide by 60 meters (198 feet) long. In the United States, shows may hold Training Level and First Level Test 1 in an arena 20 meters by 40 meters (132 feet). Two long sides and two short sides form the arena perimeter, where prescribed spots along the arena wall are marked for the standard arena by the letters A, K, V, E, S, H, C, M, R, B, P, and F, and for the small arena by the letters A, C, K, E, H, M, B, F.[8] Though not actually marked inside the arena, the centerline runs down the middle, paralleling the long sides, connecting the letters A and C. The center of the arena is the letter X.

The arena divides into one center line, two quarter lines, two long diagonal lines, and four short diagonal lines. Although they are not marked on the arena, they are used as reference points.

The head judge sits outside the arena at C. If more than one judge presides, they are positioned at E, B, M, and H. Riders perform specified movements at designated letters of the arena. The tests and the levels in which the tests fit are progressively more difficult. For example, First Level test 4 is more demanding than First Level test 1. Second Level test 1 is a progression from First Level test 4.

---

[8] No one knows why those particular letters are used or if they have any meaning.

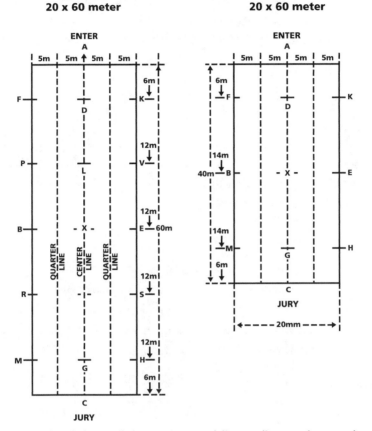

The standard and the small dressage arenas delineate distances between letters. These drawings show the quarter and centerlines which are not visibly marked in an actual arena. REPRINTED WITH PERMISSION OF USEF.

USEF regulates the national levels of Training, First, Second, Third, and Fourth, while the FEI regulates the international levels of Prix St. Georges, Intermediate (Intermediaire) I, Intermediate (Intermediaire) II, and Grand Prix, allowing shows to offer any level for which their judges are rated.

Musical freestyles may be performed at First Level and above. Set to music and featuring a pattern of the rider's choice, a freestyle test gives the rider license to express her artistic and creative side. It includes required movements and gaits of the chosen level, excluding prohibited movements. The rider may enhance her horse's good points and minimize his lesser abilities by her choice of music, choreography, and degree of difficulty in how the movements are put together.

CONDUCT OF CLASS

Dressage classes at Arabian shows are conducted in the same manner, with the same arena, using the same dressage tests as in open shows. The judges are USEF-licensed dressage judges.

All rides are scheduled for a specific time. When a competitor's time arrives, she is allowed to warm up around the perimeter of the arena until the judge blows her whistle or rings her bell. The rider then has 45 seconds to enter the arena. Every test (except musical freestyles) begins with the rider entering at the letter A, riding at either the trot or canter, depending on the test, to the letter X , halting at the letter X, and saluting the judge.[9] Every test (except musical freestyles) ends with a final salute to the judge either at X or G.

Test results appear as a total point score and a percentage score. The percentage divides the total number of points given by the judge by the total possible points in the test, as designated on the front page of the test. A score of 60 percent or higher indicates a good grasp of the level. A score in the upper 60s and certainly in the 70s might mean you are ready to move up a level.

SCORE SHEET

Just as every person puts on his or her pants one leg at a time, so every test, from Training Level through Grand Prix, is scored movement by movement in the same manner.

---

[9] In a musical freestyle, the rider may choose where to do her salute to the judge.

The score sheet is divided into three sections: movements or the pattern of the test, collective marks, and further remarks. Each movement and the four collective mark categories are scored from 0 to 10. A box next to each movement on the test sheet provides space for the judge to make a comment or two on the movement.

Each mark relates to a corresponding word:

0 – Not Executed	6 – Satisfactory
1 – Very Bad	7 – Fairly Good
2 – Bad	8 – Good
3 – Fairly Bad	9 – Very Good
4 – Insufficient	10 – Excellent
5 – Sufficient	

A studied methodology governs how a judge determines the scores. Each movement has an "essence," or a central component. For example, the essence of a trot lengthening is the quality of the lengthening itself. "Modifiers" of that score are the transitions from and back to working trot, the working trot before and after the lengthening, and how the corners of the arena are ridden.

The judge analyzes the execution of the essence of the movement and takes into account the modifiers in light of the quality of the gaits, the impulsion, the submission, and the specified criteria for the movement. Each element of the training scale fits into at least one of these four categories. For example, the judge will consider the horse's suppleness as a product of impulsion (elasticity and swing of the back). She considers the appropriate elements of the training scale and the level of the test and assigns the movement a mark.

Consider the "stretchy circle" in light of the training scale. The test directives call for the horse to gradually take the reins, stretching forward and downward while the rider maintains light contact. The essence of this movement is the stretch, in which the horse seeks the contact while maintaining balance, steady tempo, and correct rhythm. The judge asks herself, is the horse relaxed and confident in the rider's hands (relaxation and contact)? Has he made a comfortable and steady contact with the bit (contact)? Has his gait remained regular and elastic (rhythm and regularity of the gait, and suppleness)? These questions address submission and the quality of the gaits. Has he stretched forward and down, seeking the light contact (contact and balance/impulsion)? Does he maintain a circle (straightness and balance/impulsion)? Is he quickening or slowing (balance/impulsion)? These questions address submission and impulsion.

The test collective marks are four qualities that reflect what has happened during the test.

GAITS: Criteria for this score are the regularity (purity and soundness) and freedom (amplitude of range of motion of the fore and hind limbs) of the natural gaits, and, in higher level tests, of the collected and extended paces.

IMPULSION: This mark considers the thrust or the releasing of the energy stored by engagement. Impulsion derives from suppleness of the back and the desire to go forward with correctly engaged hind legs. It is associated with a phase of suspension in the gait. This phase exists in the trot and canter, but does not in the walk, so impulsion is not applicable to the walk.

SUBMISSION: The mark for submission (compliance, throughness, and obedience) reflects the horse's attention, confidence, and willingness, as well as the lightness of the forehand, ease of movements shown in the correct execution of the movements (including correct bend, acceptance of and obedience to the rider's aids, and a balance appropriate to the job at hand), self-carriage, and acceptance of the bridle. The judge rates the harmony between horse and rider.

RIDER: This mark represents the judge's opinion of whether the rider in that test on that day effectively and correctly influenced the horse with the correct use of her position, seat, legs, and hands.

And finally at the bottom of the test, the judge summarizes the positive and negative aspects of the test.

THROUGH THE LEVELS

OKW Entrigue and Patience Prine-Carr perform a medium trot at Second Level. They wear the tack and attire appropriate for the level. Compare this to their picture below with "Ricky" in a double bridle and Prine-Carr in a shadbelly coat. PHOTO BY MADDIE HOSHIZAKI.

OKW Entrigue is photographed in a trot extension as he is shown in Prix St. Georges by Prine-Carr. Notice how the higher level work has increased the horse's power, range of motion, uphill balance and musculature compared to his Second Level photo. PHOTO BY ROMNEY MAUPIN.

TRAINING LEVEL: *"To confirm that the horse's muscles are supple and loose, and that it moves freely forward in clear and steady rhythm, accepting contact with the bit."* USEF Rule Book

A good Training Level horse with correct basics is beautiful. He moves with freedom, suppleness, and regularity (regularity and rhythm refer to the correct footfalls of the horse). Though he is not necessarily "on the bit," he accepts the contact and stretches forward onto the bit. He is relaxed, obedient, and responsive to the rider and moves with a natural balance neither inhibited nor forced by strong hands.

"Acceptance of the bit is the stage of the training scale 'contact,'" explains FEI "I" judge Janet Brown Foy. "It means the horse is accepting both sides of the bit equally, with a closed mouth, softly chewing contact. For me, there is a little control or flexion of the poll in acceptance of the bit. 'On the bit' requires lateral and longitudinal flexion of the poll. The entire picture is relaxed, active, carrying with the hind legs and supple in the back. Many times at Training Level, where acceptance of the bit is required, the horse has not yet become supple through the back."

The Training Level horse travels around 20-meter circles and corners of the arena and performs transitions between consecutive gaits in a steady tempo, neither too fast nor too slow for his balance and the quality of his gaits.

In test 1 and 2, the rider may post or sit the trot. This option helps the green rider who may have trouble sitting the trot and at the same time is teaching her horse to accept the bit. When a horse resists the bit, he becomes tense and tightens his back, which makes it more difficult for a rider to sit the trot. Posting becomes the better choice.

By tests 3 and 4, horse and rider have worked through some of these problems. Bending becomes a more important element as the horse develops his ability to step with the inside leg into the outside rein. In test 4, the shallow trot serpentine tests all the critical elements:

acceptance of the bit, bend, acceptance of the leg aids, and moving off the rider's inside leg in a relaxed and obedient manner.

The "stretchy circle" introduced at Training Level further tests the correctness of the horse's training. Here the horse gradually takes the reins by stretching forward and downward with a light contact, while maintaining consistent balance, rhythm, tempo, and the quality of the gait. The amount of the stretch varies with a horse's ability to maintain his balance and step under himself while stretching. More important than how low the horse stretches, the exercise demonstrates the horse's seeking the contact with the rider's hands and the bit. It also tests the rider's ability to maintain tempo and bend with other aids than just the reins, without manhandling the horse or holding him up. If the horse is "held up" by the rider, balanced heavily with weight on the forehand (most Training Level horses are still somewhat on their forehand), or has other problems, they will show up in this exercise.

FIRST LEVEL: *"To confirm that the horse, in addition to the requirements of training level, has developed thrust (pushing power) and achieved a degree of balance and throughness."* USEF Rule Book

First Level challenges basic training and the qualities of suppleness, relaxation, throughness, and impulsion. The horse should show thrusting or pushing power from his hindquarters as he lengthens his stride at the trot and canter, while remaining elastic and in the correct rhythm of the gait. The horse must move solidly on the bit, working through his back, strong and balanced enough to maintain the same tempo during the lengthenings of frame and stride. He should demonstrate an understanding of and responsiveness to his rider's weight and leg aids without leaning on the reins to maintain his balance.

Transitions take on increased importance. The horse must now trot out of the halt without first walking. He is judged on how he moves into and out of the lengthened stride. Canter departs are precisely at the letter, not between letters as in Training Level.

The bar is raised on how responsive the horse is to lateral aids. Leg yielding is added. The amount of bend increases from Training Level, with tests now requiring 15- and 10-meter circles. First Level test 3 calls for two 10-meter half circles in succession.

SECOND LEVEL: *"To confirm that the horse, having demonstrated that it has achieved the thrust (pushing power) required in First Level, now shows that through additional training it accepts more weight on the hindquarters (collection), shows the thrust required at medium paces and is reliably on the bit. A greater degree of straightness, bending, suppleness, throughness and self-carriage is required than at First Level."* USEF Rule Book

Second Level requires the final building block of the training scale— collection. Though the expected amount of collection is minimal compared to the levels ahead, demands of this level cannot be met successfully without it. Because he must carry more weight on his hindquarters with a greater degree of self-carriage, a Second Level horse also needs greater muscular development and power than he did at the previous level.

Dressage collection is neither slow nor small. A gait ridden in collection is forward and expressive, with enhanced suspension and cadence and increased joint articulation, especially of the hip, hock, and fetlock joints of the hind leg (engagement) during the weight-bearing phase.[10] The rider enjoys the upward feeling of the shoulders and elevation of the forehand.

Several new movements are introduced: shoulder-in, haunches-in, turn on the haunches at the walk, simple changes (canter-walk-canter), counter canter, and medium trot and canter. Movements and transitions come more rapidly and require that the horse be solidly on the bit, on the aids, and bending.

---

[10] This is not "hock action" or flexion of the hock when the leg is in the air.

These movements are also gymnastic methods to improve collection. Shoulder-in creates and improves collection as the horse develops his ability to bring his inside hind leg underneath him and carry more weight on it. The same applies to travers or haunches-in. In the correct version of this movement, the inside hind leg carries more weight by coming up under the horse's midline. Incorrectly, the rider pushes the hindquarters in without thought to bend or collection.

"Second Level horses tend to have a rocking chair type balance," says Greta Wrigley, USDF gold medalist who has trained several Arabians to FEI levels. "You get them collected, get a few movements, but then you drop the ball or the horse does and he crashes onto his forehand and you have to find a place where you get him back on his hind legs. I hear all the time that the movements come so fast. If he gets on the forehand, you don't have time to get him back together."

Because of the increased demands, a rider will want to concentrate on understanding and feeling where the horse is underneath her. And she may need to improve the control and fitness of her own body. Consider her job in the turn on the haunches at the walk. She uses four parts of her body separately: the inside hand says bend, the inside leg says bend around my leg, the outside leg says move your hindquarters over, and the hips maintain the rhythm.

THIRD LEVEL: *"To confirm that the horse has achieved the requirements of Second Level. It now demonstrates in each movement, especially in medium and extended paces and in the transitions to and from collected movements, rhythm, suppleness, acceptance of the bit, throughness, impulsion, straightness and collection. There must be a clear distinction between the paces."* USEF Rule Book

Some people look at Third Level as the real beginning of dressage, a place where movements become dance and the horse blossoms into a vision of grace and effortless power. Judges hope to see an elegant horse in true lightness, with improved self-carriage and engagement. Here we meet for the first time the flying change, half pass at the trot and canter, and both medium and extended paces of the trot and canter. These movements demand correct understanding by horse and rider of dressage basics, greater lateral suppleness, and a higher degree of collection, ridden from the hindquarters to the rider's hands. At this level trouble will rear its ugly head with horses that are overridden with the rider's hands.

"The more uphill he is, the easier the work is for him," says Hilda Gurney, two-time Olympic competitor, FEI "I" dressage judge, and sport horse breeder. "A lot of horses never get beyond First and Second Levels because they can't do collected gaits. You want lightness off the ground, but not a steppy gait without suspension. In a dressage horse, collection should bring you more float and reach."

FOURTH LEVEL: *"To confirm that the horse has achieved the requirements of Third Level. These are tests of medium difficulty designed to confirm that the horse has acquired a high degree of suppleness, impulsion, throughness, balance and lightness while always remaining reliably on the bit, and that its movements are straight, energetic, and cadenced with the transitions precise and smooth."* USEF Rule Book

This very difficult level introduces the collected walk, walk pirouettes, canter pirouettes, and flying changes every fourth stride and every third stride. Many movements at this level are more about the rider than the horse. For example, the rider may be able to create balance and power in the collection, but cannot cope with the resulting impulsion. The horse will power out of the collection into an impulsive extension, but the rider cannot sit her creation, or the horse breaks because the rider is not balanced.

Half passes require that the rider sit with weight to the inside of the bend and allow enough give in the outside rein to allow the horse to move sideways and forward with an inside bend. Test 2 requires a counter change of leads from one half pass bend to another half pass bend, and flying changes must be straight, on the bit, clean, precisely at a letter, and obedient.

The collected walk "is a dead giveaway of training in the past," says Max Gahwyler, USEF "S" judge and FEI "I" judge. "It's very difficult, and if you ask too early (in the levels), you get hand riding and the horse paces. It has to come from behind. The free walk you paid for; the collected walk you created."

The hardest movement of this level is the canter pirouette, which begins as a quarter turn in test 2 and a half turn in test 3. In the pirouette, the horse turns around his inside hind leg while remaining active and in the canter rhythm, but on the spot where the movement began. He bends around the rider's inside leg in the direction he is turning.

"Think of staying in a ballet plie or deep knee bend throughout the whole movement," says Gurney. "It takes a very generous horse to do pirouettes correctly. If you have a horse that will cheat, he'll cheat on these."

PRIX ST. GEORGES: *"Test of medium standard. This test represents the medium stage of training. It comprises exercises to show the horse's submission to all the demands of the execution of classical equitation and a standard of physical and mental balance and development, which will enable him to carry them out with harmony, lightness and ease."* USEF Rule Book

Prix St. Georges calls for the same movements as Fourth Level test 3, but the pattern is more difficult. Movements come one after another, with little breathing room or places for preparation and improvement of collection. Judges expect more power and precision, with lightness created by invisible aids. They look for indicators of the horse's future skills, such as downward transitions that show a capacity for piaffe and passage, and yet they always want to see harmony, relaxation, elasticity, and energy.

INTERMEDIATE (INTERMEDIAIRE) I: *"Test of relatively advanced standard. The object of this test is to lead horses on, progressively and without*

harm to their organism, from the correct execution of Prix St. Georges to the more demanding exercises of Intermediate II." USEF Rule Book

Intermediate I adds to the mix full pirouettes at the canter, a canter zigzag (three half passes five meters from either side of the center-line with a flying change at each change of direction), and flying changes every two strides. Many horses that have reached Prix St. Georges can move up to Intermediate I in six months to a year, says Gurney. "But that's where most horses stop."

INTERMEDIATE (INTERMEDIAIRE) II: *Test of advanced standard. The object of this test is to prepare the horses for the Grand Prix."* USEF Rule Book

This giant leap calls for piaffe, passage, transitions between the two, and eleven changes of canter lead every stride. At Prix St. Georges the canter zigzag was between the quarter lines of the arena and did not require a specific number of strides. This level requires a stride count, which is four half pass strides to the right of the centerline, eight strides left, eight strides right, four strides right. (At Grand Prix the count is 3-6-6-6-3.)

At Intermediate I the half pirouette is on a short diagonal line. "You can cheat a little on size and straightness (because of the judge's viewpoint from her position at the letter C)," says Gurney. "But at Intermediate II you need a little more straightness because it's on a full diagonal. Then in Grand Prix you must be straight because the pirouette is on the centerline (directly in front of the judge at C)."

GRAND PRIX: *"Test of the highest standard. The Grand Prix is a competition of the highest level, which brings out the horse's perfect lightness, characterized by the total absence of resistance and the complete development of impulsion. The test includes all the school paces and all the fundamental airs of the Classical High School, of which the artificial paces, based on an extreme extension of the forelegs, are not part. For* *this reason, the school leaps, no longer practiced in a great many countries, do not figure in the test."* USEF Rule Book

The step up from Intermediate II to Grand Prix is not huge. Though the pattern is more difficult, the movements are the same. One third of the test score depends on piaffe and passage. Intermediate II calls for eight to ten steps of piaffe, allowing some forward progression. At Grand Prix, the test requires thirteen to fifteen steps of piaffe in place.

"Very few horses can piaffe and passage, much less get a 6 or 7 score," says Gurney. "A horse might be able to do passage, but 'stamps ants' in piaffe or can't do the transition between the two. And it takes a very athletic horse to do good straight one tempis (changes of lead every stride). The movement has to be straight, on the bit, under control, and on the right count."

Few horses have the aptitude for FEI levels, and rather than a poorly ridden FEI test, judges would rather see a harmonious, elegant, smooth, balanced Second Level test that demonstrates those all-pervasive basics outlined on the training scale.

Who to Bring to the Party

Riders who love Arabians for dressage respect their willingness, intelligence, and soundness. Dr. Hilary Clayton, a world-renowned expert on equine biomechanics and conditioning who holds the Mary Anne McPhail Dressage Chair in Equine Sports Medicine at Michigan State University, says of her horse MSU Magic J+/: "Whatever I ask, he answers yes—and he always tries 100 percent. And I like his motor. When I put my foot on the gas, I get a response from behind."

Greta Wrigley prefers Arabians because they are quick to learn and easy to teach. She also appreciates their friendliness. "I like the bonding you get with these guys. Also, being small, they are a lot handier and easier to manipulate. Try dealing with a 17.2 hand four-year-old."

MSU Magic J+// and owner Dr. Hilary Clayton demonstrate piaffe, the competitive dressage movement with the highest degree of collection. PHOTO BY JANE MANFREDI.

The Arabian hardiness and ability to stay sound play important roles especially when reaching up to the middle and upper levels.

Conformation

Basic correct conformation will protect the dressage horse from wear and tear or injury, especially at the higher levels. He should be symmetrically built, with hindquarters that can generate power to lift his forehand off the ground. He will have an advantage if his overall balance is uphill because it will enhance his agility and lightness and make it easier for him to shift his weight to his hindquarters.

More specific to this sport, he should have enough space between the jawbone and the wing of the atlas or first vertebrae to fit at least two fingers. This space will allow comfortable flexion in the poll and jaw when the horse is on the bit.

Another important connection point on a dressage horse is between the withers and the neck. Some horses have a smooth, rising connection here. Others display a dip in front of the withers. While correct work over time will fill in the musculature in front of the withers and create a stronger topline, a horse that comes equipped will have an easier time. For the same reason, a strong loin will complete the connection from back to front.

To facilitate the job of lifting the front end, the horse's neck should be neither deep set nor extend flat out from the withers.

Hilda Gurney emphasizes the importance of a long, forward-sloping femur to help put the hind legs under the horse. For a horse to reach the higher levels, he needs to undulate the pelvis and still maintain the gaits.

"Arabians can do pirouettes and piaffe, and most are fine with flying changes because they have lovely canters with jump and suspension. But often if an Arabian engages behind, he gets very flat and earthbound in his gaits and loses that lovely floating movement that is the beauty of an Arabian," says Gurney. "When he does that beautiful floating trot with spring, air time, and elasticity, he is not engaged enough for lateral movements. Then if he looses the air time and the float, his gaits become irregular.

"For example, in the half pass, you want the horse to cross the legs during the suspension phase (of the stride). The more suspension he has in the trot, the easier it is for him to float over and show crossing while in the air. If you have a flat trot and he has to cross steppy, then the one leg is going to hit the other leg. In the canter half pass, the horse springs over or jumps over in suspension. The flat canter can't jump over. That is why the quality of the gait is so important."

Preparation at Home

To perform well in a dressage test, you have to know the territory. Before competing, attend a few dressage shows. Study how riders handle the warm-up, how they ride around the arena before entering, and how many tests they ride (for the national levels, two is somewhat the norm).

In preparing for a competition, spend time working in a regulation-sized arena. You may think that your 10-meter circles are 10 meters, and perhaps they are, but you might have a surprise if you have never measured them. You also will find that movements come up faster in a 66' by 198' arena than they do if you are working in a larger one. In addition, the square corners of a dressage arena will help you balance and prepare your horse for upcoming movements.

Two schools of thought address test preparation. Some riders firmly believe that while you should familiarize yourself with test movements, riding the test more than once or twice will teach your horse to anticipate movements rather than listen to your aids.

Speaking for the other school, Wrigley says, "I feel that if he knows what's coming, he needs to learn to wait for you to ask. I need to know if I can string the parts of the test together. I need to figure out where I can snooze and when I have to hustle. Then I get pickier and re-ride a lot of movements until each movement feels good. It may take me two or three days before I can string the movements together into an acceptable test."

Through Fourth Level, you may have your test read aloud while you ride. Some people prefer to ride with a reader, while others find it distracting. Try at home to find which suits you.

For post-show homework, study videotapes of your rides. Compare the judge's scores and comments on your written test with what you see on tape. Return to the early videos at the end of the show season to see how you have progressed.

A word of caution. "Don't take tests home and try to change everything," advises Wrigley. "Stay working with someone who knows your horse and you. Maybe it wasn't the greatest test as far as this judge is concerned, but maybe it's a better test than you did last week. Or maybe the judge is correct, but at this point you can't do anything about her comments because you lack the skill at this moment in time."

And final advice: lessons, lessons, lessons. Even Olympic riders consistently work with "eyes on the ground."

Clothes and Tack

CLOTHES: Though the USEF Rule Book allows for "conservative colors" and jodhpurs for Training through Fourth Levels, a black or dark blue short riding coat and white or off-white breeches are the expectation. To complete the outfit, add a tie, chocker or stock tie, boots or jodhpur boots, a hunt cap or riding hat with hard shell, derby, or top hat.[11] While the rule book promotes conservative color gloves, most riders arrive at the arena in white. Some riders feel that if your hands are very busy and need quieting, black is a better choice.

For tests above Fourth Level, the dress code calls for a dark tailcoat or shadbelly with top hat, or a dark jacket with a bowler hat or hunt cap, white or light-colored breeches, stock or tie, gloves, and black riding boots. However, it is rare to see an FEI test ridden in anything but a tailcoat.

A whip no longer than 43.3 inches including lash is allowed except in certain championships and selection classes. Metal spurs are mandatory for FEI tests, and the accepted designs are specifically outlined in the USEF Rule Book.

TACK: Rules call for an English type saddle with or without a tree and with stirrups. At FEI level, a dressage saddle is compulsory. Saddle pads are optional. The traditional color is white. At present plain

---

[11] Years ago, top hats were only allowed at Fourth Level and above. Some people still feel you need to "earn" the top hat.

snaffle bridles with a regular cavesson or a dropped, flash, or figure eight noseband are called for at Training through Second Level. Third and Fourth Level horses may compete in a snaffle or a simple double bridle. As this rule may change, check the rule book. A double bridle is required for competition at Prix St. Georges, Intermediate I and II, and Grand Prix.

Dressage rules are quite specific about which bits are permitted. Again, check the rule book diagrams of approved bits.

CHAPTER TEN

HUNTERS AND JUMPERS

"O! for a horse with wings!"

—William Shakespeare, *Cymbeline*

DO PEOPLE LOVE TO JUMP HORSES OVER FENCES BECAUSE they cannot fly on their own? Or it is because the jumper is his own pilot when taking a fence, his will and his spirit are in command and the rider is along to thrill to the ride? Or is the joy found in seeking the perfect hunter round?

The origin of competitive jumping is in the hunt field, dating back several centuries in England, where hurdling over a neighbor's fence was a means to reaching the fox. Show jumping was born in 1864 at the Irish Royal Dublin Society's first horse show, when jumping an obstacle as an end in itself was a relatively new concept. Its early function was to assess hunters. In those days the exercise was fairly brutal for the horse, grounded in little science and research.

Methods clearly improved with the innovative riding of Italian Captain Federico Caprilli, who transformed the jumping world with his new style. Prior to 1902 and the "Caprilli Revolution," hunt and steeplechase riders in Ireland and England sat straight up in the saddle, like dressage riders. When they attempted a jump, they straightened their legs and leaned backwards so they would not bounce out of the saddle when the horse landed.

Caprilli contended that this method interfered with the horse's natural jumping trajectory and caused the rider to slam onto the horse's back and jerk on the horse's mouth. In contrast, Caprilli shortened his stirrups, leaned forward, and lifted his seat out of the saddle, imitating the jumping trajectory and body position of the horse. Because he was better balanced during the jump, he could loosen the reins and allow the horse to freely stretch out his head and neck, raise his back, and maintain his balance through the jump and landing.

The first show jumpers, especially in Ireland, were hunters bred for the stamina to hunt day after day, with tremendous jumping ability and courage to tackle huge banks, ditches, hedges, and stone walls. Thoroughbred stallions were crossed with strong local mares to produce heavy hunters. The resulting mares were then crossed with Thoroughbred stallions to produce lighter hunters suited for show jumping.

During the first half of the nineteenth century in Britain, the cross between horses of Arabian origin chosen for their endurance, valor, and soundness, and horses of the English "racing breed" (Thoroughbreds) selected for their scope and speed, proved valuable as cavalry horses. In 1836 the two breeds were united in France to produce the French Anglo-Arabian, a breed today known as outstanding jumping horses. Polish Anglo-Arabian stallion Ramzes (1930s), called "the stallion of the century," influenced warmblood breeds that have produced fine jumpers.

HOW WORKING HUNTERS AND SHOW JUMPERS COMPARE

Today, working hunters are quite different from show jumpers, and their competitions have distinct trials and appeals.

The challenge for a hunter is to produce a near perfect ride in which the horse performs a correct, mellow, and able round with style and grace. He should appear sure, safe, and a pleasure to ride over a jump course that is designed to allow the horse to maintain a steady, even pace. His scope or jumping ability should make a course appear easy. Plain-colored fences replicate obstacles found in the fox-hunting field.

The handsome appearance, intelligence, and willing attitude of an Arabian make him an ideal candidate for working hunters. When on course, he approaches the fence with his eyes looking forward and ears pointing ahead. His pace is free-flowing and ground-covering, with a horizontal, sweeping motion that remains consistent before and after the jump. He travels with suspension, grace, and fluidity. He appears strong with good quality and athleticism, moving in balance and cadence. His hind legs reach well under him. He carries his head and neck in a natural, relaxed manner.

In an ideal jumping form, the hunter meets the fence squarely at a take-off spot which is as far away from the fence as the fence is high: three feet away for a three-foot fence. On take-off, he plants both hind feet, rocks back onto his hocks, and effortlessly pushes off the ground. As he leaves the ground, he snaps his knees forward and up,

WL Intruder+//, ridden by Michelle Mahoney, shows the pretty look and correct jumping form of a hunter. PHOTO BY JIM NAISMITH.

tightly folding and tucking his legs in front of his chest. His forearm is held at least parallel to the ground. Over the top of the fence, he reaches and arches his neck and back to create an arc from muzzle to the dock of his tail, forming his body into a shape called a bascule. His hind legs extend straight behind him.

He finishes the perfect semi-circle arc over the fence by landing with ease and finesse at a spot an equal distance away from the fence as the take-off spot.

He continues on to the next fence in the same free-flowing, rhythmic, impulsive, long and low reaching stride with which he began the course. He uses the prescribed number of strides between fences and in combinations of two or three fences standing at related distances. On the correct lead for the direction of travel, he stays straight through his body when the lines and fences require straightness. He bends in the direction of travel. He maintains a good attitude, with quiet manners.

A horse that does not meet the criteria for a good hunter moves in a short stride, perhaps with high action, in a choppy, stiff manner. He may carry his head too high and hollow his back, or he may carry his head behind the vertical line, causing him to appear tense and uncooperative. He gives the impression of giving a bumpy, unpleasant ride.

"A hunter round should look like anyone could do it," explains Michelle Mahoney, winner of several national and regional hunter and jumper titles. "Spectators who ride should easily be able to see if he jumps long, or smooth, or if he's not changing leads, or that he looks too fast. It's not that hard in an average class. It gets hard to tell when everything the horse does is perfect."

"The challenge of hunters is that you have no margin for error," says Kristin Hardin, who has for many years shown in the open and the Arabian hunter and jumper classes. "One of the Arabians I ride may be playful at home, but when he goes in the ring he tries so hard to be perfect. He does everything right. Hunters have to be really broke, prepared, and rideable because every stride is judged. Style and beauty matter, but mostly you can't make a mistake. It's really harder than jumpers."

Jumpers

While hunters are judged on their form and their success over the jump, jumpers are given scores based on penalty and time faults incurred between the start and finish lines. Since jumping form is not a consideration, the jumper's mission is to complete the course faster than his competitors while not touching or knocking down a rail. The course, which tests his quickness, agility, and bravery, traditionally consists of bright-colored jumps, a greater variety of jumps, and a more difficult pattern than a hunter course.

A good Arabian jumper has the physical characteristics to be quick, cat-like, and careful, making him a match for fast and compact jump courses with sharp angles and tight turns that demand speed and agility. Generally his conformation has a bit more uphill balance than the hunter, with his withers higher than his large, strong hindquarters. The ideal neck is fairly long and well arched, to provide him with better balance. A sloping and long shoulder will give his gaits more suspension and free, ground-covering movement.

Further, his agreeable attitude, intelligence, and desire to do well endow him with the character to listen, turn, run, and jump. He waits for direction from the rider as to which way to go, responds, collects, makes a quick turn, then explodes in a big jump effort. He is always on, and yet balanced, listening, and responsive.

A jumper who does his job well likes to jump. At best, the most that the rider can do is bring the horse to the right spot before the jump with the right impulsion and speed. The horse has to want to jump and have the courage to do so.

"With any good jumper, it comes down to their attitude, their intelligence, and their desire," explains Hardin. "They have to want to jump because the job requires them to make such a great effort. When you are on course, the jumps come up fast and in tight spaces; the jumper has to be supple, flexible, and agreeable. When he jumps well, you are not making him do it."

Show jumpers are coveted for their endurance, handiness, great coordination, suppleness, and speed. They should move in a loose, free, ground-covering manner, with great mobility and suppleness. The trot should be free, active, and energetic. The canter, his most important gait, should be bounding and in an uphill balance, even when moving with increased speed. Although the jumper's movement is not judged, it does influence his success on the course. A long stride, at least 12 feet, will ensure the horse's ability meet the length between jumps. A horse with tremendous knee action and a stride which is more up and down than forward may have trouble with, for example, the in-and-out jump, over which he must take only one stride between jump elements. A horse that moves in a downhill balance will have a more difficult time rocking back on his hindquarters to lift over the jump.

And of course, he must have jumping ability.

Riding a Jump

Learning to ride a jump course begins with an elementary math lesson. Jumping calculations are based on a 12-foot stride. There was a day when stride length was adjusted shorter for Arabians, but that is rare today. The standard distance between jumps is 12-foot intervals. Six feet are allowed for landing and six feet for take-off. Therefore, a jumping distance between two jumps that should be taken in one stride will measure 24 feet (6 plus 12 plus 6); two strides equals 36 feet, three strides 48 feet, four strides 60 feet, and five strides 72 feet.

APPROACH: In approaching a jump the rider learns to evaluate the speed her horse needs to go in order to meet the fence for a balanced, clean, effortless jump. At any given time a horse may need to speed up, slow down, shorten the stride, or lengthen the stride. "The approach depends on the rider's skill to make that judgment on how many strides she needs to reach the fence. If you are cantering at a 12-foot stride, and you are four strides away from the fence, you would probably keep this same pace. If you are long, you might lengthen a little," says Mahoney. "You don't want him barreling around the corner in a 14-foot stride. Nor do you want him in a 10-foot stride up to the first fence because you will have to go like crazy to get the distance between the next jumps."

To develop skill at measuring strides, canter over poles set 12 feet apart. This exercise will tell you how your horse's stride compares to the 12-foot standard and give you experience adjusting the stride.

TAKE-OFF SPOT: Picking the take-off spot requires rider experience or an experienced horse. The higher the fence, the further away from the jump the horse should take off. Some horses take off "long," or before the spot. Others "chip," or take off too close to the fence.

To cultivate your ability to find the best take-off spot, canter up to a single pole on the ground or set a foot off the ground. Try to judge how far away you need to be in order to go over the pole smoothly. "You'll know if you are taking off at the wrong place because your horse will chip it or take off long or throw you back, off balance," explains Mahoney.

IN THE AIR: Once the horse's front feet leave the ground, the rider gives up control and allows the horse to do his job. At this point, it's important that the horse is free to use his head and neck for balance.

LANDING: Once you land, your job is to maintain the right length and speed to continue in a 12-foot stride. After a landing, some horses need to move faster to make the next jump. Others need to hold back a bit.

In these three photos, Starsearch SMA and Jane Mendelsohn show the phases of "bascule," the desirable arc formed by a horse when he jumps. In this photo the horse is in the take-off phase. PHOTO BY TIANNA HUX.

Starsearch SMA jumps in the cross-country phase of Combined Training at a show open breeds. PHOTO BY SHANNON BRINKMAN.

As he lands, this purebred Arabian unfolds in the final phase of the bascule. PHOTO BY GRAHAM PHOTOGRAPHY.

CONDUCT OF THE HUNTER CLASS

At Arabian shows USEF-licensed hunter officials judge Arabian hunter classes. Before the class, show management will post the courses, which will reveal the distances between jumps. The classes may include:

GREEN WORKING HUNTER: open to horses any age in their first or second year of showing. Courses contain a minimum of eight jumps between 2'9" and 3', with a maximum spread (width) of 3'.

REGULAR WORKING HUNTER: open to horses any age regardless of showing experience. Courses contain a minimum of eight jumps between 3' and 3'3", with a maximum spread of 3'. The Working Hunter course should include a variety of jump types and at least one change of direction.

HUNTER HACK: horses are shown at walk, trot, and canter, after which they jump two fences 2' to 2'6" in height. They are judged on performance, manners, and soundness.

UNDER SADDLE REGULAR WORKING AND GREEN WORKING HUNTER: horses are shown at walk, trot, and canter. The judge may ask for competitors to hand gallop. She will look for obedient, alert, responsive, and free-moving horses. There is no jumping in this class.

In determining the winners of hunter classes, the judge tracks how the horse performs over each jump on the course. Her evaluation begins when the horse enters the ring. The first strides and first jump are very important because the judge is mentally determining a preliminary score.

The judge credits good jumping form from a horse that moves in an even pace with a good attitude. She discredits poor jumping form, touching a rail, dangerous jumping, circling while on course, bucking, wrong leads, knockdowns (more so from front feet than from hind feet), refusals, dropping out of a gait, adding a stride to an in-and-out jump (a combination of two jumps set at one stride in between). In her mind, the greater the danger of a jumping problem or fault, the greater the penalty it deserves.

The horse will be eliminated for three refusals, going off course, jumping a fence before it is reset, bolting from the ring, illegal equipment, or if the horse falls or the rider falls off.

CONDUCT OF JUMPER CLASS

USEF-licensed judges conduct the Arabian jumper classes. For these classes, riders are permitted to walk the course before the class.

In amateur and junior classes, obstacles start at 3' and go to a maximum height of 3'3" with spreads to 4'. In open classes jumps start at 3'3" and go to maximum height of 3'6" with spreads to 5'.

On entering the arena, the competitor has 45 seconds after the judge sounds an audible signal to cross the starter marker in the correct direction and start on course. The time on course starts when the horse's chest crosses the start line. Time ends when the horse crosses the finish line.

Jumpers are scored mathematically, based on penalty faults that consist of refusals, falls, knockdowns, touches, and time penalties.[12] Jumping form is irrelevant.

Courses are given a "time allowed," which is determined by the length and difficulty of the course. If the time allowed is exceeded, a one-quarter time fault is charged for each elapsed second or fraction thereof. The show's prize list indicates which table from the USEF Rule Book will be used to calculate scores.

Tips for Amateurs

To take up jumping, a rider first needs good basic skills, balance, and confidence in her flat work. "Jumping classes are hard, and one of the most difficult sports," says Mahoney. "Other sports do the same pattern all the time. Even reining horses have the advantage of facing familiar patterns. With jumping, every time you go to a show, you face all new fences, striding, turns, and courses."

Those starting out may:

1. Become rattled in the warm-up. "I don't do a lot of jumping in the warm-up before my class because the arenas are too hectic, with too little room. They can be dangerous. The warm-up fences are too airy[13] with lots of poles," says Michelle Mahoney. "I warm up on the flat, but not a lot of jumping."

2. Lose focus on entering. "Stop before you go in the arena," says Mahoney. "Take a breath and go through the course in your mind. Go in calmly. Some riders let things go faster in their heads than they need to be."

---

[12] Which penalties will apply to a jumping round depend on which USEF table is applied to the class.

[13] Airy refers to an obstacle that has large open spaces. They are more difficult for the horse and rider to judge.

3. Get their horses going too fast, which causes the horse to lose balance and form.

4. Cut corners of the arena, which makes it difficult to meet a fence well. "In Hunters it's important to use the entire arena to make your ride smooth," Mahoney advises. "If you cut the corner, you won't get a nice, straight line to the jump. You'll be on a diagonal line, or end up on one side of the jump. The fences are set up to use the whole arena; so you need to use the rail and corners to ride a fluid, pretty course."

5. Forget their pattern, especially in the more complicated jumper courses. It is imperative to walk the jumper course before your ride to determine where you should turn and to figure out any shortcuts that will give you a faster time. "I won a National Championship because the course designer left in a shortcut. He set the course so that whoever could get through this hole between two fences, rather than go around one fence, they would save a lot of time. When I walked the course I saw the hole," Mahoney recalls. "I took it and I won."

WORK AT HOME

Flat work is as much a part of a hunter's or jumper's week as jumping fences. The horses spend training time learning to move straight through their bodies, to bend, to respond to the rider's legs both laterally and longitudinally, to willingly follow the reins, and to use both sides of their body equally.

"I want hunters to stretch down more, stay soft and on my leg. Jumpers are the same, but you are teaching them in a more elevated frame," Kristin Hardin explains.

Flat work builds the horse's back strength, which will keep them sound longer and jumping well into their late teens. "When they land after a jump, they use their backs to hold themselves and to decrease the concussion. It is critical to keep their backs strong. The better the back, the less the concussion on their legs. If they are not trained properly to use the right part of their body, they won't stay sound," says Hardin.

How often the horse jumps each week varies. Jumpers are not jumped as often, perhaps two days a week. With a jumper, you want him attentive to your directions on the course. Drilling him at home may make him less alert. Your work should keep the jumper sound, careful, and interested.

Hunter training requires fine-tuning exercises that make a horse soft and rideable. While you do not want the hunter bored by too much repetition, you want his work to become second nature. You might jump him three days a week.

"I keep my jumping consistent. I won't jump a lot and then not jump for a month. Flat work can't simulate jumping. If they are not jumping fit, they will get sore. The act of jumping keeps their backs loose. Jump a cavaletti[14] and you get the same action in their back. You don't have to do big jumps all the time," says Hardin.

Equally important, the rider should work on her position. While she cannot help the horse go over a jump, she can interfere with his success either by her balance or how she uses the reins.

"The rider must sit in perfect balance because she affects the horse by her weight distribution. If she sits too forward or sits up too early, the horse will pull down a rail. Sometimes a beginner sits a little behind the motion because she is scared that if the horse stops, she will fall off. In actuality, getting behind affects the horse's balance and makes the jump more dangerous," Hardin explains.

If he approaches a jump too quickly or too abruptly because the rider has not brought him to the right spot before the jump with the

---

[14] A cavaletti is a ground rail or pole attached to or resting in a low standard.

right impulsion and speed, he likely will knock down a rail. "Most horses want to jump clean, and most rails fall because of rider error," says Kristin Hardin.

TACK AND CLOTHING

EQUIPMENT: For hunters, a light hunter type bridle with either snaffle, Pelham, or double bit with cavesson nosebands are allowed. A breast plate or breast collar is acceptable. Martingales are prohibited in Hunter Hack, Under Saddle, and tie-breaking classes. Boots and leg bandages are prohibited. For jumpers, any type of English bridle, martingale, tiedown, boots, and leg bandages are allowed.

Although the USEF Rule Book states that a rider may use any type of English saddle, a forward seat saddle is the best choice because it is designed for jumping. Many style options are available, including the more popular type with a knee roll and a deeper seat than once was available.

ATTIRE: Hunter classes call for informal attire of suitable material for hunting (tweed, Melton, or warm season lightweight fabric coat of conservative color, breeches or jodhpurs, and boots). Conservatively colored protective headgear is mandatory. Spurs, crop, or bat are optional. In jumping classes, show management may allow riders to compete without riding coats. Formal attire calls for black, dark blue, dark green, or scarlet coats, white or light fawn breeches, a white tie or chocker or hunting stock, and a white or lightly colored shirt.

CHAPTER ELEVEN

INTRODUCING WORKING WESTERN DICIPLINES

"I guess I learned it from the horse."

—Tom Dorrance

THE HEYDAY OF THE AMERICAN COWBOY WAS BARELY A heartbeat in the history of nations, lasting less than a generation from the end of the Civil War in 1864 to the mid-1880s. Today we take the skills and techniques roughed out by these men of the West who could barely squeeze out a living and honor their talent and hardiness by turning their jobs into sport.

Today, the decked out Working Western horse and his rider for some reason don't seem costumed. Maybe it is their stance, or their calm nature, or their skill. Or maybe it is because the stories of the cattle drives from Texas to Montana, Kansas, and Missouri that piloted over 10 million cows to their destinations are ghostly shadows in the show arena. You can easily envision the trail boss who rode ahead of the cattle seeking out water and pasture. Along the way he and his horse maneuvered over and through obstacles mimicked in today's trail horse class. Starting up the herd after a night's rest or regaining control of the cattle in a stampede required reining maneuvers. In the roundup, the cowboys rein and move the cattle, separating and cutting their chosen cows and calves out of the herd on horses born with the same cow sense seen in today's working cow horse and cutting classes. The pride that cowboys and vaqueros took in the skills and success of their horses led to challenges that became rodeo and horse show competition as we know it today.

Whether competing in reining, working cow horse, trail, or cutting, Arabian Working Western horses have critical qualities in common: they are calm, they are agile, and they are pretty.

Generally Arabians have the quickness, intelligence, and trainability to pick up the complexities of the classes and deal with, as sometimes is the case in the cow classes, the confusion of these disciplines. They must be confident and not mind going alone into the arena in working cow, trail, and other classes in which horses compete before the judge one at a time. They are centered, focused, and willing to partner up with their rider.

Their smaller size, 14.2 to 15 hands, adds to their cat-like handiness so important in this tight, often staccato, work that is fast and ground-covering one instant, then immediately slow and measured. They must have well-muscled, rounded hindquarters with deep, long hips, strong hind legs, gluteal, and gaskin muscles and loins, considerable bone, and big feet. Yes, they are powerhouses.

A Western horse's front end is neither over-muscled nor high necked. The shoulders need great mobility to follow a cow's movement or perform a reining spin. This is difficult if the chest is too wide and the shoulder is massive. The neck should come fairly horizontally out of the withers.

Arabian judge Don Burt came up with the image of a well-balanced horse as a trapezoid, a four-sided geometric figure, unlike a square, with only two parallel sides. Imagine, then, a horse's body like a trapezoid, in which the shoulder and hip angles match each other, but go in the oppose direction (and therefore are not parallel). Add to the picture a short back and a long underline, and you have a trapezoid.

And the horses are pretty. After all, these are Arabians.

HALF ARABIANS

Half Arabians have proved to be a golden cross in Working Western, especially in reining and working cow horse. The Arabian/Quarter

A horse with balanced conformation has shoulder and hip angles, back and underline lengths that match the geometric dimensions of a trapezoid. ILLUSTRATION BY VICTORIA SMITH.

Horse cross ideally produces a horse with the hindquarter strength and flexibility of the Quarter Horse and the willingness to please and agility of the Arabian. Particularly golden are those Half Arabians created from the mix with the palomino Quarter Horse Hollywood Dun It, all-time leading sire in the history of the National Reining Horse Association. In addition to stellar performance, these horses often have very amusing and recognizable names such as Dun Scootin, Motor Scooter, and Sheez A Dun Deal.

TACK AND CLOTHING

The tack and clothing for all Working Western classes are the same as those outlined for Western Pleasure.

Leg and foot protection, allowed in reining, working cow, and cutting, but not trail classes, include bell, shin, splint, skid, and rundown boots and leg wraps. Proper boots on the front legs protect the horse from hurting himself and provide some leg support. Sliding or skid boots prevent one hind leg from hitting the inside of the other and sand or dirt burning the fetlock during a sliding stop. Some riders consider polo wraps dangerous unless put on by an expert who can wrap them to stay on with uniform pressure. Other riders shun the use of boots or wraps, especially on the hind legs, because sand and dirt too easily work their way inside the boot and can irritate the horse's legs.

Any Western bridle is allowed; only split or romal reins are acceptable. With these the rider must ride with only one hand. Closed reins are allowed with snaffle bits and bosals. The rider may ride with one or two hands in snaffle bit, hackamore, and freestyle classes.

Any Western saddle works, but the rider may ride better with one designed for the specific sport, such as a reining saddle for reining. Traditionally Western horses show in Navajo style saddle pads and blankets, often color coordinated with the rider's outfit. For riders, chaps are not necessary, but do give a traditional and serious look. Headwear choice depends on the season: straw for summer and felt for cooler months. To assure that it does not fall off, some riders secure the hat with bobby pins, hair spray, or golf club grips cream wiped on the front of the hat's sweatband.

The Look

If your heroes have always been cowboys, these are the classes for you—providing you remember that these are horse show classes with an emphasis on the word "show." While the Western horse may not be dolled up like a halter horse, he is beautifully groomed, his coat ablazin', his mane floatin' like a wave, his tail flashin', and his big brown eyes watchin' with calm interest.

CHAPTER TWELVE

TRAIL

*"There is no secret so close as that between a rider and
his horse."*

—Robert Smith Surtees, 1803–1864

"LIONS AND TIGER AND BEARS, OH MY!" WHISPERED THE
terrified Dorothy as she traveled through the forest in search of the
Wizard of Oz and her way home. Had she ridden an Arabian trail
horse during her adventure, she would not only have fearlessly
marched through the obstacles and terrors of the yellow brick road,
but she also would have looked good doing it.

The Arabian trail horse is unflappable, and his classes are all
about getting through the unknown in style. He and his rider maneuver with calm, interest, finesse, and precision through an obstacle course that simulates what the team might encounter on nature's
trail or in fulfilling the duties of a ranch horse.

Lou Roper, who has won dozens of national champion and reserve titles in trail, explains, "The trail horse is like the horse on a
ranch that will jump over a few things, take you to pick up letters
from the mailbox, jog down the aisleway between paddocks to see
how other horses are doing, then take you to grab a blanket drying
off a rack, and then run it down to another barn. You have all the
maneuvers of a working horse."

Trail class patterns challenge the trust and confidence shared between rider and horse by laying across the horse's path unfamiliar elements in a variety of shapes, sizes, and positions, possibly unlike any
the horse has seen before. Because a course designer has an infinite

number of combinations and options to place before the exhibitors, each trail course is a new experience and challenges the rider and the horse's knack for facing the unknown.

Each pattern tests the rider's control, training, and aptitude and the horse's agility and calmness. A good course, on the one hand, will challenge the rider's talent to direct her horse and the horse's ability to follow her instructions. In other parts of the same course, the horse's skill at negotiating on his own and the rider's trust in his ability and willingness to do so will be called into play. Take for example the manner in which the horse picks his way over a network of logs. The rider cannot tell him every step of the way where to put his feet. The rider will, however, show him where to start, where to end, and where to go next. This combination demonstrates a partnership between horse and rider.

Trail courses vary in difficulty according to the level of the show. The combination of obstacles and the spaces between them determine

This segment of a national championship trail course will require attention and precision on behalf of horse and rider. PHOTO BY LORNE ROBERTSON.

the simplicity or difficulty of the courses. A tight, compact course with obstacles in close proximity to each other requires from the horse precision and small moves. A forward motion course calls for more jogging and loping. Obstacles come up fast and test the horse's focus and engagement.

"What I like about trail is that you are able to fit into one class the skills required of the most number of disciplines," says Roper. For example, "You have to be able to show on a pitched rein (where the rider has no contact with the bit), like Western Pleasure Horse or Reiner, and jog over an obstacle on a soft rein. But then you have to be able to take contact with the bit and do a hard maneuver like a tight serpentine. So you have on contact and the off contact. You have a real feel of how much horsemanship you have or do not have."

"I think of a trail horse like a biathlete in the Winter Olympics," says Mike Damianos, Arabian judge and multinational champion in Trail. "He's the guy who cross-country skis, then stops and has to shoot a rifle at a target. The modern trail course has the gymnastic challenges that require the horse to be that athletic, but he also has to have presence of mind, resolve, and confidence to aim, point, and shoot."

A judge is looking for a horse that listens to his rider and acts on command, but not one that blindly goes along. She will study the horse's approach to the obstacle, how he negotiates the obstacle, and how he goes between obstacles. The horse should be eager, but not stressed, moving promptly toward the obstacle with authority and courage. He should carefully but willingly approach and proceed through an obstacle with a bright, inquisitive outlook, neither fretting nor rushing. He's not a robot. He's relaxed, but also responsive and light. He's calm and obedient, but interested.

The judge considers whether the horse negotiated the obstacle cleanly, without making inappropriate contact, such a hitting a pole when picking his way over a maze of poles. She wants to see an athletic horse, with the resolve to stay calm, that moves through the course with style. He picks up his feet, lopes with expression and grace, and handles the work effortlessly, as if he has to give only 70 percent because the work is so easy for him.

Different obstacles bring out specific attributes in a trail horse.

CALMNESS TESTS: Walking through water or brush, on plastic sheets, past plants, near domestic animals and other potentially spooky items in a steady, willing manner indicates a winner. Carrying an animal hide or dragging a sack of tin cans from a rope calls for calm nerves. Your horse's cool is demonstrated when you ground-tie (you dismount and drop the reins, and the horse stands as if tied to an immovable object) and walk away, confident that he will stand still for as long as the judge requests.

AGILITY OBSTACLES: Stepping through a line of car tires, trotting or loping cavalettis (wooden poles or rails attached to low standards), and walking over a bridge bring out the horse's athleticism. Logs or jump poles may be set up in a maze, a line, a serpentine, or as a box to

Flicka carefully carries rider Lou Roper over poles raised to various heights. PHOTO BY MIKE SCHRAM.

be walked over, jogged over, or loped over. They can be raised, crossed, spaced even or uneven. Bridges are set up in many ways for many uses. Some may rock, while others may have poles stretched across them.

Commonly incorporated into a trail course are "walkovers," a series of poles arranged in varying heights, widths, and shapes. To correctly navigate these obstacles a horse should drop his head slightly to look at the obstacle as he moves over without hesitation. Stargazing, dragging his nose on the ground, or stiffening at the rider's tight reins usually leads to walkover faults, from slight touches to knockdowns, whereby a portion of the obstacle is moved from its original position.

CONTROL MANEUVERS: The request to perform a turn on the forehand, turn on the hindquarters, and to side pass appear on most courses. In the last maneuver, the horse walks sideways with his front legs on one side of a pole and his hind legs on the other, without moving forward.

Passing through a gate requires several desirable moves of the trail horse. Consider the control moves required to push a gate away[15]: the horse does a side pass to line up your body with the handle, then backs until his head clears the gatepost. Then you open the gate away from you; ride through until your knee next to the gate clears the opening. Using that leg next to the gate, you move the horse's hindquarters away from the gate, and, with the leg away from the gate, you move the horse sideways to the gate to close it.

WHAT TYPE OF HORSE

A good athlete with a solid brain that is easily guided, careful, and well trained owns the trail class. And these winners come in a variety of types and ages.

---

[15] The course design may ask that you either push the gate away, pull it toward you, or that you back through it.

"I've had national champions from five years of age to early 20s," explains Lou Roper. "In trail you have a large cross section of types of horses. Some older horses that don't stand up to the athletic requirements of reining and Western Pleasure can retire into a successful life in trail because they have to only be athletic for moments at a time. I've had horses that were burned out mentally and physically turn into national champion trail horses because they got a new start. They see a reason to do what they have been asked to do. It makes sense to them."

The quality of a trail horse's gaits and conformation are important in that he must look like the work is easy. If he is lumbering and stiff, short strided and unable to engage, it's likely the job of maneuvering in and out, around, and about obstacles will be more than he can handle.

"If you want to do well, you have to look good at the obstacles. If you don't have a good mover, he won't be able to extend or shorten the stride as necessary to take the obstacles. That takes a certain level of engagement and suppleness consistent with an athlete," says Damianos.

A horse that moves with grace and beauty over the course presents the judge with a much nicer picture.

CONDUCT OF THE CLASS

To begin trail classes, horse show management draws the competitors numbers from a basket or hat to determine the "order of go" and posts the pattern for the class at least one hour prior to the class.

At a designated time, exhibitors are invited to inspect the course with the judge. Amateurs and juniors may bring their trainers. This walk-through is not to be missed. Here you can plan the line of travel and pick your approaches to each obstacle. When an experienced competitor walks the course, he tells himself where he should look, what he should do, and where he should be at specific places in the course. He thinks about how he needs to help his horse perform at his best.

Following the course walk, the judge will give competitors instructions on how he wants them to ride the course. For example, he may tell them that the gate is a "left-hand push away" and give hints as to the best approach to handling the obstacle.

Scoring

Trail Horse classes are scored events. Each horse and rider combination rides into the course with 70 points. During the performance the judge instructs a scribe to record on a score sheet a score for each obstacle. At the end, points and half points for how well the horse negotiated the obstacle are either added to or subtracted from the starting 70 points. Any penalties incurred are subtracted to arrive at a final score.

Following are obstacles scores and the criteria for that score:

+3 EXCELLENT: The horse approaches and negotiates the obstacle in correct form with definite style. He performs in an efficient manner with curiosity and athleticism, while maintaining the quality of an ideal trail horse. His performance is **visually impressive**.

+2 VERY GOOD: The horse approaches and negotiates the obstacle in correct form with noticeable style. He definitely displays many qualities of the ideal trail horse. His performance is **visually attractive**.

+1 GOOD: The horse approaches and negotiates the obstacle in correct form with some degree of style. He may display some qualities of the ideal trail horse, but lacks those qualities to the degree that are exhibited by the excellent and very good performers. His performance is **visually pleasing**.

0 AVERAGE: The horse approaches and negotiates the obstacle in correct form with minimal style. His performance as an ideal trail horse is flawed by slight errors in form and leaves a visually neutral impression.

-1 POOR: The horse fails in some way to approach and/or negotiate the obstacle in the correct form. He lacks some of the quality of the ideal trail horse. Willingness to guide or control may have been compromised, but he is safe.

-2 VERY POOR: The horse noticeably fails to approach and negotiate the obstacle in correct form. He is definitely deficient in the qualities of the ideal trail horse. He shows noticeable resistance and may not be safe.

-3 EXTREMELY POOR: The horse approaches and/or negotiates the obstacle in unacceptable form, but avoids elimination. His performance is likely reckless, careless, and dangerous. He shows significant resistance toward the rider's commands.

Here is how penalties work.

A rider may earn a **no score** penalty for abuse of his horse or another exhibitor, or for illegal equipment. (Essentially he is eliminated.) A **zero score** is given for going off course, incorrect use of the reins, equipment failure, loss of a shoe that forces a time-out, or if the horse or rider falls. These cause elimination too, but the horse and rider may advance in an event that has more than one round.

TEN-POINT PENALTY: These penalties are for naughty horses and distracted riders. They may be granted to out of control horses that stampede, run through, or jump over entire obstacles that are not designated jumps, or blatantly disobey by kicking, bucking, rearing, striking, or leaving the designated ground-tie area. Ten points are taken off when a horse steps off the side of a bridge with two or more feet. Other chances for error are side passing with the wrong end of the horse in the slot designated for the side pass or pulling a gate when the rider should push the gate (or vice versa). When the judge deems that the horse has three times refused to do the work, he may ask the rider to proceed to the next obstacle without completing the current one. Along with the request come 10 penalty points.

FIVE-POINT PENALTY: This penalty is given for each refusal. When three are added up and the judge has to ask the rider to move on, 15 penalty points are added to the above 10 penalty points given for moving on. Five points are also subtracted for placing two or more feet outside a confining element, for evading or missing an element of a series of components (for example, riding over only two of three poles), losing an object you are carrying, placing one foot off the side of a bridge, riding on the wrong lead or in the wrong gait, and obvious cueing or touching the horse in front of the forward cinch.

TWO-POINT PENALTY: These penalties are awarded for knockdowns, placing one foot outside a confining element, or skipping a slot. A slot is a space between parts of an obstacle such as in "overs" (walkovers, jogovers, lopeovers) where in the designated gait the horse negotiates a series of poles.

Problems with leads including switching leads, picking up the wrong lead, cross-firing (moving in a different lead in the front end than in back), or approaching the obstacle on the wrong lead or in the wrong gait result in two penalty points. Holding the saddle with the free hand results in this penalty.

ONE-POINT PENALTY: Double striding, adding strides or adding steps, breaking gait, and stepping on an element of an obstacle leads to the loss of a point.

Preparation at Home

A successful trail horse understands the rider's cues and thus can respond willingly. He is maneuverable, controllable, and obedient to the rider, not the obstacles. In return the rider is patient and clear. To achieve this relationship with your horse, work at home should include lateral exercises that allow you to move the forehand and the hindquarters as much and as little as you need. These exercises include shoulder-in, haunches-in, turn on the forehand, turn on the haunches, leg yielding, and side pass.

Homework also focuses on sharpening the horse's handiness by improving neck reining and turning.

If Trail Horse classes are in your future, train yourself to be a thinking observer. Attend trail classes at shows and ask yourself, what is the trail course designer trying to accomplish? What is his goal for the course? How did he bring out certain qualities in the exhibiting horses and riders?

Then duplicate his ideas at home.

First, introduce your horse to the basic maneuvers one at a time: obstacles and walkovers, jogovers, lopeovers, side passes, gates, mailboxes, bridges, back throughs, small jumps, and serpentines. When he becomes confident with one obstacle, ask him to take on two in a row. After that routine becomes a relaxed affair, add other challenges.

Then make variations in:

1. their placement in the arena
2. distances between obstacles
3. order of obstacles
4. the number of elements in one obstacle

"For my national win I had done so many things with the horse that even something new didn't affect him. And sometimes you're lucky because something unusual that you practiced shows up on the course," recalls Damianos.

At the Show

Take the course walk with the judge. Spend the time needed to learn the pattern. Rehearse it in your mind repeatedly. Then do your best to stay focused in your class. Nevertheless, anyone who has shown trail has gotten lost—it happens.

"My biggest advice to myself and to my amateurs is to never stop showing and never stop trying. You can make a mistake, your horse can make a mistake, but you still have a chance of winning," says Damianos.

RIDE THE COURSE WITH THE DESIGNER AND THE CHAMPION

2004 U. S. National
Arabian and Half Arabian
Championship Horse Show

October 14, 2004
Class 211 Arabian Trail Horse — Final
Class 646 Half Arabian/Anglo-Arabian Trail Horse — Final

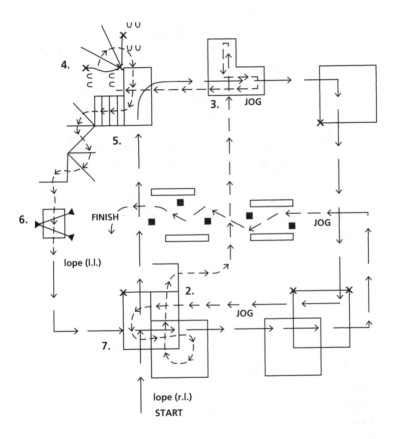

The trail course diagram and description for the 2004 U.S. National Championship Half Arabian Trail Horse Finals were designed by Lorne Robertson. The class was won by Michael Damianos.

When the course designer puts obstacles in your way, he has his reasons. To explain his thinking, Lorne Robertson, creator of the 2004 U.S. National Championship Trail courses, went step by step through his design for the final open class, in which the top ten horses from the Arabian and Half Arabian semifinal rounds competed for the titles of champion and reserve champion.

On this course Mike Damianos won the U.S. National Arabian Trail Horse Championship on PS Poison, the Reserve Championship on MFA Maverick, and the Half Arabian Trail Horse Championship on Wyatt Earp. He also commented on what he called "a high end, monster course."

As you travel through the course, keep in mind that Robertson's goal was to reward horses and riders that communicate well with one another. Success on this course called for trust, patience, and precision. It demanded collection, lengthening and shortening of stride, balance, and softness. Less an issue of talent at navigating the obstacles, what mattered most was how the riders prepared their horses for the obstacles and how the horses went into and came out of the obstacles. "The number one error by riders is that they ride each obstacle separately, not the whole course overall," says Robertson.

The Course

#1 – Enter the arena at the walk. At the marker, lope on the right lead. Lope over poles as drawn. Poles are set on 6'6" strides. Some poles are raised to a maximum of 10" at center.

Robertson: By loping around much of the arena at the start of the course, the horse can relax into his work, as he sees the entire ring, and the rider can show the judge how her horse is responsive, focused, and maintains his rhythm. Loping over poles is not hard work for the horse, but it does offer an opportunity to show the judge the team's precision, trust, and responsiveness.

Damianos: This first obstacle looks easier on paper. There are no lines on the course, and it looked like a sea of lumber. I had to know that the farthest left slot was the one to go through, and I had to do it in the prescribed two strides. As I rode I said to myself, 'There is a lot of room after the second pole, but I better be looking way up there at the next slot.' My next concern was the corner coming up; it would be easy to get in trouble if I was not angling straight. Then I needed to reach the next two poles in two strides, lope over the poles, and take two more strides to the third part. Before the sharp turn I had only a second or two to get my thoughts together. The bottom corner was particularly tricky because I had to make the sharp right turn into just a six-foot hole (a six-foot space between poles). If I didn't keep my eyes forward, I wouldn't stay in the right lane.

#2 – Jog over poles and through boxes as drawn. Some poles are raised to a maximum of 8" at center.

Robertson: The rider has about 20 feet to get the horse from the lope to the jog. She should jog immediately after the last lope pole in order to give herself room to show the judge what a well-trained, beautiful mover her horse is, letting him stretch down into a Western jog, a feat after the earlier tightness. Then she could jog right to the next pole with an adjusted, rhythmic stride. On the other hand, if the rider is loping along on long reins and thinking, 'Okay, now I'm over the last pole, what do I do now?', she is too late to take advantage of the course. This series of boxes requires precision and has to be ridden sharply, rhythmically, and fluidly—boom, boom, boom. It is pole, pole, turn, pole, turn, pole. After loping, the horse has to trot up under himself and not cover a lot of ground.

Damianos: Because the next components came up real soon, I jogged right after the last lopeover pole. This is why you have to know early on where you are going. After the first two poles, you make two left turns, and then a right circle, which makes a very tight, tough obstacle. My horse had to be able to change frames, collect easily, and be most tractable for good steering. After the last pole, I had a little time to regroup.

#3 – Jog into the chute. Halt. Back around the chute and jog out.

Robertson: Before the chute, the horse has to pass a group of trees (squares on the course map) that might distract him and cause him to hesitate before continuing to the chute. The rider has to straighten the horse and have him trot right into the chute. The horse had to trust that the rider wouldn't ask him to jump the end wall (of the three-sided chute). If he didn't have that trust, he might break into a walk. The degree of difficulty here is that you jog him all the way up to the wall, and ask him to stop and back.

Damianos: Here is a true test of a trail horse. You have done all these fast things, and now you have to plan to stop, back, and jog out. I practiced this slow and deliberate move a lot.

#4 – Open the gate with the right hand. Continue over poles. Close the gate. Poles are raised slightly.

Robertson: Here you walk over two poles while holding the rope gate. You then place it on the other standard.

Damianos: This was a unique obstacle. Holding the gate and going over the walkovers was hard.

#5 – Walk into the box and over poles as drawn. Some poles are raised to a maximum of 10" at center.

Robertson: My objective is to allow the horse to show how well schooled he is. After walking over the familiar-style poles, the horse has to walk over railway ties and big logs and junk lumber. The rider adjusts the horse for that and then lets him figure out how to do it. If the rider takes her legs off the horse or loses the rhythm turning left and turning right, the horse will add an extra step as he turns. This is a penalty. The rider needs to maintain the forward momentum around the corner left and in the bank right. The last turn, a square corner, sets up the horse to go straight for the upcoming bridge. If the rider waits to cross the last pole before getting the horse's attention, it is too late. How the rider gets out of #5 affects how she gets into #6.

Damianos: The horse can figure out how to go over these poles better than I could ever tell him. I had to tell him where to turn in a few spots, but basically he went his own way.

#6 – Continue at the walk over the bridge. Poles on the bridge are raised to 8". The distance between poles is 4' at center.

Robertson: If you get in and out right, the rest takes care of itself.

Damianos: The trick here was to go straight over the bridge, then pick up the left lead. It wasn't too difficult.

#7 – Lope over poles on the left lead, as drawn. Distance between poles is 6'6", 6'6", 6'6", 13', 6'6", 6'6", 6'6". Some poles are raised to a maximum of 10" at center.

Robertson: This lopeover requires precision: pole, pole, pole, then a break with a two-stride, then pole, pole, pole. The horse was literally bouncing over the poles. The rider has to ride the first pole so that the horse's front feet were 3'3" away from the first pole before he went over it, not up against the first pole. Otherwise he is too close. He won't see the pole because it would be too close. Horses only see what is out in front of them, not what is near their feet. The rider has to give him the chance to see the first pole, so he can essentially memorize where it is.

Damianos: These lopeovers were in a different lane than previous obstacles. One exhibitor lost concentration and loped through the wrong lane. She got a zero score. That happens. Anyone who has shown trail has gotten lost at some time.

#8 – Jog serpentine as drawn. Markers are 10' apart, guardrails @ 8'.

Robertson: The rider jogs through a serpentine of trees, ending on a positive, very pretty note with a chance to show off her horse. The guide rails on the side keep the horse from swinging out. It is tight. The rider has to know where her horse's hind end is and what it is doing.

Damianos: The course was so difficult and so big that you could make a mistake and still have a chance of winning the big prize. The trick is to never stop showing.

CHAPTER THIRTEEN

REINING

*"As a species we are fast runners, too . . . and this gives us a
common bond with the horse and a deeply rooted admiration
for its amazing pace and grace . . . Sitting on its back we
fuse with it in our minds to become one single, galloping
invincible being."*

—Desmond Morris, *Horsewatching*

HOUR AFTER HOUR SPECTATORS LINED THE ARENA FENCE
around the reining classes at the Scottsdale Arabian show. A man
dressed more for golf than for cowboy games asked the woman to
his left how the scoring of the class worked. She shrugged and
looked to the person to her left. No one knew. They acknowledged,
however, that although they knew very little about what they were
looking at, throughout the show they were lured back to this fence
to watch horse after horse.

Like the old Bobby Darin song "Splish Splash," those horses
were slippin' and a-slidin', whirlin' and a-twirlin'. They were among
the increasing numbers in the fastest growing division in the Arabian
show scene. Reining is great to watch and even more fun to do. Its
speed is a rush, and its precision is an addiction.

Drawn from a vaquero and cowboy heritage, reining began on
the West Coast in classes known as stock horse competitions. As the
sport filtered to the East it picked up the name "reining." Today its
popularity has expanded worldwide, especially in Germany, England,
Holland, Italy, Austria, Japan, and Brazil. In 2000, the Fédération
Equestre Internationale (FEI), the governing body of international

equestrian competitions, brought reining into its selective covey of sports, and reining became the first and only Western discipline invited by the United States Equestrian Team.

Reining competitions test the ranch-type horse's athletic ability in the performance of moves that allowed the cow horse to do his job. Exhibitors ride one of ten approved patterns. Each pattern consists of seven to eight groups of maneuvers, which include small, slow circles; large, fast circles; flying lead changes; rollbacks; 360 degree spins; and sliding stops. In freestyle reining, a rider creates her own pattern by choreographing the required maneuvers to music.

A successful reining horse demonstrates his willingness to be guided and controlled by his rider through the maneuvers. He is rewarded by the judge if he executes the pattern with finesse, confidence, and attitude in a quick and smooth manner. The quality of the performance ratchets up a notch if he carries out his job in controlled

AM Good Oldboy and Gary Ferguson kick up dirt performing a sliding stop. PHOTO BY HOOFPRINTS.

speed. Any movement in which he shows resistance or the rider loses control detracts from the quality of the ride, or "running the pattern."

Much of the thrill of reining is the speed and exhilarating moves, such as spins and sliding stops. Yet equally thrilling is the precise and exacting nature of the maneuvers and patterns. You ask for a great response, and the horse willingly gives it. You and the horse are hooked together, and you think "Wow, this is going to work today."

CONDUCT OF THE CLASS

Reining is conducted in a fenced arena, dotted by markers along the side walls at the center of the arena and at least 50 feet from each end wall.

An exhibitor rides individually, before a judge or judges, a pattern designated in the show's premium list and chosen from the ten official patterns found in the USEF Rule Book or obtained from the National Reining Horse Association.

As a scored event performed under the rules and guidelines of the National Reining Horse Association, AHA, and USEF, each exhibitor enters the arena with a starting score of 70. The judge evaluates each maneuver group against an ideal and gives it a score ranging from minus 1½ points to plus 1½ points, either adding (called "plused" or "credit") or subtracting (called "minused) from 70, which denotes an average performance. He also may give it a penalty, with points ranging from one to five. (See sidebar.) Therefore, the final score will be 70 points plus or minus maneuver scores, minus penalties. A final total score of 76 is outstanding.

Maneuver scores represent the following:

+1½	Excellent	-½	Poor
+1	Very good	-1	Very poor
+½	Good	-1½	Extremely poor
0	Correct		

In determining where those pluses and minuses belong, the judge will consider three factors:

1. On pattern: Are the horse and rider performing the correct maneuver at the right time and place according to the designated pattern?
2. Correctness: Do the horse and rider fulfill the basic elements of the maneuver? If they fail to perform correctly, negative points are assigned.
3. Degree of difficulty: Does the team shine in their work? Do they perform with smoothness, finesse, attitude, quickness, authority, and controlled speed? If so, plus points are awarded.

After each run, the score is announced. The horse with the highest score wins.

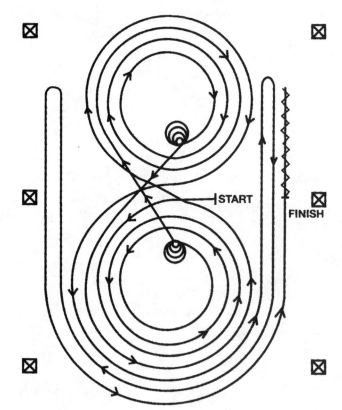

Reining pattern #5 (facing page) calls for:

1. Beginning on the left lead, complete three circles to the left; the first two circles large and fast; the third circle small and slow. Stop at the center of the arena.
2. Complete four spins to the left. Hesitate.
3. Beginning on the right lead, complete three circles to the right; the first two circles large and fast; the third circle small and slow. Stop at the center of the arena.
4. Complete four spins to the right. Hesitate.
5. Beginning on the left lead, run a large fast circle to the left, change leads at the center of the arena.
6. Continue around the previous circle to the left, but do not close this circle. Run up the right side of the arena past the center marker and do a right rollback at least twenty feet from the wall or fence—no hesitation.
7. Continue around the previous circle, but do not close this circle. Run up the left side of the arena past the center marker and do a left rollback at least twenty feet from the wall or fence—no hesitation.
8. Continue back around the previous circle, but do not close this circle. Run up the right side of the arena past the center marker and do a sliding stop at least twenty feet from the wall or fence. Back up at least ten feet. Hesitate to demonstrate completion of the pattern.

REPRINTED WITH PERMISSION OF THE NATIONAL REINING HORSE ASSOCIATION AND THE NRHA REINER.

Choosing a Reining Horse

Consider a pasture of yearlings. They hear something in the distance. One youngster shoots his head and neck up in the air, throws his tail over his back, and trots off. Another one drops his head, gets back on his hocks, wheels around, and gallops off in a flat stride across the pasture. Yearling number one might best find a job in the English Pleasure arena. Sign up youngster number two for the reining ring.

Arabian reining prospects today often start their careers under saddle directly on a path toward becoming reining horses. They may, however, have early training in Western Pleasure in order to learn a solid foundation. They are taught to be comfortable in the bridle, and to willingly move their shoulders. They learn to relax under saddle. This training also improves their movement. "In today's highly competitive show world, they should be good movers. Wouldn't the judge rather see a good mover than not?" says John O'Hara, a multi-national champion reiner.

"I like prospects that track up (the back foot steps beyond the point where the front foot previously landed), and the front end gets out of the way of the hind end. It's important they be fluid movers. And the bottom line is that if they move well, they will be able to stop and do better lead changes and spins," says Tony Boit, Arabian reining competitor, national champion, and retired judge.

Temperament

A good reining horse has a distinct mental attitude. He walks into the arena calm and cool. He is secure working in an arena alone and prepared to please his rider. As soon as he receives the cue to start running the pattern, he turns on, and he stays on until he understands that he is done. He walks off as if his big effort was no big deal.

"He's like a light switch: one moment it's on, and the next moment it's off," relates O'Hara.

"Some horses can't take the heat. They get too stimulated by the work, such as the horse that is going 90 miles an hour around a large fast (circle), and 10 miles an hour in the small slow (circle) but he's fighting the rider the whole way. You can't pay him with points because it's not a willing ride," says Boit. "You don't want a horse that stimulates and gets tighter and higher as his run goes on."

Conformation

A horse built for reining has stout loins, powerful hindquarters, well-muscled gaskins, especially inside, and strong hock and fetlock joints to take the pressure and stress of sliding stops. The neck is not too long. "With the rapid pace of the spins and flying changes, if you have a too-long neck, it's going to be awkward," says Bazy Tankersley, reining horse breeder.

A horse with a massive front end tends to fall on his forehand, making spinning difficult. A wide chest and massive shoulder make it difficult for the horse to cross his outside front leg over his inside front leg when spinning, and he may not have the reach needed to stretch out his front legs in a rundown and stop.

Arabians usually have free-moving shoulders and carry them up nicely. This feature lends to excellent lead changes, spins, and circles. "I don't care what division you're in, if you lose the horse's shoulders, you lose the class," says Boit.

On the other end, some Arabians have more difficulty articulating the hind end joints and are not always built to "sit" or squat with their hindquarters as is needed in a sliding stop. Today, however, more Arabian breeders have bred specifically for reining horses and improved this characteristic.

Age and Size

Compared to some other breeds, Arabians are mentally and physically slower to develop. For that reason, the reining training does not really take off until the horse is four or five. NRHA futurities, dominated by Quarter Horses, are for three-year-olds. Arabian futurity entrants are five years old.

Another factor to consider is the horse's size. Most reiners prefer a smaller horse, feeling that the smaller package makes a more agile, quicker, handier, and balanced horse. A horse that is too small, under 14.1 hands, may not have the physical strength, muscling, and bone to do the job.

REINING PENALTY CHART

Deductions from scores include zero, $\frac{1}{2}$-, 1-, 2-, and 5-point penalties. Exhibitors who receive a zero score or a "no score" penalty are ineligible to place in single-round classes. Exhibitors with a zero penalty may advance in multi-round events. Those with a "no score" penalty may not advance.

WALK-IN OR RUN-IN PATTERNS

Failure to walk or stop before executing a lope departure	2-point penalty
Jogging in excess of half a circle	Zero score penalty
Failure to be in a lope prior to the reaching the first marker	Zero score penalty

STOP/SLIDE

Failure to completely pass the specified marker before initiating a stop	2-point penalty
Failure to remain a minimum of 20 feet from the wall or fence when approaching a stop	½-point penalty

SPIN

Freezing up or brief refusal to start a spin, or complete stoppage in a spin	2-point penalty
Over-spin or under-spin enough that the horse's shoulder is not touching the centerline where the spin began or a full ⅛ of a turn	½-point penalty
Over-spin or under-spin more than ⅛ of a turn and up to ½ of a turn	1-point penalty
Over-spins of more than ½ turn	Zero score penalty

ROLLBACK

Freezing up in rollback	2-point penalty
When exiting a rollback:	
– jogging up to 2 strides	½-point penalty
– jogging more than 2 strides, but less than ½ the length of the arena	2-point penalty
– jogging in excess of ½ the length of the arena	Zero score penalty
– failure to remain a minimum of 20 feet from the wall or fence when approaching a stop	½-point penalty

CIRCLE

Performing a circle or figure eight on the incorrect lead	1-point penalty for each quarter circle on the incorrect lead
When starting a circle:	
– jogging up to 2 strides	½-point penalty

– jogging more than 2 strides, but less than ½ the circumference of the circle	2-point penalty
– jogging in excess of ½ a circle	Zero score penalty

BACK UP

Backing up more than two strides if the maneuver is not included in the pattern	Zero score penalty

LEAD CHANGE

Delay of lead change by one stride	½-point penalty

Where a change of lead is specified immediately prior to a half circle and followed by a run to the end of the arena:

– failure to change leads by one stride	½-point penalty
– failure to change leads by one stride and up to ½ of a circle	1-point penalty
– failure to change leads by the next maneuver	2-point penalty
– failure to change beyond ½ of a circle	2-point penalty

RUNDOWN AND RUN-AROUND

Failure to be on the correct lead when rounding the end of the arena

– for ½ turn or less	1-point penalty
– for more than ½ turn	2-point penalty

GENERAL

	No score penalty
Infraction of any state or federal law which exists pertaining to the exhibition, care, and custody of horses within the state or country where a reining is being held	
Abuse of the animal in the show arena and/or evidence of abuse prior to or during the exhibition of a horse in competition	
Use of illegal equipment, including wire on a bit, bosal, or curb chain	
Use of illegal bits, bosals, or curb chains	
Use of electric shockers, whips, bats, tack collars, tie-downs, or nosebands	
Use of any attachment which alters the movement of or circulation of the tail	
Failure to dismount and/or present the horse and equipment to the appropriate person for inspection	

Disrespect or misconduct by the exhibitor	
The judge may excuse a horse at any time for unsafe conditions or improper conduct	
Use of more than index finger or first finger between split reins	Zero score penalty
Use of two hands or changing hands except in snaffle bit or hackamore classes	
Any finger between romal reins	
Failure to complete the pattern as written	
Performing the maneuvers out of order	
Including maneuvers not specified in the pattern	
Equipment failure that delays the completion of the pattern	
Failure to display correct exhibitor number	
Balking or refusing a command which delays completion of the pattern	
Running away or failing to be guided, making it impossible to discern whether the entry performed the pattern	
Horse or rider falls to the ground	
Failure to wear proper Western attire	
Spurring in front of the cinch	5-point penalty
Using the free hand to instill fear or praise	
Holding the saddle with either hand	
Blatant disobedience, including kicking, biting, bucking, rearing, and striking	
Breaking gait	2-point penalty

MANEUVERS

The rider is required to show his skill and his horse's obedience by riding maneuvers with only one hand on the reins, a style that derived from the cowboy's need to use his other hand for roping and other ranch jobs.[16] Extremely loose reins will not earn extra credit with the judge. On the other hand, heavy contact tells the judge the horse has taken over the program. "The ideal horse is on a semi-loose rein, and you don't see the rider's hand lift. He steers off the legs. You don't want a drape in the reins. You want a light to medium contact," O'Hara describes.

WALK-IN: The horse walks to the center of the arena to begin the pattern, appearing relaxed, confident, attentive to his rider, and giving and flexible through his poll. Though the walk-in is not a maneuver scored on its own merit, any signs of intimidation or tension are considered a fault that is taken off the first maneuver score.

Reining judges at the Scottsdale Arabian Show watch from atop elevated chairs for a better view of reining maneuvers. PHOTO BY PATTI SCHOFLER.

"Here is where you see a lot of checking, jerking, and bumping (with the reins). It's a red flag that tells me the rider's having trouble keeping the head down," says Boit.

RUNDOWNS AND RUN-AROUNDS: In the rundown, the horse lopes through the middle or along the sides of the arena, depending on the pattern. The rundown is usually the preparation for a sliding stop. In

---

[16] In most classes the horse is ridden in a standard Western or curb bit. If he is ridden in a snaffle bit or hackamore, usually limited to young horse classes, the rider may use two hands.

the rundown, the rider needs full control of the horse's speed and straightness. A crooked rundown will lead to a crooked stop. Running in an uphill balance, not on the forehand, will also lead to a better stop. The best speed is the speed at which the horse stops best.

The horse must pass the center marker before stopping, but not go so far that it looks like the rider is using the arena fence to assist the stop.

In the run-arounds, the horse lopes around the ends of the arena.

STOPS: The dramatic sliding stop, the hallmark of reining, is an exhilarating picture. The horse runs down the side of the arena building his speed to a great pace, then puts on the breaks by crouching down his powerful hindquarters and melting into the ground as he slides on his hind legs. A good sliding stop may travel 15 to 25 feet. A great one may cover 40 feet.

In a correct stop the horse rounds his back, drives his hind legs low and under his body in a locked position. His hind feet slide under him, burying his tail in the dirt. His front legs walk along maintaining forward motion, ground contact, and cadence (a uniform rhythm or tempo). His head stays in a relaxed, unfettered position because he has the power and muscle to hold his position throughout the slide, remain straight in his body, on a straight line and in contact with the ground. His mouth is closed because he has responded to the rider's body and leg position, and the rider hasn't pulled too much on the reins.

To create the stop, the rider sits deep in the saddle ("sits on her pockets"), takes her legs off the horse's sides, pushes her feet hard into the stirrup, softly says "whoa," and smoothly, slowly takes up the reins. As soon as the horse stops, she releases the rein contact.

You don't want an abrupt, tense stop. You don't want the horse to bounce off the ground a few times, or his front legs to jam into the ground or prop like pogo sticks. Some horses try to protect their mouths by diving into the stop, or throwing their heads up and bracing, or "scotching," the term for a horse stopping before the rider has asked.

"Reining is not a pulling contest. It's all about body position," says O'Hara. The lighter the rider can cue the horse to achieve the desired response, the greater the accomplishment and the better the result. The horse should ideally begin his stop when the rider says "whoa." He reaches out his neck and takes up the slack in the rein. How much pull the rider uses depends on the horse. The less pull, however, the longer the slide.

A horse that does not walk with his front legs when he slides behind, but instead stiffens his front legs, is likely scared or nervous about stopping because the rider might pull too hard during stops.

The rundown to the slide also affects the quality of the stop. Tony Boit wants to see a smooth rundown. "The horse might anticipate the stop and rush, but you want every stride to build, build, and build, to gradually and smoothly get up to speed. Make it pretty. It doesn't matter how fast as long as they don't run off. The first priority is that it be correct. If the horse slides 40 feet with his head upside down and the guy's knuckles are white from pulling on the bridle, or if the horse runs off and then gets pulled off his feet, that's really bad. Anything that looks dangerous is bad."

SPINS: The spin is another crowd-pleaser, especially when the horse turns like a blur, flowing through 360-degrees at extreme speed. In this maneuver the horse should flatten out, plant his inside hind leg (the leg on the inside of the bend), and turn his shoulders around his hindquarters. The propulsion of the spin comes from the driving of the horse's outside hind leg. The outside front leg crosses over the inside front leg, which moves to the side, out of its way.

Spin styles vary. A good reining horse just feels the touch of the outside rein on his neck and he is hot off it to make his turn. Some horses look a bit to the inside. "You'll see riders shorten the inside rein to lead the horse into the spin, and the horse turns like a blur. But that's like riding with two hands, and it takes away from the maneuver score," Boit comments.

Equally problematic is the use of so much outside rein that the horse's head tilts to the outside. This position makes it difficult for the horse to turn his shoulders around his hindquarters because he is leaning on his inside shoulder.

Some horses spin a little straighter in their bodies or step a little higher with their front feet. Some stop the spin with their head up higher. "These horses might need to put their heads up for balance. Instead of bumping the head down, you have to live with that," says Tony Boit.

Speed in a spin is a plus if everything else is correct. "You see horses going around so fast they loose their hind end and are turning on their belly buttons," says Boit. Instead of bringing the shoulders around the hindquarters, this horse has no bend in his body and is turning from his center. "I like to see a horse drop down, round up, get flat, and really step around, step around, step around."

Each reining pattern has at least four spins in a row both to the right and left. Over- or under-spinning a revolution will garner penalty points. "Anyone who has done reining has over-spun or under-spun," O'Hara contends. "You get lost. Or the horse stumbles getting into the turn and you miss your count."

Many riders use the help of a trainer or a sharp-eyed friend to let them know when to stop. That person will let out a "hoot" or some other prearranged sound to tell the rider she has spun 3¾ revolutions, giving her time to hear it and prepare to stop.

The horse depends on the rider to cue the horse when to stop. In addition to pressure from the rider's outside leg to maintain the motion, many riders use the "cluck" sound to keep their horse moving. The horse has learned at home that this sound means to speed up. To let the horse know to stop spinning, the rider says "whoa."

Once the spin has stopped, a rider will let the horse stand five seconds to let him relax and get his bearings before moving to the next maneuver. "Wait and make sure he's settled. He can go to sleep for all I care," says O'Hara. "Then when I lift my hand, he goes on."

This technique demonstrates to the judge that your horse guides willingly.

CIRCLES: Reining patterns ask for two types of circles performed at the lope: the large circle that is ridden at a fast pace and the small circle that is ridden at a slow speed. In the pattern, the circles are related to each other. For example, Pattern 7 states: "Complete three circles to the left: the first two circles are large and fast; the third circle small and slow. Change leads at the center of the arena."

The circles must be clearly different sizes performed at clearly different speeds. They must be executed in the center of the arena, with a common starting or center point. The transition between the two types should be quite clear. The circles should show the rider's control, the horse's willingness to be guided, and a degree of difficulty in speed and speed changes. If the pattern calls for a set of circles in both directions, they ideally should be equal in size, speed, and arena position. And they should be round, not egg-shaped or ragged.

Circles test the horse and rider's precision. They show the judge how well the horse moves, how he stays straight between the reins, how he responds to the rider's speed requests, how well he follows his nose, and how well he bends in his body. The horse should be straight on the circle, meaning he should bend throughout his body.

LARGE, FAST CIRCLE: On this circle the horse is lengthening his lope and covering more ground per stride than when he is not lengthening. The closer to the starting point the horse begins his faster stride, the higher the score, because he will gain points for a degree of difficulty. Yet the execution must look fluid and soft. An abrupt burst of speed may interfere with the horse's balance and steering ability. However, taking longer than a quarter of the circle to reach speed may be too slow.

"I have the horse settled and quiet before I start," states John O'Hara. "It's not how fast I get to speed, but that it looks good getting there and being there."

The rider should also place the large circle at least 10 feet away from the arena fence. "If you hug the rail, the arena becomes an overexaggerated round pen. You must show the judge that you are guiding the horse, not using the rail to steer," O'Hara adds.

TRANSITION: The ideal transition happens at dead center. The horse comes back clearly, hard, instantly, but maintains the forward motion. "We call the center home plate, and it's hard to drop him into the center and start up the small slow (circle)," says Boit. "It will win you points, but it may cause other problems." The horse may switch leads or stop or get into a tug of war that tells the judge that the horse is not being willingly controlled.

If you ask the horse to slow down slightly before the center point, he has the time to respond and collect, thereby giving a smoother picture. This can be accomplished by sitting up straight, deepening your seat into the saddle, and riding in a slower rhythm. The horse feels the change in your body. You take a light hold of the reins, he collects and slows his stride, and you release the contact.

At the Scottsdale Arabian Show this purebred Arabian performs the fast circle of a reining pattern. PHOTO BY PATTI SCHOFLER.

SMALL, SLOW CIRCLE: The size and the speed of the small, slow circle should contrast with the large, fast circle. The greater the contrast in speed in the two circles, the better the score. Ideally the small circle is exactly half the size of the large circle. Each horse, however, has a length of stride and a degree of collection in which he is comfortable and performs his best. Going beyond his ability may not create a pretty picture. If the circle is too small, the horse's correct three-beat lope may become four-beat or the stride may become choppy. If you go too slowly, he may drop into a trot.

"To get to the pay window, you want the circle to be perfect. Know where the center marker is. Pay attention to the markers to help your geometry," Tony Boit suggests.

Too much inside rein will also plague the rider's geometry. If a rider shortens the inside rein, she shows the horse is not willingly guided. While the judge might not notice the shorter inside rein, he will notice that the circle is not round and the horse's outside shoulder leads.

LEAD CHANGES: "Kiss of death," John O'Hara calls this maneuver because it offers up so many ways to lose points.

Simply put, a lead change executed at the lope changes the leading legs of the front and rear pairs of legs when changing the direction of travel. The judge, however, wants to see more than the horse going from one lead to another. The horse must change the front and back legs at the same time, not front, then back, or vice versa. The horse should not dive into the change, bounce the rider around, speed up, or slow down to accomplish the feat or after it's done.

"I like pretty, smooth, balanced, and willing," Tony Boit points out.

The points really peel off when the horse does not make the change at the designated spot. If he goes one stride past the center without making the change, he loses ½ point. He then loses 1 point for each ¼ circumference of a circle that he goes on the wrong lead. This is only the penalty accruement. The judge will likely also give a poor maneuver score.

ROLLBACK: In a rollback, the horse crisply turns 180 degrees by rolling the shoulders back to the opposite direction and turning over his hocks. To complete the maneuver, the horse immediately, without hesitation, without walk or trot steps, takes off into a lope. It is not a stop, then a circle, then a stop.

"A rollback is so hard to do and takes a real talented horse. You can groom the maneuver and make it better, but he has to do it naturally, and not all horses can lock their hocks," says Boit.

BACKUP: The horse backs up in a straight line for at least 10 feet.

HESITATION: All the patterns call for a hesitation at the end of a pattern to show the judge that you have finished the pattern. It appears in other parts of the patterns as well. To do a hesitation, the horse stands in a relaxed manner.

SHOEING

Often reining horses are shod with sliding shoes on the hind feet. These are $7/8$ to $1\frac{1}{4}$ inches wide, wider than other shoes, and with extensions of the shoe (called trailers) behind the heel, to give the horse the maximum surface on which to slide. Some farriers will rasp or file back the toes so they don't dig into the dirt at the start of the stop.

SHOW SCENE

Arabian reining has increased its presence on the Arabian show scene through the efforts of the Arabian Reining Horse Association, an affiliate club of both the National Reining Horse Association and the Arabian Horse Association. ARHA has raised prize money and increased the number of classes at shows.

To succeed in Arabian reining, you and your horse must do well and look good doing it. Gone are the days when a rider pulled her horse out of pasture, tore the knots out the mare's long mane, and arrived at a show expecting to win. The horses have gotten so good that you must pay attention to every aspect in order to come out on top. "The horses are as fit and slick as halter horses," says John O'Hara. "Top condition, strong and pretty. Ten years ago it wasn't like that."

Professionals also advise:

1. While the controlled speed may bring up the score, correctness and smoothness are the first priority.
2. Study the pattern. Walk through it on foot. Go over it in your mind several times. To keep your horse from anticipating maneuvers, practice the pattern in segments, rather than always practicing the entire pattern.
3. Make sure your horse is really warmed up before going into the arena.
4. If you see someone in the warm-up arena doing something you like, don't try to put it in your program at the show. Try it at home first.
5. Learn to focus on the moment. Focus on one maneuver at a time. And don't let one bobble affect the rest of your ride.
6. If your horse can only give you 90 percent and you're asking for 92 percent, you're overriding him. Your horse will let you know as he becomes tense and struggles to do the work you ask him to do. This is a common problem for amateurs and professionals.
7. Often a horse is good at one thing and not another. If you have a big stopping horse and an average turning horse, don't try to get a plus on the turn. Go for a clean maneuver on the turn and a plus on the stop. Remember correct form, conducted in a controlled, smooth, and pretty manner, is more important than speed. Capitalize on your horse's good points and smooth over his weaknesses.
8. Since the sport is so specific in its demands and skills, find a trainer who specializes in reining.

WORK AT HOME

While you may not want to practice every maneuver every day, do work on some maneuvers daily. The intensity of the work should vary each day as well. Develop your horse's suppleness. Improve his responsiveness and maneuverability. The key to good reining is your control of the horse's entire body and your ability to put any part where you want to put it when you want to put it there.

Focus on your balance and posture. Ride often with one hand because that is the skill you need in the show arena.

STOPS: "Don't do hard and heavy stops every time," John O'Hara advises. "Go to schooling shows and make the sacrifice of your score by not stopping too big. This will teach him to be honest and not just tear down there and stop."

To keep your horse from anticipating the stop, teach yourself to always look up in your rundowns and in your stop. Look at the arena fence, a tree beyond the fence, or something to keep your head up and your sight beyond where you will be stopping.

SPINS: Most people have their own method for preventing dizziness in a spin. One technique is to look through the horse's ears. Others focus on the fence or a cone. Concentrating on counting the number of 360-degree revolutions helps some people from becoming dizzy.

Spotting an object also helps in counting the turns. Pick an object, perhaps the center marker, and stay aware of where it is at all times. When you look at it, be sure you are looking straight at it. After completing each full spin, count the object.

Focus on maintaining your body control in the spin, and avoid leaning or any extreme movement. This will help your horse keep his balance. Some riders inadvertently wobble in a spin and throw the horse off balance.

To keep your horse from anticipating the end of spinning, vary the number of spins, sometimes doing only one or two. Experiment on how far ahead of time you need to say "whoa" to stop your spinning. Or try thinking "one, two, three, stop" and then say "whoa."

LEAD CHANGES: John O'Hara does a lot of counter canter so that when he gets to the center of the arena to change directions, the horse does not anticipate the flying change.

ROLLBACKS: "If you have access to cattle, let the horse learn a rollback from working the cattle. Then it makes sense to him. Otherwise you can use a fence," says O'Hara.

FREESTYLES

Reining freestyles are a highlight at the Arabian Youth National Championships. Here is a chance to dress in an outrageous costume, ride to your favorite music, and make up your own dance with your horse. Years later people still remember one reiner who dressed as Santa Claus and performed to "Grandma Got Run Over By a Reindeer."

Within a four-minute period, the freestyle horse and rider demonstrate the required maneuvers, plus others that enhance the presentation. Their work is judged on technical and artistic merit.

The required maneuvers include a minimum of four consecutive spins to the right and four to the left; three stops; one lead change from right to left lead and one left to right lead. The exhibitor may add other reining maneuvers and non-classical maneuvers that enhance the performance.

CHAPTER FOURTEEN

WORKING COW HORSE

*"Riding is a partnership. The horse lends you his strength,
speed and grace, which are greater than yours. For your part,
you give him your guidance, intelligence and understanding,
which are greater than his. Together you can achieve a richness
that alone neither can."*

—Lucy Rees, British equine behaviorist

THREE PLAYERS PARTICIPATE IN THE WORKING COW HORSE
class: the horse, the rider, and the cow.

In this sport, the horse plays a hard, fast, and aggressive game.
He is a cat and the cow is a mouse whose every move he controls
until his rider signals that it is time to move into another playground.

For the working cow rider, this game is an adrenaline-pumping,
sweat-pouring challenge of speed, intensity, and quick reactions. She
stays in the moment, reacts, and rides with a mix of muscle memory
and purposeful intent. If she thinks too far ahead, she misses the moment and the cow is gone. If she has no plan, her ride is helter-skelter.

In large part, the difficulty of this class derives from the unknown character of the cow. On first seeing the cow, the rider's
question is, will this run be a dance, a race, or a standstill? The cow
may be wild, dull, herd bound, fearless, fearful, strong, weak or have
poor vision. If the cow merely jogs around, like a partner who will
not dance, the horse and rider team cannot demonstrate its fancy
footwork. Nor can the team perform if the cow is wild, does not notice the horse, or bangs into the fence. But if the horse, through his

rider's instructions, can make the cow move at a fairly fast speed along designated sections of the arena, turning and circling in response to the horse's body language, the score could reach a spectacular 75 out of 80 points.

To play this game, the horse and rider control the moves of a single cow through three segments of a pattern, and they are judged on how well they control the cow and the style in which that control is done. The required pattern includes boxing, going down the fence, and circling. To play this game well, horse and rider need "cow sense," or the ability to read a cow and understand what it will do next. What escape mechanism will it use? Why does it turn now? Why does it not turn now? If the cow is pushy, how will you get to the correct spot and still be able to turn the cow? How close can you get before the cow gets too wild? The signs are there. For example, a raised head indicates that the cow is about to move, and a dropped ear indicates where it will go.

In order to figure out what will happen next, the rider needs to know how a cow moves and read it as quickly as her horse does. Horses learn about cows fairly quickly, and Arabians pick it up quicker than most breeds. Another plus for Arabians in this sport is their agility and catty attitude. They like to play games. "I have one mare that is pretty hot, and when we get to a show and the cattle aren't there yet, she lopes around kind of ditzy," says Bob Hart, Arabian trainer and National and Scottsdale Working Cow champion. "But as soon as the cattle get there and she sees them, she settles right down."

Arabians have the right components for the job: they are intelligent and brave, and the well-conformed, balanced individuals have the coordination for this work. They should have an alert, responsive attitude, with the ability to work at a reasonable speed and yet respond to a light rein contact.

A smart horse that thinks the work is fun will do well. "The dull ones think it's too hard. Their brains don't catch up with the speed of what they have to do. They can't get it or don't care or can't remember that long. So then the riders pick at them and it's not fun for anyone," says Debbie Compilli, Arabian trainer and National and Scottsdale Working Cow champion. The good ones like the challenge, the game, and telling another critter what to do.

Above all, a working cow horse must listen to his rider. Though he knows his job, he must not take over. If the rider indicates the team is not going to turn now, he should comply.

In the pattern, the horse should "rate" the cow, or stay at the same speed as the cow, until the rider tells him to change. He should run just at the cow's hip so that cow and horse move together. He should not run past the cow. If he moves in too close, the cow will run faster. If the horse lags behind, the cow will run ahead or spring across the arena. If the horse is at the cow's head, the cow will not, for example, run the full length of the fence. Should the cow refuse to run down the fence, the horse has to get behind it to get it moving, but stay on the hip so it stays on the fence. For the cow to turn, the horse has to get up to the calf's eye.

"You work a cow as if you have to stay within a bubble made up of you and the cow," Hart advises. "You can't be too far out, in, forward, or back."

RIDING THE PATTERN

The cow work is scored between 60 and 80 points, with 70 denoting average. Penalty points are taken off the score as determined by the judge. The rider completes the three segments of the pattern, continuing to work the cow until the judge blows a whistle to end the performance.

The exhibitor has 20 seconds after the cow enters the arena to request a new one if he does not like the one he drew. If a cow blows right past the horse as if it did not notice him or is too wild, it might be better off returning to the herd. The judge may also give the exhibitor a new cow for several reasons, including lameness and blindness. "I try not to ask for another," says Compilli. "If you send one back because it's too wild, there's a chance the next one will be its big, bad brother."

BOXING: A good working cow horse shows enthusiasm as he works the cow at the end of the arena, moving it back and forth between the ends of the short side, attempting to keep the cow near the center of the fence. Most horses like this boxing because they are playing with the cow.

The objective is to keep a cow contained in a specific area. "Imagine being in a 300-acre pasture and your boss tells you not to let this calf get away from this area. Your job is to keep the cow in one spot, by itself," Compilli explains. "In the box you first get the cow to acknowledge your horse and that the horse is stopping it from running across the arena. If the cow never looks at the horse and turns away from him, the horse is not making the cow turn. He is only mirroring the cow. So a cow that doesn't obey the horse will never honor the horse on the fence."

In proper work, the horse is training the cow. After the horse stops the cow on the fence line several times, the cow understands that when the horse approaches him, the cow turns the other way. This is how points are earned. They are not earned by excessive movement by the horse. For example, if the cow is standing still and reluctant to move, but the horse jumps back and forth in front of it in an attempt to move it, he is wasting energy and risking losing a working advantage over the cow.

How long the rider stays in the box depends on how her work has progressed. If she stays too long, the cow may tire or "run out of air" by the time she gets to the rest of the pattern and will not have enough speed to give the horse valuable points. Also, the judge may take off points because the cow is exhausted or breathing too heavily. On the other hand, if she leaves too soon, especially if the cow is too fresh or wild, the cow may outrun the horse on the fence.

Debbie Compilli and DA Janic move the cow to the opposite direction during the "Down the Fence" segment of the Working Cow Horse class.

"The box is when you and your horse are learning about the cow. It takes experience to know how long to stay. People tend to stay too long and take more air out because they don't know if they can handle the cow going down the fence," says Bob Hart.

TURNING ON THE FENCE: Reining maneuvers come in handy in this segment. Horse and rider take the cow down the long side of the arena fence at a gallop past the center marker. Near the opposite end, before the cow reaches the corner penalty marker,[17] the horse overtakes the cow, blocks it, and turns it in the other direction and back down the same fence. The horse passes it, blocks it, and turns it for the second time. The team must make at least one turn each way before moving to the next segment.

---

[17] In this segment, if the horse and rider use the corner to help in turning the cow, they will receive a penalty.

199

For this fence work, the horse and rider move aggressively and fast to maintain their position with the cow and not allow it to run off the fence. The horse, not good fortune or the cow's decision, must clearly cause the cow to turn.

"You want to make a long run because the cow will be more de-termined when you turn him and he is running toward the entrance. If you only have 70 feet to turn him, you might not make it," Com-pilli advises. "If you have the whole arena, and you're riding a horse with any stuff, you can turn it again before it gets to the far corner. If you have a young horse and the calf is still running hard, you might run it down the fence further. Or if you get a bad left-hand turn and you want to try again in order to gain points and you have enough cow left, you do another turn. Rarely does anyone do more than four turns because they won't have enough cow left."

CIRCLES: Circling is the most difficult segment of the pattern because both horse and cow are growing tired. The horse and rider take the cow away from the fence at an advantageous time, maneu-ver it to the center of the arena and turn it at least 360 degrees in each direction without the assistance of the fence.

The team demonstrates their control of the cow by the circle's size and symmetry, the speed at which it is made, and the similarity of the right and left circles. They circle the cow by starting in a fairly large circle; the circle should then grow smaller and smaller, or "tighten down." Care should be taken not to make contact with the cow.

"Circling is the most dangerous part of the pattern," Bob Hart warns. "If the cow bumps you just right, it can tip you over. A horse is at his weakest point, and if he loses his footing or catches a toe, he can tumble over."

Compilli recommends circling more than you think you need. "It's better to do two circles right, then change, and do two circles to the left, because sometimes what the rider thinks is a full circle the judge might not." She also suggests that the first circle direction cause the cow to look away from the herd.

Bob Hart Jr. and Bar-Fly+/ tighten down the circle in the last segment of the Working Cow Horse class. PHOTO BY JIM BORTVEDT.

"Ride up," Hart advises "Sit up tall. Don't lean. If you're at a high rate of speed, you're a little out of air, and your horse is not as surefooted as you'd like. You have to keep your balance so that your horse doesn't have to balance you too."

JUDGING WORKING COW

WORKING COW CREDIT/FAULT/PENALTY CHART

COW WORK	CREDITS	FAULTS	PENALTIES
BOXING	Maintains working advantage Head-to-head working position	Excessive reining and/or spurring Horse lacks interest in cow; horse makes unnecessary movement	Loss of working advantage (-1 point)

COW WORK	CREDITS	FAULTS	PENALTIES
TURNING ON THE FENCE	Rates cow down fence a reasonable distance	Shoulders into cow	Loss of working advantage; switches sides; makes first turn before center marker; uses corner or end of arena to turn cow; or changes sides of the arena (-1 point)
	Tight turns	Drops into the cow for a turn in improper position	
	Holds cow close to fence when coming out of turns	Outrun by cow	
		Reluctant to drive to the front of cow	Runs past cow (-1 point for every horse length)
			Passes corner before turning cow (-2 points)
			Hangs up on fence; knocks down cow without working advantage (-3 points)
			Does not turn cow each way (-5 points)
CIRCLING	Drives to the front of cow	Makes very large circles	Loss of working advantage (-1 point)
	Tightens down circles; or makes circles of equal size and symmetry	Circles cow on off lead	Exhausts cow prior to circling; or knocks down cow without working advantage (-3 points)
		Fails to circle close to cow or in working advantage	
	Circles when the cow is still fresh		
GENERAL	Degree of difficulty of cow	Horse shows bad manners, resistance to rider, or fear of cow	Bites, strikes, or exhausts cow (-3 points)

COW WORK	CREDITS	FAULTS	PENALTIES
	Horse exhibits courage, responsiveness to rider, interest, and natural cow sense and quickly counters cow's moves	Horse swaps ends or turns on forehand	Blatant disobedience (-5 points)
		Responds slowly or fails to respond to cow's moves	Turns tail, balks, or fall of horse and/or rider (zero score)
	Light contact		Out of control while working cow, or runs over cow and causes horse to fall (no score)

WORKING COW SCORING GUIDELINES

75 AND HIGHER: Excellent form and position on animal; high degree of difficulty; excellent eye appeal

73–74: Good form and position on cow; good control of cow; high degree of difficulty with good eye appeal

71–72: A credit-earning run with correct form and position, better than average control of animal, with some degree of difficulty and eye appeal

70: Correct form, average degree of difficulty

68–69: Slight loss of form or position on cow; average degree of difficulty and eye appeal; good work with major penalty or average work with minor penalty

66–67: Trouble controlling cow and/or horse/rider out of position; loss of eye appeal

65 OR BELOW: Major penalties, loss of control and position; no credit

How to Ride Working Cow

In an ideal performance, the horse shows a working advantage over the cow by demonstrating control and forcing movement, maintaining a head-to-head position with the cow, all the while listening and responding to direction from his rider. The degree of difficulty is raised according to the cooperation of the cow and the ability of the horse to control the cow while at speed. In a faulty performance, the horse shows little interest in or too much aggression toward the cow. Similarly, fault is found with the rider who uses excessive rein-ing or spurring.

"With a Cow Horse class, it's best if you create the move, rather than respond," says Hart. "A good cow will be responsive to what you do. You make a move, and the cow makes a countermove."

The rider needs a solid, balanced seat so she does not hinder the horse's ability to respond to her instructions and to rate the cow. Working a cow happens at such fast speed that a rider who flops around may fall off or throw the horse out of balance so they may both hit the dirt.

"The rider has to think 100 percent of the time, but have the experience so that she doesn't have to think how she will do some-thing. In golf, a good tournament player doesn't have to think about how he swings a club. In the show arena, you have to react," says Compilli. "There are times when we fall down. If you don't like that, you shouldn't do this sport. You can't ride and be thinking about what might happen."

Working Cow attracts an intense, brave, and aggressive person-ality who is mentally sharp and physically fit. "Be aggressive, but save your life," advises Bob Hart. "You have to know when it gets dan-gerous and to back off. The rider is usually the one who puts the horse in a bad situation. An aggressive person thinks quickly and changes quickly. If you're not, you'll be behind. It's rare that I don't come out of the arena wringing wet and out of breath."

Since the cow you work influences how well you perform, un-derstanding cattle is fundamental. You need to know how to move a cow, how much pressure to put on it, how to judge its personality, and how it is affected by the herd, the weather, or the arena, and what breed it is. Bob Hart suggests assisting at a ranch with vacci-nating cattle. "You don't have to work cattle all the time, but be somewhere that you can learn that a cow will do certain things when you do something. You'll learn pretty quickly how they react when you have to run them into a squeeze chute for their shots."

Learning to ride for this event is best started with a trained horse that understands cattle and has experienced the intensity of the arena work. To avoid the expense of leasing cattle with which to practice, you and your horse can learn on a "flag." Attach an object to a pulley system, which allows a helper to move the object at varying speeds. You can learn to ride your horse while he follows the object. If your horse is having a problem turning over his hocks or turning to the right, you can set your flag work so that you can focus on just those problems. A cow will not give you options.

When you start working with cattle, begin with an older cow and just follow it around the arena. "This will teach you and the horse to rate an animal," says Debbie Compilli. "When the calf stops, you stop. If it turns, you go with it. When it trots, the horse trots. If the cow slows down, he slows down. In a couple of days, you can feel the horse thinking that if the cow stops, he should stop. He's starting to match what the calf is doing. He is supposed to rate the calf until you tell him to do something else. This is a good way to start learning."

Advice to Amateurs

1. When you arrive at the show, inspect where you will be "cowing," or showing. Study the arena, the ring size, the fence, where the cattle enter the arena, and where people are sitting. If people are sitting on one side, the cow likely will not want to go there.

2. Inspect the footing. A sand and soil mix allows a horse to catch an edge with his foot for a more solid turn. Shavings are slippery. If necessary, Bob Hart suggests having cleats welded onto your horse's shoes to give him better purchase.

3. Study the cattle. Are they wild? Sensible? Dull? Which are good prospects? Check their eyes for spots and blindness. If you see a problem, tell show management. Also suggest

that if cattle have not already been pushed around the rail of the arena before the classes, they should be. "The cattle need to know the arena too. If someone was chasing you into a strange room and you didn't know where things were, you might be quite difficult to deal with," Hart points out. "Why make the odds so bad that the horse can't show his talent?"

4. Have a plan, but be flexible. You may get in the arena and find that you have to change the game plan because the cow did not read the playbook.

5. Style matters. "If the horse stops on his front feet and his hind end flops around, but he happens to be where the cow is, he's not going to get style credit," Compilli says. The judge wants to see the horse work in a smooth, effortless, forward manner. He should work hard, but not struggle. In the same vein, the rider who sits a horse well allows her horse to do a better job. When the two are in sync, eye appeal credit goes up.

6. The cow cannot be mistreated. Any horse is capable of getting into bad position, and a horse may run over the top of a cow. The more experienced the horse, the less likely this will happen. The rider is responsible for guiding the horse into a good position. "In training, any horse with an aggressive attitude may try to bite a cow. I find this happens when the inexperienced horse starts feeling more confident," Compilli points out. "As he learns that his movements make the cow move or turn, he feels dominant, and he uses his body parts to dominate. Then the rider makes it clear there are boundaries the horse shouldn't cross; he cannot bite, strike, or kick the cow. The horse has to learn restraint, just as he must learn that the rider can rein him away from the cow at any time."

7. You may get lost. Even champion Bob Hart has come out of the arena telling his crew he got lost. "You lose where you are because it's so fast."

8. If the horse and rider are doing their job, the speed will be fun, but not out of control. "He is not running away. That's dangerous. He is just running," Debbie Compilli advises.

9. You may hold the saddle horn with one hand to help you stay in the middle of the saddle to prevent yourself from interfering with horse's action and to keep yourself from falling off. Excessive use of the horn may lead to a penalty.

CHAPTER FIFTEEN

HALTER AND BREEDING

"A gold jewel cannot be made except from gold."
—General E. Daumas (1803–1871)
from his book
The Horses of the Sahara

IN THE LATE EIGHTEENTH CENTURY, FARMERS BROUGHT their breeding animals, cows, pigs, and sheep to agricultural shows where judges compared the owners' horses to their neighbors'. Similarly, the Arabian halter arena today asks judges to compare breeding stock and their offspring in their abilities to produce great Arabians as both breeding animals and future performance candidates.

In an ideal world, a presentation in a halter class is a dance between horse and handler, who move together stride for stride, as if they are of one mind. When the horse trots beside his handler and when he poses for conformation inspection, he demonstrates his willingness to work as a teammate with his handler. He epitomizes the beauty and exquisite quality of Arabian type, the vitality and expressive temperament and movement of the breed and the correct conformation that is the goal of the breeder.

In reality, the Arabian halter division continually struggles over its status as a showcase for the best Arabian breeding horses and a razzmatazz exhibition by the show handler and "show-off" horse. Showmanship has become as much a part of the halter class as is conformation study. The horse's presence and charisma are rewarded along with straight legs and strong hindquarters.

Showing a horse at Halter is a specific skill with which a handler seeks to maximize her horse's strengths and minimize his weaknesses, requiring an astute judge to make an accurate evaluation. "If the class were based purely on the horse's merits in his natural state," says Greg Gallun, Arabian judge and international halter trainer, "we would tie them to a post and leave them there for the judge to look at."

JUDGES' CRITERIA

When evaluating a purebred colt, stallion, filly, or mare, judges employ the following criteria in order of priority: Arabian type, conformation, suitability as a breeding animal, quality, movement, substance, manners, and presence. For geldings, judges consider in order of priority: conformation, type, quality, movement, substance, manners, and presence.

Half Arabians and Anglo-Arabians are judged in classes separate from purebreds. The criteria are conformation, quality, substance, and, lastly, Arabian type. The horses may show characteristics of the other breeds that make up their breeding.

Further, show management may separate Half Arabian halter classes into stock/hunter and saddle/pleasure type horses. Stock type horses show conformation qualities important for Working Western disciplines such as reining, and for Western Pleasure. Hunter types show qualities important for hunt seat classes. These horses may naturally carry their heads and necks lower than saddle/pleasure types and have a more ground-covering, forward movement. They are shown in a more relaxed manner in a less elevated stance.

Saddle/pleasure horses have conformation qualities important to saddle seat classes. These horses generally have a high set-on, well-arched neck. They move in a flowing, animated trot. They are more refined and animated than the substantial, quieter stock/hunter types.

Shows also offer specialized halter classes. Most Classic Arabian classes focus on type, presence, animation, carriage, and conformation, in that order. For Classic Head classes, entries appear in plain, un-marked sheets or coolers. Only the uncovered head is judged and as-sessed for Arabian type.

CONDUCT OF CLASS

A Halter class begins with horses and handlers entering the arena one at a time. The handler walks her horse through the in-gate. She begins to run and her horse picks up the trot. The lead line she holds does not control the horse—her cues do. The pair moves in partner-ship. The horse maintains the same speed as the handler, staying shoulder to shoulder. The further out the lead line, the better the judge can see him and he can show off. He trots with his tail arched and his neck and head aloft, with animated strides, joy, and natural expression, unintimidated, yet obedient to his place with his handler.

The Gladys Brown Edwards painting has become the standard by which to stand up a horse for Halter class inspection.

He moves with lightness, balance, and cadence, straight and forward, with grace and freedom, appearing not to touch the ground.

The judge watches each horse enter the arena and creates his first impression.

Horses and handlers stop at the area designated by the judge for lining up the exhibitors. The group then forms a circle around the judge and parades at the walk. Their manner is relaxed and natural, on a loose lead line, the handler at her horse's side, her whip and arms held low. The judge evaluates both conformation and movement.

After walking in both directions, the horses line up to meet the judge for individual inspection. The handler "stands up" her horse in front of the judge. She takes a position that reflects her personal style, and the horse's comfort level and experience. She will likely stand several feet away from her horse and face him. She will raise one or both arms, one holding up the end of the lead line, the other holding up the whip above and behind her. Her stance signals to her horse to "stand up," or strike a pose that has become the standard for Arabian Halter presentation and which replicates the Gladys Brown Edwards painting of the classic Arabian horse.

The horse ideally stands with four feet flat on the ground. The front legs are even. One hind leg stands slightly back. The other is perpendicular to the ground. The neck arches and stretches forward and upward. Opening the throatlatch, the head lifts high and toward the handler.

After the judge inspects her horse from several angles, the handler resumes her position beside her horse's shoulder. At the judge's instruction, the pair walks a few steps, then trots straight and actively away from the judge to a designated point in the arena, after which they return to the lineup.

Once all horses stand up before the judge, he may walk the lineup and review the horses as a group. When the judge reaches a horse in the lineup, the handler again stands up her horse. She lets her horse relax after the judge has finished his review.

While the class may seem fairly straightforward in its conduct, showing a horse in hand for a Halter class requires considerable and distinct training, conditioning, and grooming.

Training Walk and Trot

The handler's goal is for the horse to clearly understand and follow her body posture and voice. Her success relies on her ability to communicate with her horse through his innate language of position, gesture, and sound.

Taught in a step-by-step, consistent, and repetitive manner, the horse first learns to walk next to and to stop next to the handler. When the handler makes a clucking sound and walks, he walks off with her. When he walks off, he stays at the handler's shoulder even though she loosely holds the lead line. When she says "whoa" and stops, he stops. He stands quietly waiting for further instruction.

The horse next learns to trot in-hand. The handler may only need to initiate a faster pace herself, and the horse will trot. Or she may have to hold a whip in her off hand (the one away from the horse), reach around behind her own body, and tap him on the hindquarters. Usually just a tap will suffice. At the same time she makes a clucking sound to reinforce her cues. The horse soon will learn that if she moves her body as if to tap him, he must move off. Eventually, she has only to cluck or move forward and he will trot.

The trotting horse should be bright and animated, moving forward as if trotting on his own. If the handler has to drag the horse across the arena, the horse is not able to show his best gait. On the other hand, the handler who has to keep circling the horse to keep him under control slows down the class and does not make the judge very happy.

If the horse gets excited while trotting and breaks into the canter, ideally he will come down to a trot in response to his handler's quiet voice command, saying either "trot" or "whoa."

Most importantly the horse learns that the handler has a space and he has a space and never the twain shall meet. If he comes too close and the handler moves toward his shoulder with her shoulder, he is to move away. This response actually comes quite naturally to a horse. If you watch a mare and foal in the pasture, the mother will move the baby over by pushing it with her shoulder or nudging it with her nose.

"I want the horse to learn that when trotting in-hand, he can relax and be himself, but he can't get on top of me," says Kim Potts, judge and national champion halter trainer. "He needs the confidence to walk and trot in his space, do his job, and hold up his own carriage. I teach him to move away from me when I step into him. That way when I'm showing he knows to move away. I don't have to be there yanking and flapping.

"Horses need guidance and they're happier with boundaries. You set boundaries when you school them. You don't want them so restricted that they can't show off. You want their training to enhance their best features. But you want some limits. On the other hand, you certainly can take away those best features if you're too hard on them. If they understand to stay at your shoulder, you don't need to pull or jerk on the halter."

Because a halter horse is often young or inexperienced, training at home should introduce him to circumstances that might frighten or upset him at a show. At home he can learn a safe way to react and become comfortable with and eager for new adventures.

For example, spectators are often quite noisy when they shout approving hoots and hollers for their favorites. This noise can frighten a horse. If, however, he hears these sounds in a familiar setting when he is working with his trusted handler, he will know that he is safe staying at her shoulder. He may even become indifferent to the ruckus at a show.

To judge how your horse is responding to his halter work, consider that a horse that enjoys his work will carry his tail high and still, not swish or flick it around. When he is animated and brilliant, he carries his head up high and his ears forward. He maintains his speed and balance with the handler. If his ears are askew or held flat back and he is running ahead of the handler or circling around, reacting against, instead of responding to, her, the horse is not comfortable or happy with his situation.

The Pose

The manner in which an Arabian is shown individually before the judge for conformation evaluation is unique to the breed. Performed correctly, the pose has evolved as a way to show the Arabian's best features. When carried out to extreme, the pose can be detrimental to the horse's appearance and overly stressful to his body and mind. On the other hand, when the pose is attempted without requesting that the horse demonstrate his athletic and performance abilities, the result can be lackluster at best.

To visualize the correct pose, imagine a handler putting a halter on the horse in the Gladys Brown Edwards painting and following

Greg Gallun stands up this young horse that has been immaculately groomed and conditioned for this Halter class. PHOTO BY JEAN PIERRE BISILLIAT.

the lead line out in front to give him cues. This is ideally how the horse should look in the halter pose, or "stand up." It looks as if the horse were walking along and something caught his eye a quarter of a mile away.

Greg Gallun recalls the first time he showed a horse that would months later go on to become U.S. Reserve National Junior Stallion Champion. "We had high hopes for him, but until you're in the ring, you don't know. I was worked up and nervous before going in. On the reverse part of the walk, something caught his attention. He planted his four feet, flipped his tail up, arched his neck, tightened his topline, snorted, and looked incredibly regal. I thought, 'This is a great horse, and he's going to win.'" And he did win, as Scottsdale Champion Junior Stallion.

Before you can teach the horse to take the pose on cue, he must be solid in his foundation work. He must walk, halt, and travel in response to the handler's cues. He knows voice cues: "whoa" is stop; a "cluck" means walk or trot off. He will stand quietly next to the handler.

In the next phase he learns to walk toward the handler as she is in front of him walking backwards. When she stops and says "whoa," the horse stops with his hind legs flat on the ground and under his body. This takes time and lots of repetition before the horse has the confidence to walk up and stop with his hind legs squarely on the ground.

The subsequent step focuses on teaching the horse to stop with his front feet fairly even and under the point of the shoulder. He also learns to accept the handler's efforts to position his legs by moving him forward, back, or sideways. These cues become more subtle as he understands.

The horse next learns to follow cues to stretch his neck forward while holding his body still. When the handler pulls on the lead line and the horse feels pressure on his poll from the halter or on his chin, either from the halter or a chain attached to the halter, he learns to yield to the pressure and reach his neck forward. He also may learn to bring his nose toward the handler by following a treat she offers him.

The handler may then teach him to bring his neck forward toward the butt end of a whip. The latter will be a cue in the show arena.

"It's very awkward for them to learn to keep their body still and move their head and neck. It's hard," Kim Potts explains.

In the final phase the horse learns to elevate his head and neck while straightening and tightening his back and hindquarters to hold that frame.

"The art is for the horse to show intensity and show a shapely neck while keeping his balance," says Greg Gallun.

Gallun finds it critical to teach the horse to stand flat footed, bearing weight on all four legs, with his hind legs directly underneath his body. The USEF Rule Book requires that at least one front foot and one back foot must be perpendicular to the ground. The inner hind leg (on the judge's side) should line up with the hip. Legs should neither stretch out behind the horse's hindquarters nor be slung under him.

"You want all four feet bearing weight in the proper position and balance," Gallun describes. "If you sit relaxed in front of the TV, your body is different from when you sit up at a formal dinner. You bear weight on your thighs and butt and straighten your back. When a horse bears weight on all four legs, he raises his head, elevates his neck, lifts his shoulders, and flattens and tightens his topline. It's not a magic trick." A correct pose is a biomechanical response.

In contrast, a head that sticks straight up in the air counteracts qualities of Arabian type, creating a ewe neck instead of an arched neck, one that is longer on the underside than on the topside. On the other hand, a neck that stretches straight out on a horizontal plane has little of the neck arch and bend at the throatlatch needed to complete the look. The horse likely has more weight on his front end than on his hindquarters and cannot lift his shoulders in a more regal posture.

The pose will vary with the natural frame and structure of the individual horse. However, to emphasize the horse's strengths and minimize his weaknesses, the handler needs to develop an eye for what improves the horse's stance. She might turn a plain head a bit to the side to give it a more attractive look. She might minimize the appearance of a long back or a shorter neck by adjusting the pose. She might have determined that the horse looks better standing slightly to the right or to the left, or that his croup and loin look better if he stands in a wide or narrow stance behind.

To simulate this part of the show situation when training at home, have a friend stand in the judge's position. Stand up your horse and have the "judge" walk around him. Follow this inspection by lots of petting, and maybe treats. If you plan to take your horse to one of the larger shows that uses three judges, increase the number of your practice judges. This role play is particularly important for young horses that often associate people approaching in groups with bad things like shots and worming. The horse can better focus on his job if he isn't afraid.

Once the horse's foundation is solid and he knows what his handler expects from him, encourage him to be playful. "If there is no play, the horse isn't going to want to do this. If he enjoys himself, he will last longer and make a better show horse," says Potts. "After schooling, there is play. What you do depends on the horse. Some just like walking and looking outside the arena. Others get jazzed up. Let him know its okay to show some expression, to not be perfect all the time. He learns that he has a job, and sometimes it's hard, but it's not all work."

Conditioning Horse and Handler

Halter horses are very fit and well muscled. Since many of them are young and have not been ridden, they are often conditioned by free lunging in an arena, a limited amount of longeing on a line,[18] or being led (poned) from a golf cart or an older, reliable horse.

---

[18] Longeing in a circle stresses the inside legs, especially the hind leg, and may not be appropriate or should be limited with young horses.

Working out in an equine swimming pool with an experienced trainer three or four days a week for 7 to 12 minutes is a very healthy regimen that builds strength and endurance without stressing young tendons and ligaments.

Arabian Halter horses usually work out in sweat gear, which might consist of equipment ranging from a throatlatch sweat to a neck sweat to a full body sweat. Sweating cannot alter a horse's conformation or turn a fat horse into a thin horse, but trainers believe it minimizes water retention and tightens the skin, giving a finer look to the area sweated. Care must be taken not to overheat the horse or develop fungus in humid, hot climates. Some trainers leave sweat collars on all the time. Others use them only at night, or for a limited number of days a week, or for part of a day to accommodate for the horse's comfort.

After building the horse's condition, the handler wants her horse to trot out to his fullest capability. To keep up with the horse or to show in several classes a day, a handler should be fit. Greg Gallun will get on the treadmill before U.S. Nationals, where he will show several horses through semifinal and final heats. Kim Potts regularly bikes, practices tae bo, and takes Pilates classes.

"Halter, especially with the babies, is about agility, and if you're strong, you will be a lot quicker," says Potts.

Grooming

COATS: Every professional has a formula for maintaining a beautiful, shiny, healthy coat, but they all begin with good food, grooming, worming, and regular exercise. While coat products can enhance the quality of the hair, most trainers agree that they are useless without diligent currying and brushing before and after work.

Too much bathing will dry out the coat and strip it of natural oils. On the other hand, sweat will carry the natural skin oils through the pores. "After a workout we put on a cooler, let the horse completely dry, and then curry him out, or hose off only the legs and between the legs," says Gallun. Mixing Avon Skin So Soft with water keeps moisture in the coat. Others use a combination of liniment, oil, and vinegar to condition it.

Keeping the show coat blanketed also helps.

MANE AND TAIL: Most halter horses are shown with loose, long manes and long unbraided tails. For care information, see chapter 17.

CLIPPING: Depending on the length of the hair coat, the time of the year, and the level of the show they will attend, Halter horses may have their coat shaved or clipped from head to hind end. This is referred to as "body clipping." To end up with a smooth, lustrous coat after clipping takes skill, timing, and the right tools. Clip too early and the hair starts to grow back. Clip too late and the oils have not returned to the coat. Kim Potts prefers a number-15 clipper blade (a number-10 clips too short and the hair grows back too quickly; a bigger blade tends to leave lines). A variety of products found in tack stores will bring back the oils and shine to the coat after clipping.

Clipping the head with care and artistry may take up to two hours. "It's like a gal putting on her makeup," says Potts. "You don't want to see any rigid lines. I will use five to six different blades to blend the lines because it makes

Kim Potts shows a well-clipped Halter horse, MA Windsong, wearing a classic halter worn in the show ring. PHOTO BY JERRY SPARAGOWSKI.

their faces so much prettier. It's fun to take a horse that is average looking and make him really look the best you can. It's very individual about how it's done and what is important."

The face is closely clipped to define and highlight features there, especially the eyes, muzzle, ears, and the facial crest bones, or protruding ridges along each side of the face that run below the eye and parallel to the jaw. Comparable to human cheekbones, the ridges are composed of two adjoining skull bones, the maxilla and the zygomatic bones and are sometimes referred to as "tear bones."

SHOW GROOMING: For the show arena, handlers apply varying amounts of oil and grease products on the horse's face, especially around the eyes and muzzle, to bring out the black skin, giving the horse a more exotic look and making the eyes look larger. Judges can eliminate a horse with excessive amounts of oil and grease.

"It's a fashion trend. Some judges hate it. You have to decide how far you want to go with it," says Potts.

"It's the same as the way a person presents herself. You can dress in a classy understated fashion or dress like a street walker," says Gallun.

Tips on Presentation

Preparation at home:

Take the time to train, condition, and groom. It pays off.

On entering the show arena:

1. Focus on your accomplishments and how well you have done. Kim Potts shares an important lesson. "I showed at Nationals with a mare I knew was not champion material, but I wanted Top Ten so badly. I was so happy and excited and relaxed because I made the finals. I wasn't worried about what if this, what if that, and those silly human things we bring to the arena. I looked happy; my horse looked fantastic and she rose above herself. I think about that so often. We need to have a little faith in ourselves."

2. The horse knows you one way at home. If you are different when you walk into the arena, your horse is going to feel insecure and worried. Showing is exciting and everyone gets nervous, but because the horse depends on you, you owe it to him to keep your concerns under control.

3. Learn to read your horse. Does he need to get to the arena early so he settles down? Or if he gets to the arena early will he be a nervous wreck? Or be too dull? Does he need calming? Or does he need a reminder to behave?

4. "Be clean, efficient, and professional," advises Greg Gallun. "You want a look that is simple, elegant, and respectful of your horse, the judges, and other exhibitors. Too much grandstanding makes the show ring an unattractive situation. I am not the focus of attention. I want my horse to be."

5. Focus on supporting and taking care of your horse, not the surroundings. "My goal is to remember the keys and cues to the horse I'm showing that will allow him to show and behave the best in the class," says Gallun. "I know his strengths and weaknesses both physically and emotionally, and I need to cater to them."

6. Walk your horse until you have a clear gait. Then trot. In fact, the handler has the option to walk the horse to the lineup, though most do trot.

7. "Over-showing is trotting back and forth, taking three minutes to get to the lineup. That bothers a judge, and it's discourteous to other exhibitors," Greg Gallun points out.

In the lineup before and after individual presentations to the judge:

1. "My job is to show my horse to the judges. I don't stand a horse up for someone in the audience," says Gallun. "The horse will stand up every time you ask, but he only has so

many good ones. It is a physical exercise, and they can't do it well over and over. It's like asking you to do a model's walk as opposed to your normal flat-footed walk. With a model's walk, you're intensely using different muscles."

2. Be aware of where the judges are looking. If you need help, especially in a multiple judge class, have someone in the audience keep you posted on where the judges are. That way you can focus on your horse.

3. Don't pick and yank on your horse. Let the horse relax and stand still. "The less the handler does, the better," says Potts. "Sometimes you have to get to shucking and jiving because your horse is really quiet, but you can give cues and let the horse do the work. Amateurs get nervous and overcompensate. When the judge is looking around the arena, be sure the horse looks pleasant and aware, but not standing up, like a person looks better if he's at attention and not a slob."

4. Maintain a good distance from other exhibitors. Gallun keeps 15 feet away.

Before the judge:

1. The USEF Rule Book allows you to stand up your horse when there are two horses between where you are and your turn to present him to the judge, and when you are before the judge. Otherwise, you must allow the horse to stand in a natural manner.

2. Walk the horse straight to the judge. After the standup, trot away straight from the judge so she can evaluate how straight and true the horse tracks and the correctness of his legs.

3. "A good handler shows a horse from the back legs forward. If you concentrate on the neck forward, the pose

falls apart because they are bearing too much weight on the front legs," says Gallun.

4. When you are trotting away from the judge, keep your horse trotting for as long as the judge is looking at him. Then return to the lineup and let your horse relax.

Clothing and Tack

For men and women alike, a professional look beats a unique appearance. Women wear blazers or business pant suits. Hair is neat. Shoes are sensible for running. Some women wear black running shoes. Others prefer paddock boots for more support. Both types allow the handler to be safe and agile. Men appear in suits or sport coats and ties. They rarely wear hats. Some wear dress shoes; others have turned to soft spike golf shoes for better support and traction.

The USEF Rule Book stipulates that the horse wear a "suitable headstall equipped with a throatlatch." The halter of choice today is a delicate headstall with a thin throatlatch and a gossamer noseband that is completed under the chin by a chain that attaches to a leather lead line. Few horses appear in Syrian halters, which are decorated by a colored fabric studded with beads and cowry shells. Most, however, wear a halter of a thin patent leather, plain leather, or leather with decorative metal. The noseband may be wider on a bigger horse with a longer head.[19] "Elegance is the key," says Kim Potts.

The chain may be long or short and should be clean and in good repair. Like a bit, a chain that is too fine is weak and severe. On the other hand, you don't want one that is too thick and heavy. Some trainers use a braided rope bought at the pet store on youngsters.

---

[19] The vast majority of Halter horses are shown with long, loose manes. Horses shown with braided manes must show in hunter, show hack, or dressage bridles, or leather stable halters.

Carefully introduce the horse to the chain at home and spend a lot of time practicing with it. "A show halter feels different to the horse than a barn halter," says Gallun. "As a judge, I've had horses react poorly in front of me because it's their first time in a chain."

Handlers have the option of carrying a whip no longer than six feet, including snapper or lash. It should serve as an extension of the handler's arm, not as a tool to punish the horse. A handler who uses the whip on the horse in the show arena will be eliminated. Handlers also may use grass, a hat (Arabians are very curious and eagerly sniff such items), or treats to keep the horse's attention in the stand up.

THE EUROPEAN VS. AMERICAN JUDGING SYSTEM

The system described in this chapter refers to the American system of halter judging, in which the judge determines which horse in her opinion comes closest to the ideal Arabian when compared to the rest of the class.

A few U.S. shows employ the European judging system, in which horses are awarded points from 1 to 20 in five categories: type; head and neck; body and topline; legs; and movement. Each horse is compared to an ideal, as opposed to the other horses in the class. The horse with the highest total score out of 100 wins the class. Final scores are usually announced immediately after the horse is judged and the complete scores are posted.

The Egyptian Event employs a modified European system, whereby the "type" score is multiplied by five. Every other category is multiplied by four. Scores represent the following:

20 points	Excellent, or the "Standard": ideal, perfect, could not improve
17.0 thru 19.5 points	Above Average: very good, with room for slight improvement
13.0 thru 16.5 points	Average: obvious need for improvement
1.0 thru 12.5 points	Below Average: poor, with very obvious need for improvement

The conduct of a European system class differs from the American system, which is noted for the speed in which a class can be completed. In the European system, the horses as a group are presented to the judge at the walk. They are then sent out of the arena. Each horse is brought back individually to trot in, stand up in the center of the ring, walk away and back, trot and stand up one more time.

CHAPTER SIXTEEN

SPECIALTY CLASSES

"Hast thou given the horse strength? Hast thou clothed his neck with thunder? Canst thou make him afraid as a grasshopper? The glory of his nostrils is terrible. He paweth in the valley and rejoiceth in this strength; he goeth on to meet the armed men. He mocketh at fear, and is not affrighted, neither turneth he back from the sword."

—Job 39:19–22

SPECIALTY CLASSES ARE VARIATIONS OF ENGLISH, WESTERN, and Hunter Pleasure disciplines and are testimonies to the individual Arabian horse's versatility. Horses that enter the arena in Driving, Native Costume, Side Saddle, Equitation, or Youth Halter Showmanship are likely to compete in other classes as well.

DRIVING

Driving a horse-drawn cart has its own set of pleasures and challenges. Drivers get a kick out of seeing their horses moving while drivers and horses are working together. In addition, sitting in a cart makes fewer physical demands than sitting on a horse does. It does not call for the leg strength and balance necessary for riding.

Some horses, especially mares with sensitive ovaries, enjoy being driven more than being ridden. Thus, driving serves as an effective alternative for conditioning a horse's body and mind. Without weight on her back and with less physical pressure on her body, she has a better sense of well-being and freedom.

Driving is especially suitable for teaching a young horse that is not yet under saddle about discipline and obedience, to move forward with impulsion, to drive off his hocks, and to respond to the bit without the unbalancing effect of a rider. Driving a horse builds strong lungs and muscle, while giving his tendons and ligaments time to develop without deleterious stress.

On the other hand, since a driver cannot feel the horse's movement, her ability to read whether her horse is moving correctly takes a different skill. "You have to correlate what a horse looks like in profile to what he looks like from behind," says Tim Goggins, judge and trainer.

Some drivers feel safer in a cart than on a horse's back, though in truth, driving can be riskier. With only the reins and a whip as aids, the driver has less control of the horse's body than a rider. And since the driver cannot make fast moves with a horse and buggy, maneuvering takes more time and thought.

Arabian driving classes are split into four sections: formal, pleasure, combination, and carriage. Formal and Pleasure Driving are equivalent to Saddle Seat. In combination classes, the horse is first shown pulling a cart and he then is unhitched, saddled, and ridden as a saddle seat horse. Carriage Driving falls within the Arabian Sport Horse division.

Formal and pleasure driving horses are animated show horses from the fine-harness-and-light-cart tradition. They have the characteristic high neck set, laid-back shoulder, round motion, ability to elevate, and go-forward attitude of their ridden counterparts. On the other hand, they are calm, quiet, and mannerly enough to handle being hitched to a cart.

The formal driving horse pulls a four-wheeled cart, performs the walk and trot, stands quietly, and backs readily. He has the brilliance and the bold, animated, highly impulsive gaits of a park horse. His performance and presence carry greater weight with the judge than his manners, quality, and conformation.

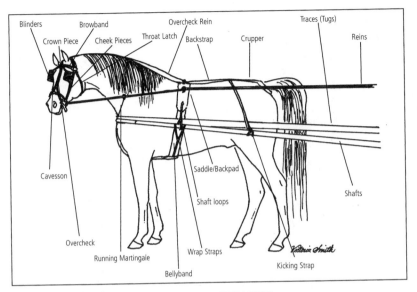

The parts of a fine harness. ILLUSTRATION BY VICTORIA SMITH.

The pleasure driving horse simulates the grace, elegance, and upward carriage of a bright, confident, responsive, and powerful English Pleasure horse. He may pull either a two- or four-wheeled cart, and he performs at the walk, normal trot, and strong trot. He is asked to stand quietly and back readily. The judge looks for manners, quality, and performance, in order of priority.

The country pleasure driving horse is comfortable and calm, with impeccable manners. A two-wheeled cart follows him, and he performs the same gaits as the pleasure driving horse. He moves brightly and alertly, with the easy and free-flowing movement of a Country English Pleasure horse. Attitude and manners take priority over performance, quality, and conformation.

Drivers in these classes dress in informal saddle seat suits. After 6 P.M. or for championship classes, formal drivers dress up in tuxedo-type jackets, formal jodhpurs, and top hats, or dark saddle seat suits and derbies. The horses are shown in light show harnesses, bridles with blinkers, an over check or side check, and a snaffle bit.

Each horse and driver is allowed one header, who acts like the person on the airport tarmac who guides the plane into its gate. The header, dressed in a plain, unmarked smock, usually white, helps the driver to line up safely by guiding the horse into a clear spot next to the other horses. The header then stands in front of the horse to ensure that the animal remains quiet and calm until the class is over.

COMBINATION CLASSES

In the demanding Combination class, the horse first shows in harness at walk and trot in both directions of the arena. He then lines up and, with the help of one or two headers, the driver unhitches the cart and saddles the horse for the ridden segment of the class.

Formal Combination involves a formal driving horse who becomes a Park horse under saddle; in Informal Combination, a Pleasure Driving horse becomes an English Pleasure horse under saddle; and in Country Pleasure Combination, a Country Pleasure Driving horse becomes a Country English Pleasure horse under saddle.

Pleasure Carriage Driving

The Carriage Driving class evolved from horses that pulled hansom cabs or carriages for a living. While the Pleasure Driving horses are upright and animated in their gaits, the Working Carriage horses typically move in a more relaxed frame, with more natural extension. They may be the hunter or country pleasure type, depending on their turnout (the term for the horse, harness, and vehicle).

"Their temperament is such that they could quietly and safely drive down the road in traffic. The horse and carriage was the automobile in the past, and they had to be very safe and steady under all conditions," says Wanda Funk, chair of the AHA Driving and Eventing Committee, and a competitor in carriage driving.

The attractive vehicle is compatible with the horse's size, type, weight, and way of going. For example, a low-stepping hunter-type mover might look prettier with a country-style vehicle. A more high-stepping horse will match better with a formal vehicle. All carts must have wooden wheels.

Grooms may ride with the driver in the appropriate class and vehicle. For example, a groom's presence is optional for a single-horse turnout, but required for a four-in-hand carriage.

Unlike for English and Country Pleasure Driving, the driver must sit to the right; if she sits in the center, the judge will mark her down.

Though these classes have a traditional feel, drivers and grooms are discouraged from wearing period costumes. A man wears a conservative coat or jacket, hat, driving apron or knee rug, and gloves. A woman dresses in a conservative dress, tailored suit or slacks, hat (floppy hats are discouraged), apron or knee rug, and gloves. Drivers must carry a driving whip at all times.

A groom wears "stable or full livery," depending on the formality of the vehicles. Stable livery is a conservative suit or jacket with jodhpurs, derby or conservative cap, white shirt, paddock boots or dark shoes, and leather gloves. Full livery is a close-fitting body coat with metal buttons that match the furnishings of the horse's harness, white breeches, black tall boots with tan tops, black top hat, and brown leather gloves.

Pleasure Carriage Driving was first introduced at the Sport Horse National Championship in 2005; exhibitors competed in a sampling of the classes, including pleasure driving-working, reinsmanship, and pick your route obstacle driving.

In working classes, the judge focuses on the suitability of the horse to provide a pleasant drive in the walk, slow trot, working trot, and strong trot. She judges 70 percent on performance, manners, and the horse's way of going; 20 percent on the condition and fit of the harness and vehicle; and 10 percent on the neatness of the driver's outfit.

In the slow trot, the horse is on the bit and maintains forward impulsion, with a steady cadence. He travels in a slower, more collected manner, but not to the degree shown in dressage collection. The working trot ranks between the slow and strong trots, but in a shorter, rounder frame with overstep.[20] The horse moves freely forward, rhythmic and straight, on a taut but light rein contact. He is balanced and unconstrained. In the strong or extended trot, he increases the speed and length of stride while maintaining his balance and lateral flexion on turns.

Reinsmanship focuses on the driver's skill at handling the reins and whip and her control, posture, and overall appearance. The condition of the harness and vehicle and neatness of the attire account for 25 percent of the judge's evaluation.

Obstacle Driving is a test of speed. At the starting signal, the driver winds through a course outlined by a series of paired markers, usually traffic cones, either on a prescribed route or one of her own design for the pick your route class. Course faults, such as knocking down cones, are scored as penalty seconds and are added to the driver's elapsed time. The lowest total time wins the class.

Showing and Safety Tips for All Driving

1. The horse must be solid in "go and whoa" before he is hooked to a buggy. Bombproof him before he is hooked to the cart. The first few times he is hooked to the cart, have a header lead him on a longe line until he is comfortable. Use kicking straps or a kicking bag to prevent him from kicking higher than the shafts, which could cause a wreck.

2. Because you haven't the benefit of legs, be sure your horse responds in a forward manner to a tap from the whip. For that same reason, he must steer well and respond to "whoa." "The worst things that can happen to a buggy are

---

[20] The hind feet touch the ground in front of the footprints of the forefeet.

for it to go sideways and to back up," says Goggins. "When going sideways, the buggy can tip over. When going backwards, the buggy can hit something. If the horse doesn't realize he hit something, he may keep backing, trapping the driver between the horse and what the buggy hits."

3. Never remove the horse's bridle before the horse is unhitched.

4. Be sure your harness is properly adjusted and all equipment is in good repair.

5. Use blinkers (also called blinders or winkers)[21] to prevent the horse from becoming frightened by the sight of the turning wheels following close behind him. They also shield him from distractions.

6. Spend plenty of time driving your horse before showing. "Unbroken harness horses at a show are really dangerous," says Goggins.

7. Be aware of your surrounding in the show arena. Think ahead. Glance around to see whether any horse is misbehaving so you can give it extra room. "Amateurs often over-steer and don't space themselves in the ring. You have to think ahead because your reaction time is delayed by the fact you're not feeling the horse. You have to be better at reading him. That skill only comes with more driving," says Goggins.

8. Keep a good distance from other horses. Positioning yourself in the arena is trickier than under saddle because a horse in harness is less maneuverable. Once on the rail, don't do a lot of jogging for position. Take care not to drive too close to the rail or tires may hit the rail.

---

[21] Leather-covered metal plates attached to the check pieces of the bridle.

9. Don't sacrifice form for speed. Maintain control of your horse at all times.

10. A good performance is the demonstration of good gaits: a true, flat walk and a clear distinction between the slow, normal, and strong trots.

11. Focus in front of yourself to keep your horse straight. Sit centered in the cart and look through his ears. You might sit slightly to the inside on a turn to keep the cart balanced. You can help maneuver the cart and horse as a unit by adjusting your weight a little to either side, but keep your horse's head square in front of his body.

12. If your horse's tail gets over the top of your reins, bring your hands forward and unloop it. If he begins to make manure while you're driving, widen your hands to keep the tail from coming down over the reins.

MOUNTED NATIVE COSTUME

There is no doubt which breed owns the Native Costume class. This spectator favorite holds all the excitement and drama that you might expect from horses of the desert. Dressed in a rich, elaborate, flowing costume, the horse seems to revel in the simulation of a chase across the sand. He is animated and spirited, evoking images of his heritage.

The Bedouin's horse walked in the desert to preserve energy for the gallop needed to raid an enemy's camp or to escape an enemy's raid. Bedouins trotted very little, in part because most rode in saddles without stirrups. Just as did his ancestors, the costume horse walks, canters, and hand gallops in a beautiful, dramatic way of going, elaborated by a well-arched neck and lofty tail carriage. He is eager and alert and yet quiet in the bridle and mannerly, even at top speed in an exciting, stimulating class. He performs with correct form, cadence, and freedom of motion.

No matter how many times you see a Native Costume class, there is something ethereal about an Arabian who is well conformed, carefully groomed, with a full mane and tail, who moves with power and balance in big, bold, uphill gaits in rich, elegant attire.

Fifty years ago, when the Scottsdale show was born, costumes were made from bed sheets. Today horse and rider's outfits are made of gorgeous and strong materials: velvets, brocades, silks, and satins, with elaborate trims and tassels, beads and glass gemstones, sequin appliqué and cowry shells.

Some costume pieces are authentic or based on the authentic Bedouin clothing and tack, but for the most part they have been adapted to exhibit a showbiz tone. For example, in reality, desert camels wore more elaborate outfits than horses did. Many tassels were attached to camel blankets to flick away insects, but not usually to horse tack.

Both women and men's outfits may consist of:

1. Top piece: an aba, which means "cloak" in Arabic, is a caftan-type piece that may cover the rider from neck to toe. Instead of an aba, the rider may wear a cape, robe, or long vest with a shirt.
2. Pants: pantaloons or harem style.
3. Head piece: a keffiyeh consisting of a scarf held on by wrapped cord (the number of cords indicated a Bedouin's wealth) or a variation of the cord. The scarf wraps under the chin or over the mouth and nose.
4. Shoes, hunt boots, sandals, or ballet slippers.

The horse's outfit may consist of:

1. Bridle: Western or English bit, or hackamore and matching reins. The bridle may be decorated in the style of a Syrian halter, with a silver chain noseband adorned with silver crescent-shaped charms. The cheek pieces of the bridle are

decorated with designs formed by beads and cowry shells, or the bridle may be covered with material that matches the horse's blanket.

2. Breast collar: made of wool or lined with manmade fur for the horse's comfort and decorated with single or multiple layers of tassels, beads, and cowry shells.

3. Blanket: Seen in many fabrics, shapes, and trims and usually outlined with tassels, running from the horse's tail to wither. In Syrian-style costumes, the blanket runs under the saddle. In other styles, the blanket runs over the saddle.

4. Saddle: The rider may ride in any style saddle. The saddle is covered in fabric. Stirrup leathers and stirrups are decorated with fabrics.

The horse's color determines the costume colors. Black and gold work well for most horses. Silver and turquoise show off a gray. White and camel colors bring out the red tones in a chestnut. Jewel tones look handsome on a bay.

The costume should not hinder the horse's motion or hide his outline. Test drive every part at home so that you do not

The Native Costume horse enjoys a ground-covering hand gallop that shows off his costume and his flair. PHOTO BY DOMINIQUE COGNEE.

get in the arena and then have the tassels on the bridle cause your horse to flip his head or your head scarf slip over your eyes while you are in a hand gallop. Be sure that your shoes allow your foot to stay in the stirrup. If you are wearing a cape, sew drapery weights into the bottom so that it billows but does not fly about like a giant tent.

When you are considering various fabrics, take them out into daylight to see how they will really appear to the judge. Stand back 70 feet. Some that might appear striking close up may look faded at a distance.

LADIES SIDE SADDLE

Two centuries ago, only Annie Oakley types rode astride, with one leg on either side. A proper lady rode side saddle, with both legs on one side, and those legs were carefully and fully covered by her long skirt. Such a woman was in good hands with a mount that had the manners of an angel, thus allowing her to look elegant and at ease to the onlookers whom she hoped to attract.

Today, the elegance and romance of riding side saddle attracts women to this class that encourages period authenticity. Like the riders of the 1800s, they ride in saddles with one stirrup, usually on the left side, and two crescent-shaped padded pommels, or horns, also on the left. The left pommel curves downward and provides a place for the rider's left leg to snuggle up against. The rider curls her right leg around the right upward curving pommel. She may carry a whip in her right hand to act as her right leg.

Arabian side saddle divided into English and Western styles, are essentially pleasure classes with an emphasis on manners, comfort, and ease, out of concern for the ladies. The horse's walk should be ground-covering, the trot or jog-trot comfortable, and the lope or canter smooth. The horse is well trained and "finished" in his work in a regular saddle so that he is not confused by his rider's variation in the aiding system. Most English horses have moved up to a double bridle, and Western horses go in a curb.

Showing in saddle seat side saddle clothes and tack, Wendy Potts and Berried Treasure trot a victory pass after winning the Half Arabian Side Saddle, English. PHOTO BY MIKE FERRARA.

More importantly, to create a pretty picture the horse must accept the slightly uneven weight of the rider and the cues from one leg of the rider. For that reason, not all horses are candidates for side saddle. The horse should be balanced and straight. If he is very much right- or left-sided, the rider has the added difficulty of making him straight with aids limited to her weight, one leg, and a whip.

A horse with good size withers will help keep the saddle in place. "For horses that have round withers, you have to strap the saddle on so tightly. You don't want to make the horse uncomfortable," says Patience Prine-Carr, a trainer and competitor who teaches side saddle.

Keeping your weight centered will help your horse maintain his balance and provide you with an easier ride. From behind, your body should look as if you are riding astride: straight, leaning to neither one side nor forward or back, with your back centered and perpendicular to the horse's spine. Your arms, elbows, and hands are in the same position they would be were you riding astride.

"Your seat bones rest on either side of the horse's spine and do not put more pressure on one side. People make their back or their horse's back sore by riding crooked," says Prine-Carr.

The tools for riding side saddle are the rider's weight, left leg, a riding crop, and voice commands. For example, the horse should learn to bend from the weight of the rider's inside seat bone. If he does not, the rider can teach him to bend to the right by tapping with the whip on his right side where the rider's leg would push him over. At the same time, she puts more weight on her inside seat bone. To keep the horse on the rail, the rider reminds him with her whip. To ask the horse to canter, some riders rely on the normal head position as the cue to canter. Others use voice command, either saying "canter" or making a kissing sound.

In Western side saddle classes, riders sit the jog-trot. English riders have the option of sitting or posting. "If you post, you should barely come out of the saddle. You just rock with the horse," says Prine-Carr. "Some people post by pushing off the one stirrup, which causes them to twist their hips to the right. It's not very pretty. When I teach, I take away the rider's stirrup. The stirrup is not there to push off; you rest your toes there. It's there in case of a problem. But if you step too much into it, you'll push the saddle over."

"Your horse needs to maintain his impulsion to help you at the trot," says Shiloh Bishop, 1999 open and amateur National Side Saddle Champion. Her horse's impulsion allows her to post instead of sitting his big moving trot, which creates a more comfortable, pleasant picture.

Costumes enhance the beauty and grace of this class. How far to carry each costume is the rider's choice. Fifteen percent of the judge's determination is based on the costume. For the Western class, the rider dresses as she would for a Western Pleasure class. In the English class, the rider wears either hunt seat, saddle seat, or show hack attire.

As a minimum requirement, each rider must wear a skirt, divided skirt, or an apron that matches her pants, jodhpurs, or breeches and covers the rider's Western, jodhpur, or hunt boot on the right leg. The apron should hang parallel to the ground. For hunt seat, the apron sits above the left ankle; for Western, it ends at the ankle or the arch of the rider's foot; and for saddle seat and show hack, the apron may reach the lower level of the left heel, long enough to hide the toe of the boot.

Boots are required. Hats are mandatory: for hunt, the hat is usually a black silk top hat at least four inches high; for Western, the traditional Western hat; for saddle seat, the traditional derby, top hat, or soft hat; and for show hack, either a hunt cap, derby, or top hat.

Most traditional is the hunt seat attire. To meet historic standards, the rider attaches to her saddle a leather sandwich case that carries a watercress sandwich with its crust cut off and wrapped in

Note the two-sided pommel of this antique hunt seat side saddle and how it sits off center. PHOTO BY PATTI SCHOFLER.

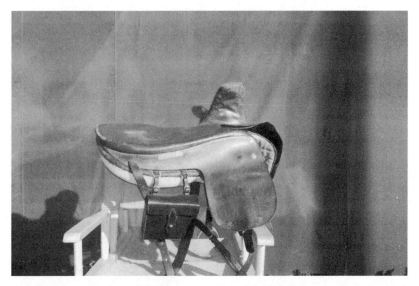

Typical of the properly outfitted hunt seat side saddle, this one totes a box designed to carry a sandwich and a flask of sherry or tea. PHOTO BY PATTI SCHOFLER.

waxed paper. The case also carries a flask three-quarters full of tea or sherry.

Horse and rider should appear as if they can go for hours—not as if the rider can't wait to get out of the saddle. Well-made Western and English style side saddles may be bought new or custom made. Buying an antique side saddle at a garage sale without the eye of an expert may not put you in the best seat.

"A lot of the old saddles were plantation or Victorian saddles made in the U.S. before we had saddle makers that knew what they were doing. They are uncomfortable, don't fit the horses well, and belong hanging on the wall," says Prine-Carr. "Beware of saddles made with steel sides. They sit you crooked, and they make you look like you're sitting in a bucket."

On the other hand, some side saddles built in England in the late 1800s and early 1900s are wonderfully built. Prine-Carr has a favorite: a 1910 Champion Wilton, which is engraved under the saddle flap with the words "By Appointment of His Majesty the King."

This honored designation, called a royal warrant, indicates that the tradesman or tradeswoman was a preferred supplier of goods or services to the King of England.

EQUITATION

Equitation is the act or art of riding a horse; a simple description fraught with complexity. Consider that a horse in his natural wild state has perfect form, balance, and beauty. Add the human on his back, and he struggles to return to that natural state. Being the more intelligent member of the partnership, the human is responsible for showing him how to succeed with his new burden.

She does this through principles of equitation, a system of balance, body alignment, and use of aids or cues that has proven effective in restoring natural balance and in fulfilling the horse's greatest potential in a chosen discipline. The horse, by his nature, responds in a positive way to the correct signals and combinations of signals. His amazing sensitivity reacts to a spectrum from the smallest change in a seat bone to the larger deepening of the rider's weight, from the action of a little finger on the rein to the opening position of an arm, from the shift of an ankle joint to the pressure of the whole calf. He responds to the large and the small if these requests make sense to how his body works.

Though not always called equitation, the term now also refers to the biomechanics of the rider, or "the way muscles move bones to produce and sustain various forms of action," as described by dressage trainer Baron Hans von Blixen-Finecke sixty years ago.

When a rider's biomechanics mesh with her horse's, the result is a beautiful picture. The rider seems to do nothing, and the horse travels softly, actively, rhythmically, and in balance, as if on his own. His rider, who is no longer an encumbrance, may in fact improve upon his natural state.

All eyes and judgments in equitation classes are on the rider to determine not how pretty she looks, but how well she positions herself to give aids or cues to effectively influence the horse. Certain basic principles apply to all disciplines of the Arabian equitation classes, which are Western/Reining Seat, Western Horsemanship, Saddle Seat, Hunter Seat Not To Jump, and Hunter Seat Over Obstacles.

BALANCE: The rider seeks to maintain a compatible balance between her center of gravity and that of her horse's. She neither falls forward nor backward when her horse moves, but stays in balance with his motion. The base of support for this balance and the foundation for the back, arms, and legs is the seat, which stays deep, secure, and elastic. The seat, thighs, and hip joints absorb the motion and allow the rider to maintain her balance so she can follow, feel, and influence the horse's movement and stay in harmony with her horse.

BODY ALIGNMENT: With her eyes looking forward and level with the horizon, the rider's neck and head extend upright as if someone was pulling a string from the top of her head. Her shoulders are slightly drawn back, straight and directly over her hips. Her entire back is straight. Her upper back leans neither right nor left, forward nor back. Her lower back neither slouches nor arches. She, however, is not stiff and rigid.

Her arms drop easily beside her body. Her hands meet a soft, rounded wrist, neither cocked nor horizontal as if playing the piano. The bend of her elbows and the height of her hands depend on the horse's head and neck carriage. A line from the side of her horse's mouth through her hands and to her elbows is correct.

The rider's thighs lay flat against the side of the horse. Her knees, slightly bent, rest flat against the saddle without gripping, so they can work with her calves and thighs as an aid and to secure her balance. Ankles are loose and supple. The balls of her feet are on the stirrups. Her heels are lower than her toes. Her feet point forward or slightly outward to help the inner knee bones and the inside of the calves maintain contact.

She could draw another line from her shoulder to her elbow to her hip to the back of her heel.

USE OF THE AIDS: The rider's aids include her seat, legs, hands, and voice, which work both independently and in conjunction with each other. Her seat creates impulsion, gives direction, signals gait changes, and controls tempo, rhythm, and speed. It transfers the rider's weight to the horse and influences his movement.

Her legs create bend, forward motion, and suppleness. They activate the horse's hindquarters and create energy that travels through his body to the mouth and the bit. There it is controlled by the rider's hands to give the horse effective head and body carriage. Legs guide the horse and, when combined with other aids, create impulsion for the gaits, transitions, circles, stops, spins, collection, and extension. Legs improve balance, form, elevation, and softness.

Her hands act to guide the horse. They determine the degree of bend. They restrain or receive aids.

The rider's voice provides instruction on gait changes, increased impulsion, and stopping.

While these basic principles apply to all seats or styles of riding, each discipline has its own needs.

SADDLE SEAT: For this elegant riding style, the rider sits evenly in the middle of the saddle with her pelvis forward and seat bones on the saddle. She is balanced, not gripping, on the inside of her thighs. While the back is straight, it must yield to the motion of the horse and allow him to perform.

Her leg drops in a natural position directly under her so she can use her leg aids to guide the horse and maintain impulsion, balance, and cadence. Some saddle seat riders who keep their lower leg off the horse cannot then influence or direct him with their calves.

Her hands are held slightly in front of the horse's withers and slightly inside the vertical line, neither perpendicular nor horizontal to the saddle. They maintain a sympathetic rein contact with the horse's mouth, not pulling the head into position with the reins.

A common fault in Saddle Seat Equitation is when the rider's upper body leans behind the vertical line and she raises the reins too high, losing both the proper alignment of head, shoulder, hip, and heel and the line from the bit to her elbow.

At the walk, the rider sits straight while slightly moving her hips individually forward and back in rhythm with the horse's gait. When posting the trot, she follows the gait's cadence with her hips under her body for better balance. At the canter, her seat follows the horse's motion.

The judge wants to see a rider as an active participant whose horse works in a lively, willing way.

REINING/WESTERN SEAT: The rider maneuvers the reins with only one hand held above the saddle horn, with the forearm parallel to the ground. She uses the hand, the wrist, and bent elbow to work the reins. The hand that is not holding the reins may rest in a relaxed manner on the rider's thigh or in a position that allows the rider to keep her body straight and her hand still. She may hold the romal or the ends of the split rein with her free hand to keep them from swinging or to adjust the position of the reins, provided it is held with at least 16 inches of rein between her hands. Her upper arms align with her straight body.

She may ride in either split or romal reins. She holds split reins by running the leather across the palm of her hand from the index to the little finger. The index finger may lie between the reins if the reins hang on the same side as the reining hand. If the ends of the split reins are held in the other hand, she cannot put a finger between the reins.

She holds romal reins with a loose fist, in a vertical position, with the reins running from the little finger, through the hand, and over the thumb. With the thump facing up, the knuckles point toward the horse's ears. She cannot put a finger between the reins.

A common fault is the rider's leading with the shoulder of the rein hand.

In all gaits the rider sits straight, with a slight motion in her seat to follow the horse's rhythm. In sitting the jog and the lope, she takes care not to pop out of the saddle or to lean back. Judges frown on obvious shifting of the rider's weight, leaning to direct the horse, abrupt or heavy hands, loss of forward motion, or overuse of spurs. When riding a pattern or tests assigned by the judge, the performance should be accurate and smooth, with the rider showing control and balance.

HUNTER SEAT EQUITATION NOT TO JUMP: The hunter seat is designed to give the rider balance, security, and control to meet any emergency on the hunt field. The workmanlike position derives its flexibility and control, lightness and suppleness, from the lower leg and seat.

The leg is the rider's security and anchor. Her inner knee bones contact the saddle, but not so tightly that her calves and heels pull away from the horse or her upper body falls forward or backward. Her calves maintain contact with the horse in a supporting, but not a gripping, driving manner. Her heels sit slightly behind the girth, flexed in and down to act as a shock absorbers.

Lauren Christensen wins a U.S. Reserve National Championship in Hunt Seat Not to Jump Equitation Walk/Trot on Deborah Johnson's horse Couquette+. PHOTO BY ROB HESS.

The rider sits close to the saddle pommel with her thighs flat against the saddle. Her seat is flexible and follows the horse. Her upper body is erect, her chest raised, her shoulders back, and her back straight, without being stiff, hollow, or sway backed. Her head is lifted and straight, her eyes looking ahead, never down to find a lead or diagonal. This position is called three-point contact: her two legs and her seat make contact with the horse.

The hand position is similar to that of the saddle seat rider, only lower because the horse carries his head and neck lower. Knuckles turn 30 degrees inside the vertical and hands are about two or three inches apart.

When the horse stands at the halt, the rider's body is straight. When he walks, trots, and canters, the rider slightly closes her hip angle and moves her body in front of the vertical line a couple of degrees. The inclination is greater at the posting trot and at the hand gallop than at the walk, slower sitting trot, and canter. The rider closes her hip angle to no more than 20 degrees in front of the vertical. She shifts forward into two-point contact as the horse gallops, taking her weight off the horse's back by lifting her seat out of the saddle and putting the weight into her legs. Her flexed ankles reflect the downward distribution of weight, with the lower leg maintaining contact with the horse at all times. This position enables the rider to stay with the motion of the horse by increasing her agility and smoothness in following her horse.

HUNTER SEAT EQUITATION OVER OBSTACLES: When the rider enters the arena, she picks up the canter, rises into two-point position, inclining her upper body about 20 degrees in front of the vertical, allowing her to ride over the horse's center of gravity. Her ankles reflect a deep, downward weight distribution. The lower legs remain fixed to the horse's side when she rides between and over jumps.

With a purposeful look about her, she establishes the pace she will maintain as the horse canters throughout the course.

Her eyes focus beyond her position, looking around the corner before her horse turns the corner. Approaching a jump, she spots a focal point thirty feet beyond the jump. Her shoulders are up, her chest open, elevated, and straight over the horse. Her back is straight. Her two-point position has freed the horse's back so he can arc over the fence. She should not throw her upper body to get the horse to leave the ground for the fence.

As the horse leaves the ground to jump the fence, his thrust and lift further closes her hip angle in a smooth motion. She allows him freedom to balance himself by following his head and neck forward with her hands. She may rest her hands on the crest or sides of his neck, about a third of the way up the mane. This crest release gives her upper body support and the horse freedom to jump. The rider's eyes look ahead. Her shoulders are up; her chest is open and elevated. Her back and shoulders are straight.

On landing, her heel flexion provides shock absorption and allows her to maintain her position unjarred. Her hip angle opens back to the two-point contact. She rides forward to the next jump.

This rider is balanced and secure, which gives her the ability to follow the horse and accommodate his jump, staying out of his way. She keeps her center of gravity balanced with that of her horse to create a smooth, fluid, and controlled ride.

A judge evaluates her position between and over jumps. She also wants to see accuracy and smoothness to and over jumps. The rider should be in total command, with the horse in balance and control, moving with impulsion, bending and on the bit. A team that looks disciplined is rewarded.

On the other hand, a judge will penalize a rider that allows her horse to refuse a jump or trots on the course when trotting is not a part of a test. A judge considers it the rider's responsibility to place the horse at the correct distance to the jump and take-off spot (as explained in chapter 10) and will penalize riders who place their horses in poor spots or who fall behind the motion on take-off.

CONDUCT OF CLASS

Class A shows may offer classes in Saddle Seat, Hunter Seat Over Obstacles, Hunter Seat Not to Jump, Western Seat, and Western Horsemanship. The exhibitors perform as a group walk, trot, and canter in both directions of the arena. The judge may then ask the competitors to individually ride at least two tests, which he chooses from a list outlined in the USEF Rule Book. In Western Horsemanship, the horse and rider perform at least four tests. They vary in the degree of difficulty. For example, the Saddle Seat rider may have to drop her stirrups and regain them or trot a figure eight. The Hunter Seat rider may be asked to halt and back or canter a serpentine with a flying change of lead on each change of bend. The Western Seat rider may have to back her horse or perform a sliding stop.

In Hunter Seat Over Obstacles, competitors jump a course of at least six obstacles.

Though the Arabian Horse Association encourages shows to hold equitation classes for adults, most classes cater to riders 17 years old and under. Often classes are divided into 13 years old and under, and 14 to 17 year olds. Also, walk/trot classes for 10 and under in each seat are available in most shows.

Riders 17 years old and under may compete in AHA Medal classes at Class A shows in order to qualify for equitation classes at the Arabian Youth National Championships. Medal classes include Saddle Seat, Reining Seat, Hunter Seat Over Obstacles, and Hunter Seat Not to Jump.

In AHA Saddle Seat and Hunter Seat Not To Jump Medal classes, exhibitors perform rail work as a group. Individually they ride a pattern designed by the judge and based on the tests listed in the USEF Rule Book. For the Reining Seat[22] medal, the judge may

---

[22] In Class A shows Western equitation is called Western seat; in AHA medal classes Western equitation is referred to as reining seat.

choose one of the ten USEF/NRHA reining patterns. Hunter Seat Equitation Over Obstacles riders are required to jump a course.

A pattern is designed to test the rider's ability to control the horse at different gaits on lines and circles and in transitions. The judge is looking to reward the rider who understands her horse's biomechanical and mental characteristics. She is not a robot running through the judge's requests; she is a thinking rider. Life is grand with a "pushbutton" horse, but the rider has to know which buttons to push and how to push them. Horses are living creatures who become crooked, or distracted, who have different thoughts from their riders, and who as individuals respond to one degree or another. A judge would rather see a rider correct a problem in an appropriate way than a rider who travels along in perfect form, but who for all her awareness of what is going on under her might as well be riding a wooden horse.

As with all disciplines, a judge likes a smooth, accurate, balanced, and controlled ride. While equitation classes evaluate the rider, a horse that is not going well indicates that the rider is not doing her job correctly.

Whatever the discipline, an equitation rider who demonstrates confidence and a positive attitude and who is relaxed and has a good relationship with her horse stands out no matter how big the field or who else is in the class.

FOR KIDS

The goal of Youth Halter Showmanship is for young people to demonstrate their grasp of the foundations of safe, correct horse handling, with a touch of elegance. Like equitation, this class focuses on the person's ability to show her horse, but from the ground. The appearance of the handler and her horse are a significant part of showmanship. The horse's condition, grooming, and tack reflect how well the handler has presented his horse.

Young handlers are asked to lead their horses in a prescribed pattern devised by the judge, who looks for precision and control. The pattern may include walking and trotting in a straight line or around a marker, stopping, backing up, and turning or pivoting the horse 90 to 360 degrees. The handlers also will stand up their horse in the style and techniques of showing an Arabian at halter.

The handler who shows complete control over her horse and performs the maneuvers of the pattern promptly, safely, and correctly earns credit in the judge's eye. The judge will find fault with a handler who drags her horse along, excessively jerks on the halter, or is not aware of her horse's actions or the position of other competitors. The judge wants to see a handler who is poised and alert, not posing and over-showing.

The handler should present her horse with style and control, holding herself in a natural but upright position as she leads her horse and stands him up. Her clothes should be neat, clean, and appropriate to the manner in which the horse is being shown, such as Saddle Seat, Hunt Seat, or Western.

A horse is shown in a show halter, headstall with a bit and throatlatch, or a leather stable halter. His mane is braided appropriate to a hunter, show hack, or dressage horse, depending on how he is shown.

CHAPTER SEVENTEEN

THE SHOW SCENE

*"I believe that if you own a horse, especially an Arabian, you
can't celebrate too often. We need to think of how glorious they
are and how much they mean to us."*

—Bazy Tankersley

TALK TO TEN PEOPLE AT THE END OF A HORSE SHOW AND
each is likely to have a different reaction to the experience. Showing can be: fun, hard work, scary, exhilarating, valuable, the best
day of your life, or the worst day of your life. Showing can be an
opportunity to spend quality one-on-one time with your horse and
to grow the relationship between you two. From the show experience you learn more about your horse, your discipline, and yourself.
Just preparing for a show, you probably work harder, longer, and
with greater focus, and as a result, you upgrade your skill. If a
trainer shows your horse, you have the great pleasure of seeing your
beautiful Arabian in action and likely become a larger part of your
horse's team.

To avoid that "deer in the headlights" feeling when you hit the
show road, even if you have a trainer who holds your hand every
mile of that road, attend a few shows without a horse and study what
goes on. Catch on to the rhythm of the show: what people do when
they arrive, how they settle in their horses, how they groom and
bathe their horses away from home, how they prepare and warm up,
when they go into the arena when their class is called, how they
show in their class, what they do when they are not showing or
preparing to show, and who the show officials are and what they do.

Study the outfits appropriate for each discipline: quiet and subtle for hunter; a little flasher for Western and English.

Better yet, improve your comfort level by volunteering for a show. You will start in a beginner's job that will allow you to observe and learn. In no time you may graduate from being a runner for the show secretary to the person who opens and closes the arena gate. This gives you a place to watch the mechanics of a show. After a while you may move up to ring steward and assist the judge. This position gives you a bird's eye view from inside the show arena.

To participate in an Arabian show, either as a spectator or exhibitor, contact the Arabian Horse Association (AHA) for information on clubs, shows, and appropriate contacts in your area. If your plans entail competing in a recognized Arabian show, your horse must be registered with AHA. This is not necessary for an open or schooling show.

When you want to compete, request a show "premium list" or "prize list" from the show secretary. This booklet details the rules, regulations, and specifics of that show and provides the entry form. No, the first step to entering a show is not to tear your hair out. There is a method to this madness.

The first page of the premium list outlines the dates of the show; the closing date when all entries and fees must be postmarked and mailed to the show secretary; the names of judges and show officials; the show secretary's phone number, address, and e-mail address; the location of the show; and the horse show office phone number.

The next page lists classes and the days on which they will be held. This listing gives you the information you need to fill in the entry form. A typical class list will look like this:

35	$25	Arabian Trail Horse—Novice Horse
60	$25	Half Arabian/Anglo-Arabian English Show Hack—Open

89	$20		Arabian Native Costume—AAOTR 18 and over
90	$10		Western Seat Equitation—JTR 17 and under
115	$20		Arabian Hunter Pleasure—Junior Horse
165	$20		Arabian Country English Pleasure—ATR
170	$20		Arabian Western Pleasure—JOTR 17 and under
190	$25		Arabian Stallion Breeding—3 years old
220	$35	$100	Arabian Mounted Native Costume Championship
224	$20		Arabian Sport Horse Mares—AOTH
228	0		Half Arabian/Anglo-Arabian Gelding In-Hand Champion and Reserve

The first column is class numbers. The second column is the entry fee charged to ride in the class. The third column is the prize money for class winners. The last column gives the name of the class, followed by any restrictions.

Some restrictions pertain to the horse:

1. Maiden: a horse that has not won a first place in a recognized show in that particular discipline.
2. Novice: a horse that has not won three first places in a recognized show in that particular discipline.
3. Limit: a horse that has not won six first places in a recognized show in that particular discipline.
4. Junior: A horse five years old or younger.
5. The class description will specify whether it is open to only Arabians, only Half Arabians/Anglo-Arabians, or both.
6. In-Hand or Breeding Champion and Reserve indicates that this championship class is open to the first- and second-place winners in qualifying classes.

Those restrictions pertaining to the rider, driver, or handler are:

1. JOTR/JOTD/JOTH—Junior Owner to Ride/Junior Owner to Drive/ Junior Owner to Handle. A junior is a person who hasn't turned 18 by December 1 of the current competition year.

2. JTR/JTD/JTH—Junior to Ride/Junior to Drive/ Junior to Handle.

3. AAOTR/AAOTD/AAOTH—Adult Amateur Owner to Ride/Adult Amateur Owner to Drive/Adult Amateur Owner to Handle. An amateur is a person who, after his or her 18th birthday, does not engage in activities which make him or her a professional in the horse business. An amateur/owner is an amateur that owns the horse competing in the class.

4. AOTR/AOTD/AOTH—Amateur Owner to Ride/Amateur Owner to Drive/Amateur Owner to Handle.

5. ATR/ATD/ATH—Amateur to Ride/Amateur to Drive/ Amateur to Handle.

6. Select—AOTR, AAOTR, JOTR, JTR. This category is for riders, drivers, or handlers who have not won in that discipline a regional top five, reserve champion, or champion award; a national top ten, reserve champion, or champion award; two regional top five, reserve champion, or champion awards in a select class; or a national top ten, reserve champion, or champion award in a select class.

7. Open—Anyone entered in the show may compete in this class.

On the entry form, you fill in your horse's registered name and AHA registration number, and if he has them, his USEF and USDF numbers. Once you have filled in the classes in which you wish to show and their entry fees, you complete the section requesting the names, addresses, phone numbers, social security numbers, AHA numbers, and USEF or CEF (Canadian Equestrian Federation) number of the horse's owner, trainer,[23] and rider/handler/driver, and if dressage is offered, the rider's USDF number. Numbers for local organizations may also be requested.

Copies of the following documents must accompany your entry and payment that you mail to the show secretary: both sides of your horse's registration papers or proof of sale[24]; and current AHA and USEF membership cards for all trainers, riders, handlers, drivers, and owners.

If you do not belong to AHA and you choose not to join at a Class A show, you may pay a single event fee at each show. You must belong to AHA to compete at regional and national shows and to win points or placing in AHA programs. If you choose not to join USEF, you may pay a non-member fee at each show. If you show frequently, it is more cost effective to join these associations.

On the back of most entry forms are lines for mandatory owner, exhibitor, trainer, coach, and parent/guardian signatures.

The fee schedule in the premium list outlines all potential charges, including stall fees, trailer-in fees, cattle charges, and the USEF drug fee, which pays for the services of the USEF's horse drug testing program. Check with USEF for the current list of illegal drugs.

The remainder of the premium list supplies information specific to the show, such as directions to the show grounds, local hotels, footing in the arenas, how the prize money is divided, special awards, the type of stabling and bedding, information on the show farrier and veterinarian, and other rules and definitions.

---

[23] For the show entry, the trainer is the person responsible for the horse while he is on the grounds. This may be you, your trainer, or in the case of a minor, a parent or guardian.

[24] If you are exhibiting in an amateur owner or junior owner class, the horse must be registered in the name of the competitor or a member of the competitor's family.

When deciding which classes and how many to enter, keep in mind that although Arabians have remarkable endurance and willingness to do more for their riders and handlers, some exhibitors ask too much and sign up for too many classes. Judge and trainer Gordon Potts advises, "In an ideal setting, I would only show a horse two times at a show. When I take him into the ring, I want him to do his best, and it's hard to get that level of performance time and time again, especially in a two- or three-day period. You can't expect them to be in peak every time you get on. It needs to be fun for them too. When showing becomes drudgery or more work than fun, they won't do as well."

PREPARING FOR THE SHOW

Preparing for the show begins months before. Only in this way can you ensure that your horse is in his best physical condition, at the top of his game, and understands his job. This lead time also gives you a good period in which to get fit. Spend time in the saddle or behind the buggy, and do your homework. Reestablish your strengths. Work on the places you are weakest and practice the things that make you nervous.

"The thrill of showing is seeing the success of my preparation. I know that when I go through that gate, I am prepared," says Russ Vento, an amateur competitor who has won several national titles.

Once you have entered your show, make a list of everything you think you might need for your horse and yourself, laminate it or slip it into a plastic sleeve for safekeeping, and store it in your trailer, in your show file, or with your show clothes.

Review your horse's tack and your clothes. Is the fit proper? Is everything in good repair? Are the clothes appropriate for your classes? If you buy anything new, try it out prior to the show and be sure it fits right and is comfortable for you or the horse. Get your show clothes cleaned and put in garment bags. Your hat belongs in a hat box. Don't forget safety pins to attach your show number to the back of your jacket, shirt, or vest.

Be sure your farrier has your horse properly shod for the show.

"I have it all figured out ahead of time," says judge and trainer Mike Damianos. "I even know ahead of time how I'm going to prepare and decorate the show stalls. That gives me the best peace of mind."

Grooming

Arabians are the horses of beauty and type. Naturally their owners, trainers, and exhibitors want them to look like glamorous stars. However, beautiful grooming is more than surface deep. Pulling a horse out of pasture a week before a show just will not produce the picture of a lustrous, brilliant horse. Planning and advance work will.

COATS: A horse's coat is the story of his past life. No matter how many hair products you spray on a shabby, dull coat, they will not make up for poor conditioning, nutrition, and care. The coat that calls attention to its brilliance results from good feeding, regular exercise, worming, dental care, and elbow grease.

A diet enhanced by green grass, corn oil, or rice bran adds luster to a coat. Too much shampooing dries it out. Sweating is good for the coat, but leftover sweat is not. To remove sweat, either let the horse dry and curry it out or hose him off with plain water. The massaging effect of good brushing assists muscle tone as well as healthy coat growth.

MANE AND TAILS: The trademark long, flowing mane and tail of an Arabian do not come without time and effort.

Not unlike human hair, the mane and tail do best when kept clean, conditioned, and dry. Human hair conditioners work well and are cheaper than horse products. Unlike human hair, though, the less you brush your horse's mane and tail, the fuller and longer they will remain. Tangles are better removed by hand so that hairs will not break. Silicone sprays will keep the hairs separated, but can dry out the hair.

To keep the mane from knotting or becoming snagged on fences or buckets, you might braid it. Braid the tail, roll the braid into a ball, and then secure it with gauze. Do not wrap it closer than two inches from the end of the tail bone and take the wrap off at least every two weeks to freshly shampoo and condition the tail. Allow the tail to dry before wrapping it, and then keep it dry. Without proper care, hair may rot and the tail may actually fall off. Consider leaving some hairs out or braiding into the tail strips of cloth so your horse can flick off flies.

CLIPPING: How much clipping and where you clip your horse are individual preferences. For example, for a show in Minnesota in the winter, you might not want to body clip. Similarly, for a show in Minnesota in the summer where the bugs are plentiful, you might not clip the hair in the horse's ears. And the amount of clipping will depend on how your horse lives when he is not at a show. Is he in a stall or out at pasture, where he will need a fuller coat?

Generally, different clipper blades do different jobs: a #40 blade clips short; a #10 leaves the hair a bit longer. Clipping takes practice. Some horses' coats look better immediately after clipping, while others do better by being clipped a week in advance of a show. If your horse's coat is dry after clipping, mix a solution of one part bath oil to fifteen parts water and apply it to the coat after clipping.

How you clip the horse's bridle path will not determine if your horse wins or loses. Its purpose is to clear a place for the crown piece of the bridle. Some people do clip it fairly far down the neck because they believe it shows off the neck shape better. It also was a fashion trend at one time. The usual length is eight to ten inches. "If your horse flexes nicely at the poll, you can clip the bridle path back a bit to accentuate his ability. For a horse that breaks too much at the poll or breaks at the third vertebrae in his neck, you might have a shorter bridle path," says trainer Greta Wrigley.

The removal of facial hair varies. "Trimming whiskers off the nose and chin and the long eyebrow hairs is acceptable. Taking a razor and shaving cream to the horse's face is not acceptable," says Russ Vento.

"Actually in summer when an Arabian sheds out around the eyes and nose, the black skin shows and gives more definition to the face, which is a very pretty look. It's not a look you get in February. So in order to get that look, you would have to do more trimming."

How much hair is removed along the outline of the horse's ears or inside the ear is individual preference, often based on the horse's lifestyle. Since the hair keeps bugs and dirt out of the ear, a horse that lives in pasture will not do well with his ears closely trimmed.

FEET: Movement, good shoeing and nutrition, and the proper amount of moisture contribute to healthy hoof growth. If the hooves need attention, hoof dressing will help. Bacon grease also adds to the hoof health.

GROOMING AT THE SHOW: Many exhibitors at larger, competitive shows, especially for halter classes, use oil on the horse's face to enhance the pigments and bring out the darker skin around the eyes and muzzle. Baby oil gives a natural look. Heavy gloss is more extreme and a problem in heat. The guidelines for the Egyptian Event state that a horse must be presented "without makeup, dye, heavy oils, grease or artificial appliance which distract from their natural beauty. Any horse(s) suspected of such will be given a 'white towel test,' and if anything shows on the towel, the handler will be asked to remove it. If not, the horse will be excused."

Applying a light amount of baby oil around the horse's nose and eyes at night will highlight his features. By morning it will be absorbed. Leaving baby oil on during the day may cause sunburn. Hair cream or a little petroleum jelly also works. Baby oil will remove manure stains under the tail. Baby wipes do the job as well.

Performance horses may appear in a light coat spray to keep the hair down and the dust off, everywhere except where the saddle sits. Often products that slicken the hair cause the saddle to slip. Coat products that have less silicone are the best choice, as silicone dries out the coat, mane, and tail. A way to repel dust is to wipe the horse with a clothes dryer sheet with fabric softener. Some say it also repels flies.

Braids for sport horse classes stay in best on a mane that is not very clean or conditioned. The look of a brilliant English horse is enhanced by a flowing mane and tail. The forelock is oiled and tucked under and to the side of the brow band. Western manes are often oiled down to keep them from blowing.

For glossy manes and tails, fill a spray bottle half with white rice and half with water, then let the mixture stand for 24 hours. To use, shake the bottle, spray the mix on a slightly damp mane and tail, and comb the hair through, let it dry and brush it out. Or you can rub petroleum jelly on your hands and run your fingers through the tail for a thicker, shinier appearance.

There was a day when Arabian show hooves were so glassy you could put on makeup or shave your beard in their glow. Some exhibitors, especially for regional and national shows, still will use electric sanders on hooves to even out the wall and remove ground-in dirt. Done too often and too deeply, however, this method may wear down the nail heads, weaken the shoe's hold on the hoof, and weaken the hoof wall.

A healthy, shiny look can be gained without harming the hoof wall by cleaning the feet first with a small hand scrub brush and a bluing shampoo, followed by a scrub by hand with steel wool or fine sandpaper.

To prevent the drying effects from hoof polishes that contain alcohol, first protect the hoof with wax paste polish used for shining shoes. Then apply hoof polish. Another method is to use a clear hoof "enhancer" product that is not drying. Apply one coat, let it dry, lightly sand, and then apply a second coat.

AT THE SHOW

Your first job upon arriving at the show is to take care of your horse. If you are stabling on the show grounds, look for the stall chart posted at the barns or at the show office. When you find your stall, carefully check the walls for nails, broken boards, and other potential dangers. Remove any leftover moldy hay or manure from the last resident. Bed the stall to your satisfaction. Set up your horse's water, and if food helps him to relax, feed him. Place on the front of the stall your name and the phone number where you can be reached in case of emergency. If the stalls are the portable variety, latches are sometimes more moveable than you might like. Hook your lead rope through the latch for protection against horse lips that might jimmy the door open.

After your horse settles in, consider taking him for a hand walk around the facility. However, be certain that you can handle him in a lively environment populated by garbage cans, water trucks, trailers, and more horses than he likely has at home.

You are establishing a routine at the show that will serve you and him for every show. With time, he will understand that this is what you two always do, and the routine's regularity will give him comfort. "Try to simulate his home environment. If he is nervous about his neighbor, make adjustments. Make him feel secure," says Vento.

If at all possible, bring your horse's hay from home. Since he is under the stress of new surroundings and routines, it is better for his digestive system to not have to adjust to new feed. Electrolytes added to his water or feed will encourage him to drink different-tasting water. Though classes may interfere, try to feed him around the same time he is fed at home.

Arabian shows can be very busy. And being intelligent, curious creatures, Arabians are by and large interested in everything that goes on. For a good part of the show, some will stand at the stall door with their heads out and watch everything. They may not take the time to eat or take their usual cat naps. They exhaust themselves. For this reason many trainers will close the top of a stall door or put up stall curtains to encourage the horse to relax, eat, and drink.

"Your horse will tell you if he likes privacy. Horses don't normally have a grumpy attitude. So if he has a happy, friendly attitude and after a day or so he has his ears back, he might want to be left alone," says Russ Vento.

As soon as you can, check in with the show office to pick up your number and pay any fees you might have missed when you filled out your entry.

Take care of yourself too. Remember to eat and to drink plenty of water. Try to set up a place, either at the stall or at your trailer if you are not stabling, where you can chill out, relax, and get out of any direct sun.

Keep your clothes clean and intact. A nice appearance shows respect for the judge, your horse, and yourself. Be certain you have a plan for how you will wear your hair that works with your hat. For shiny boots, heat the tin of boot polish until it melts slightly by holding a match to its bottom. Replace the lid for a few minutes. Then apply the polish to your boots with a piece of wet cotton. A final rubdown of boots with pantyhose does wonders.

"If your horse is so fantastic and doing everything right, you probably could wear a sack and win, but at the big shows where everyone looks so good, it makes a difference to be well groomed," says trainer Jim Lowe.

Stress

Everyone, even the pros, gets nervous. The adrenaline rush is part of the problem and part of the fun. But the only way to improve your showing skills is to show. From those experiences you develop the confidence, the routine, and the attitude that can make showing addictive.

Here is advice from some pros.

MARY TROWBRIDGE: "This is a sport for people who enjoy the process and not just the destination or the prize, because you're never there forever. Even with success, after you're pinned the winner, the next moment brings about new challenges. You make a lot of mistakes along the way, but happily they don't end up with death and destruction. Keep in your mind your ultimate goal, then evaluate where you are that day and give yourself a realistic immediate objective. Focus realistically on what you want for this horse in his life: next year, this show season, next month. Is it a schooling show, a Class A, regionals, an appearance at nationals, a run for Top Ten, or a run for the roses?"

KRISTIN HARDIN: "At the show, remember you're just riding your same horse on a different piece of dirt."

RUSS VENTO: "The joy of showing is reaching a goal I have set and doing well. We have to start believing in ourselves. I have a friend who rode in a championship in which out of twenty-five horses, hers should clearly have won. But she looked nervous, she rode nervous, her body was tight, and her balance didn't work. She rode without confidence. And she didn't win. If you're so worried about your hair or the competition or getting your leads that you're not concentrating on what you worked so hard to achieve, you won't make it. You have to get to the point where you believe that you have done your homework."

MICHAEL DAMIANOS: "I have taught PhDs, a Nobel Peace Prize winner, doctors, and attorneys. It doesn't matter how scholarly you are; one thing about showing horses is that it will bring out the idiot in you. Common sense leaves your body when you enter the show ring. Showing is being able to control your nerves and still use common sense."

GRETA WRIGLEY: "We have a good support system, a big team thing where everyone helps each other make showing fun. No matter what happens in the ring, everyone is going to be there for you when you come out of the ring. And I don't send my students in the ring until they know their dressage tests well and their basics are strong. There have been days when I've had bad scores. It is not cool, but you go back into the ring and clean it up. It's not the end of the world."

WENDY GRUSKIEWICZ: "Exhibitors often look at judges as the enemy. But we are your biggest fans. We want to see exhibitors do well."

Most importantly, you are the leader of a team who must listen to your teammate. You will find your comfort level if you know who your horse is and how he feels mentally and physically at a show. Some horses wilt when they enter the show arena. Some get hot. Some are overachievers; others are underachievers. Since you have done your work at home, your job will be to figure out the right amount of warm-up, not under- or over-riding him or asking him to do more than he can at the moment or waging a battle over it. Likely he will enter the arena relaxed. But ready to show.

If confidence and attitude ride with you through the entry gate, you will make that critical good first impression on the judge. You will be happy to be there, and excited and proud to exhibit your Arabian. That way you may have the ride and the show of your life.

FINDING YOUR SPECIAL ARABIAN

While you were reading this book and looking at its pictures, you might have been certain that you wanted a hunter pleasure horse. When you moved to another chapter you thought, "What fun to show in trail classes." You may have had a picture in your mind of just what your ideal horse will look like, how he will act, the way he will move, and how you will relate to him. You may have snuggled up to a few prospects. He is out there somewhere, but where?

Begin your search by joining the AHA and one of its local clubs. Membership will put you in the loop. Through AHA and your local club you will find people who have horses for sale. You will also find out the dates and places for shows where you may also find horses for sale. *Arabian Horse Magazine*, which comes with AHA membership, runs classified ads and advertises training and breeding farms with horses for sale. Subscribe to other magazines such as *Arabian Horse World* and *Arabian Horse Times*. Through these sources you will become familiar with trainers in your area and perhaps find one who fits your style. He or she can take you under his or her wing to teach you about horse buying, how to make wise, informed decisions, and lead you to the right horse for you.

Another source for sale horses is the Internet. Google "Arabian horses" as a start.

On the other hand, AHA's Discovery Farms program may be more comfortable. You, your family, and friends can visit a farm in your area for a no-pressure, no-selling outing to look at, pet, and experience the Arabian horse up close and personal. Similarly, AHA's Mentor Network program couples potential or new owners with more experienced Arabian fans who can help new owners start out on the right path.

Two other resources are the university facilities that breed Arabians and are both beneficiaries of cereal magnate W.K. Kellogg's generosity.

Michigan State University in East Lansing received its first purebred Arabian gift from Michigan native Kellogg in 1932. Others followed, and today MSU has a herd of over 100 purebreds. Its Horse Research and Teaching Center breeds between twenty and forty mares a year with the goal of producing world-class Arabians. The horses are the stars of the classroom, where students take hands-on classes in equine reproduction and breeding, equine science, equine behavior, starting two-year-olds under saddle, showing and training, and advanced riding.

Kellogg's horses came from his ranch in Pomona, California, which he donated to the state of California in 1949 with two stipulations: the property had to be used for education purposes and for Arabian horse shows. The result was the founding of California Polytechnic State University and its W.K. Kellogg Arabian Horse Center. Approximately eighty-five purebred Arabian horses are the core of the equine science teachings, outreach, research, breeding, and training programs.

Wherever you find your Arabian and whatever you do together in the show arena, you will soon realize your good fortune to have in your life a horse with such beauty and exhilaration, such tolerance and perception, one that will return to you the love, affection, and devotion you extend to him.

SWEEPSTAKES AND FUTURITIES

International Arabian Breeders Sweepstakes Program (IABS)

The Breeders Sweepstakes Program was conceived to promote the Arabian and to provide financial incentives to breed Arabians. As an addendum, this system has given owners an incentive to buy horses eligible for sweepstakes prize money and to show them at the local, regional, and national levels.

Two segments produce a payout to the horse owner. To participate in the points payout, the owner pays an annual $100 enrollment fee. Her horse then earns points in designated sweepstakes classes and recognized distance rides at local, regional, and national events. At the end of the year, AHA announces the dollar value assigned to the points.

On or before January 1 of each year, the IABS committee announces which classes will receive allocated monies that will be awarded to sweepstakes-nominated horses at the national and regional shows and certain designated non-show events, such as endurance rides and competitive trail rides. The horses must qualify for the regional or national competition to be eligible for sweepstakes-allocated prize money, except entries in regional yearling sweepstakes and two-year-old gelding sweepstakes classes, in which entries need not meet any class qualifying requirements.

To win sweepstakes prize money in either segment, a horse must be "sweepstakes nominated," which means he or she falls into one of the following categories:

1. Breeding Entry: This horse has been "nominated" or enrolled by his breeder in the year that he was conceived (not necessarily in the year he was born). This unborn foal was sired by a "nominated sire" or a "non-Arabian nominated sire" that was bred to an Arabian mare. Or

he could be out of a "nominated mare" bred to either a non-Arabian stallion or a "nominated sire."

2. Original Entry: If you have a registered Arabian that was not nominated before he was born, but you would like him to be eligible for sweepstakes prize money, you may enroll him to compete for sweepstakes cash in any payback event except the regional yearling sweepstakes breeding classes and the two-year-old Arabian gelding in-hand class.

Both these entry methods are lifetime enrollments with no additional fees. The first is more economical as a means to encourage breeders to nominate their unborn foals, rather than to see whether their babies fulfill their expectations.

The "nominated mare" category is open to any living registered Arabian mare that is bred to either a non-Arabian stallion or a "nominated sire" to have the resulting in utero (unborn) foal eligible as a "breeding entry." The owner pays a one-time entry fee.

The "nominated sire" category is open to any living registered Arabian stallion whose owner pays a one-time entry fee. Stallion owners earn payback based on 5 percent of their offsprings' sweepstakes earnings.

The "non-Arabian nominated sire" category is open to any living non-Arabian stallion.

Futurities

Futurities are about imagination and dreams coming true.

Imagine that you are certain that you made an amazing match between a stallion and a mare; even before your foal is born, you just know that colt or filly is going to be better than any other gambler's fantasy. So you put your money where your mouth is and nominate that unborn foal for a futurity, declaring that when the gleam in your eye is between a year and five years old, he or she will undoubtedly win the futurity and take home a boatload of cash.

On the surface, the attraction of futurities is the pot of gold at the end of the class. Yet futurities return more than a chunk of change as they evolve into a wide variety of styles, with varied payouts and eligibility requirements.

Some futurities aim for glitz and glamour, with large payouts. The Medallion Stallion Futurity organized by the Minnesota Arabian Horse

Breeders hosts a dinner dance. Others shoot for a style befitting their local club and welcoming to the local, at times non-horse related, community. For example, the Arabian Horse Association of Michigan Breeders Arabian and Half Arabian Futurity sponsors an evening in which spectators can come into the arena to meet the stallions close up. They then move to another venue to enjoy an elaborate sweets table. Some cater to amateurs, while others focus on the opportunities for members to show off their youngsters, look at what other area breeders have accomplished, and visit with friends. Some stick to halter classes. Others offer performance classes for the three- and four-year-olds, and in the case of reining, five-year-olds. Still others have classes for halter and performance youngsters.

Enrollment criteria reflect the versatility of the breed. Prerequisites might center on geography, bloodlines, relationship to nominated stallions, purebreds only, or membership in the organizing body.

Whatever the criteria, take as an example the procedure for the U.S. and Canadian National Futurities. For the breeding and in-hand programs, the dam of the future foal is nominated by December 31 of the year prior to the foal's birth. Then, in order to show, a futurity entrant pays a yearly renomination fee for the foal as it grows up. Halter futurities include classes for three-year-old Arabian fillies, colts, and geldings and Half Arabian/Anglo-Arabian fillies. Performance Futurities include classes for three-year-old Arabian and Half Arabian/Anglo-Arabian horses in Western Pleasure, Hunter Pleasure, English Pleasure, Country English Pleasure, and, for five-year-old and under horses, in reining.

Other futurities include the California Futurity held in conjunction with the San Fernando Valley Arabian Horse Association Class A Show, the Scottsdale Signature Stallion Futurity, and the Scottsdale Half Arabian and Purebred Arabian Reining Futurities.

SHOW ASSOCIATIONS

Arabian Horse Association
10805 East Bethany Drive
Aurora, Colorado 80014-2605
Phone: (303) 696-4500
E-mail: info@ArabianHorses.org
www.ArabianHorses.org

Arabian Professionals and Amateur Horseman's Association
P.O. Box 40
Vail, Colorado 81658
www.apaha.com
E-mail: apaha1@gmail.com

The Pyramid Society
P.O. Box 11941
Lexington, Kentucky 40579
Phone: (859) 231-0771
www.pyramidsociety.org
E-mail: info@pyramidsociety.org

Canadian Arabian Horse Registry
Canadian Partbred Arabian Register
#113
37 Athabascan Avenue
Sherwood Park, Canada AB T8A 4H3
Phone: (780) 416-4990
www.cahr.ca

Arabian Reining Horse Association
c/o Eleanor Hamilton
Phone: (763) 786-8750 days; (763) 767-1381 evenings
E-mail: h.hamilton@microcontrol.com
www.arha.net

National Cutting Horse Association
260 Bailey Avenue
Fort Worth, Texas 76107
Phone: (817)244-6188
www.nchacutting.com

National Reining Horse Association
3000 NW 10th Street
Oklahoma City, Oklahoma 73107
Phone: (405)946-7400
www.nrha.com

United States Equestrian Federation
4047 Iron Works Parkway
Lexington, Kentucky 40511
(859) 258-2472
www.usef.org

United States Dressage Federation
4051 Ironworks Parkway
Lexington, Kentucky 40511
(859) 971-2277
www.USDF.org

INDEX

Abd-el-Kader, Emir of Mascara, 1
Abeyan, 10, 12
ACS (Arabian Community Show),
    29–30
age of horse, 161–162, 179
AHA. *See* Arabian Horse
    Association (AHA)
aids, 128, 244
American Arabians, 22–23
American Remount Service, 19
American vs. European system of
    judging, 225–226
AM Good Oldboy (horse), **174**
And Miles to Go (Smith), 17
Anglo-Arabians, 12–13, 210
Apoloz=// (horse), **45**
appointments. *See* clothing
    requirements; tack
*The Arabian: War Horse to Show
    Horse* (Edwards), 11
Arabian Community Show (ACS),
    29–30
Arabian Horse Association (AHA)
    contact information, 271
    history of, 12, 23
    membership and show fees, 257
    overview, 29
    purchasing horses and, 266, 267
    for show information, 254
    sport horse classes and, 94
Arabian Horse Association of
    Michigan Breeders
    Arabian and Half Arabian
    Futurity, 270

Arabian Horse Magazine, 266
Arabian Horse Registry of America,
    21, 22–23
Arabian horses, overview
    age and, 161–162, 179
    color of, 9–10, 236
    country of origin, 14–23
    description and character, 2, 5
    gender preferences, 7
    history of, 4–6, 14–23
    legendary, 44, 57–58, 90–91
    mythology of, 3–4
    names, interpretations of, 23–25
    physical attributes of, 7–10
    strains and substrains, 10–13
    versatility of, 27–28
The Arabian Horse World
    (magazine), 57
Arabian Quarter horses, 13,
    154–155
Arabian Reining Horse Association
    (ARHA), 190, 271
Arabian Triple Crown, 31
Arabian Youth National
    Championships, 193, 249
arenas, 98, 175
arena strategy, 39–42
ARHA (Arabian Reining Horse
    Association), 190, 271
attire. *See* clothing requirements
attitude, 38
auctions, public, 32
The Authentic Arabian Horse
    (Wentworth), 11, 15

baby oil, 261
back of horse, 8
backup, 190
balance, 154, **155**, 243. *See also*
    Equitation
Balkenhol, Klaus, 118
Bar-Fly+/ (horse), 201
*Bask++ (horse), 57–58
Bedouin, 3–4, 5, 10
Berried Treasure (horse), **238**
Bey, Hasem, 6
biblical references, 227
biomechanics of rider, 242. *See also*
    Equitation
Bishop, Shiloh, 239
bits
    curb, 74
    dressage and, 126, 138
    Hunter Pleasure, 66
    reining, 183n
    snaffle, 88, 89, 183n
    Sport Horse Show Hack, 112
    unconventional, 112
blinkers, 233, 233n
Blixen-Finecke, Hans, 242
Blunt, Lady Anne and Sir Wilfred,
    1–2, 15
Bocelli, Andrea, 97
Boit, Tom, 178, 183, 185, 186,
    189, 190
Bolshevik Revolution, 17, 20
Bonaparte, Napoleon, 14
boxing, 198–199, 201
braids
    for Hunter Pleasure
        grooming, 67
    maintenance of, 262
    manes, **113**, 113–115, **115**
    tails, 115–116, **116**

breeding
    breeders and stud farms, 15–16,
        17–18, 23, 24, 267
    pedigree and, 10–13, **22**
    for show, 28–29
    sweepstakes programs for, 268
    university programs and, 267
    U.S. Army and, 12
bridles
    braids and, 224
    dressage, 138
    English Show Hack, 74
    Hunter Pleasure, 66
    hunters and jumpers, 152
    Ladies Side Saddle, 237
    Mounted Native Costume,
        235–236
    Saddle Seat Arabians, 55
    Sport Horse clasesses,
        111, 112
    Western Pleasure, 87
    Working Western, 156
Burkman, Cynthia, 61–62, 63,
    64, 68, 75–76
Burt, Don, 154
button braids, 114, **115**
Byerley Turk (horse), 14

California Polytechnic State
    University, 11n, 267
Calvary Endurance Ride, 12
Canadian National Championship
    Show, 31
canter, 51–52, 72–73, 131, 132
canter pirouettes, 131
Caprilli, Federico, 139–140
Carlin, Kathryn, **104,**
    105, 106
Carriage Driving, 228, 230

cattle and cows, 195, 197–198, 204–205, 205–206. *See also* Working Cow Horse

cavalettis, 151, 151n, 160

Cavalry Endurance Ride, 12

chains, 111, 224–225

chaps, 90, 156

character, color indicating, 9–10

Chicago World's Fair (1893), 21

Christensen, Lauren, **246**

circles, 187–188, **188**, 189, 200–201, 202

circuits, Arabian, 29

Class A, B and C-rated shows, 30–31

classes, 28–29, 34–35. *See also specific classes and disciplines*

Classic Arabian, 210–211

Classic Head, 211

Clayton, Hilary, 50, 51, 133, **134**

clipping, 220–221, 260–261

clothing requirements
  costuming, 38, 235–237, 239–240
  dressage, 137
  driving, 229, 231
  English Show Hack, 74–75
  grooms, 231
  Halter, 224
  Hunter Pleasure, 67
  hunters, 152
  jumpers, 152
  Ladies Side Saddle, 240–241
  Mounted Native Costume, 235
  Saddle Seat, 55–57
  Sport Horse In-Hand, 111
  Sport Horse Show Hack, 112
  Sport Horse Under Saddle, 112
  Western Pleasure, 90

Working Western, 155–156
Youth Halter Showmanship, 251

coats, grooming of, 219–220, 259, 261

Colon, Don Cristabal, Duque de Veragua, 21

color of horse, 9–10, 236

combination classes, 228, 230

Compilli, Debbie, 197, 198, **199**, 200, 204–207

conformation
  balanced horses, dimensions of, 154, **155**
  dressage, 134–135
  English Show Hack, 69–70
  Hunter Pleasure, 61–62
  judging description, 38
  reining, 178–179
  Saddle Seat, 49–50
  Sport Horse In-Hand, 98–99, 100–102
  trail, 162
  Western Pleasure, 77–78

continental braids, 114

Coquette+, **246**

costumes, 38, 235–237, 239–240. *See also* clothing requirements

Country English Pleasure, 44–45, 47, 48–49

country of origin, 14–23

Country Pleasure Combination, 230

Country Pleasure Driving, 229

cowing. *See* Working Cow Horse

Crabbet Park, 15

croup of horse, 8

Culbreth, Chris, **46**, 47, 82–83, **84**

curb bits, 74

cutback saddles, 55

Dahman, 10
Damianos, Michael
  Saddle Seat, 44, 46, 48–49,
    50–51
  show preparation, 259
  stress, advice on, 265
  trail, 159, 162, 166, 167–171
dam line, 25
Darley, Thomas, 14
Daumas, Eugène, 209
Davenport, Homer, 6, 16
D.B. (desertbred), 25
Dean, Jimmy, 15
Dearth, Gary
  Arabian shows, 35
  area strategies, 41
  Saddle Seat, 45, 52–53
  shoeing rules, 52
  show photographs of, **45, 80**
  Western Pleasure, 81, 83, 86
desertbred (D.B.), 25
diets and grooming, 259
disciplines, show, 28–29, 34–35.
    See also specific disciplines and
    classes
Discovery Farms, 267
Dodge, Theodore A., 1
Dorrance, Tom, 153
double bridles, 55, 74, 138
dressage
  Arabians and, 133–134
  arenas for, 120, **121**
  clothes and tack, 137–138
  competition and judging,
    120–122
  conformation, 134–135
  grooming, 114–115
  home preparation for,
    135–137

overview and history, 117–118
  term translation, 117
  tests and score sheets, 122–124
  training levels of, **125,**
    125–133
  training scale, **119,** 119–120
dressage judges, 111–112
Dressler, Willi, 19
drivers, 229, 231, 256
driving classes, 227–234, 229
drug testing, 257
Duncan, Ronald, xiii
The Dynamic Horse: A
    Biomechanical Guide to
    Equine Movement and
    Performance (Clayton), 50

Eclipse line of Thoroughbreds, 14
Edwards, Gladys Brown, **8,**
    11, **211**
Egyptian Event, 31, 225
English Pleasure, 45–46, 48–49
English Show Hack
  champions of, **69,** 75–76
  clothing and tack, 74–75
  compared to other classes,
    68–69
  conformation, 69–70
  elements, emphasis of, 37–38
  gaits, 70–73
  origins of, 59–60
  overview, 67–68
  training for, 73–74
entry fees, 255
equipment. *See* bits; bridles;
    saddles; tack
Equitation, 242–250
European system of judging,
    225–226

Fantine (horse), **13**
Fédération Equestre Internationale (FEI), 94n, 137, 173–174
feet of horse
  grooming of, 261, 262
  of Saddle Seat horse, 50
  shoeing, 52, 190, 205
  Sport Horse In-Hand judging and, 110
Ferguson, Gary, **174**
FF Summer Storm (horse), 58
The Five, 3
Flicka (horse), **160**
Forbis, Judith, 11, 16, 93
forelocks, 115, 262
Formal Combination, 230
Formal Driving, 228
Foy, Janet Brown, 110, 126
French Anglo-Arabian, 140
French braids, **113**, 113–114, **116**
full livery, 231
Funk, Wanda, 230
futurities, 269–270

Gahwyler, Max, 131
gaits
  dressage, 124, 125–133, 135
  English Show Hack, 70–73
  Saddle Seat, 50–52
  trail, 162
  Western Pleasure, 80–81
Gallun, Greg, 210, **215**, 216, 219, 222–224
gate maneuvers, 161
Get of Sire and Progeny of Dam group classes, 99–100
Godolphin Arabian (horse), 14
Goggins, Tim, 228, 233

Grand Prix, 132–133
Grant, Ulysses S., 15
grooming. *See* also braids
  clipping, 220–221, 260–261
  coats, 219–220, 259, 261
  diet and, 259
  English Show Hack, 75
  feet, 261, 262 (*see also* shoeing)
  forelocks, 115, 262
  Halter, 219–221
  Hunter Pleasure, 67
  at shows, 221, 261–262
  Sport Horse In-Hand, 110
  Youth Halter Showmanship, 251
grooms, 231
Gruskiewicz, Wendy, 40, 65, 67–68, 265–266
Guarmani, Carlo, 4–5
Gurney, Hilda, 130, 133, 135

hackamores, 87–90, 183n
hack attire, 74
Hadban, 10, 12
Haj, Salim Abdulla, 93
Half Arabian Registry, 23
Half Arabians, 12–13, **13**, 154–155, 210
half passes, 130
half pirouettes, 132
Halter
  clothing and tack, 224–225
  conditioning for, 218–219
  conduct of class, 211–213
  European *vs.* American judging systems, 225–226
  grooming, 219–221
  judging criteria, 210–211
  overview, 209–210

the pose ("stand up"), **211,** 212, **215,** 215–218, 223, 225
presentation tips, 221–224
training walk and trot, 213–215
halters, 111, 224, 251
Hamdani, 10, 12
hand gallop, 81
handlers, 103–111, 209–218, 256. *See also* Halter
Hardin, Kristin, 142–144, 150–151, 152, 265
harnesses, 229, **229**
Hart, Bob, 196, 197, 199, 200, 204, 207
Hart, Bob, Jr., **201**
hats, 56, 156
headers, 230
head of horse, 7
Helprin, Mark, 59
Henry, Marguerite, 14
hesitation, 190
HF Mister Chips+ (horse), **46**
hojjas, 10
Hollywood Dun It (horse), 155
hoof polishes, 262
hooves. *See* feet of horse
The Horses of the Sahara (Daumas), 209
hunter braids, 114, 115
hunter judges, 112
Hunter Pleasure, 59–67, **61, 69,** 75–76
hunters. *See* Working Hunters
Hunter Seat Not to Jump, 246–247
Hunter Seat Over Obstacles, 247–248, 249
Hurlbutt, Earle E., 19

IABS (International Arabian Breeders Sweepstakes Program), 268–269
impulsion, 124
Informal Combination, 230
In-Hand. *See* Sport Horse In-Hand
Intermediate (Intermediaire) I and II (dressage), 131–132
International Arabian Breeders Sweepstakes Program (IABS), 268–269

Jacob, G., 5
Janow Podlaski, 17–18
jibbah, 7
jog-trot, 81
judges, 98, 111–112, 122, **183**
judging, 38–39, 225–226. *See also specific disciplines and classes*
jumpers. *See* jumping, competitive
jumping, competitive
amateur tips for, 149–150
bascule, phases of, **146, 147**
clothing and tack, 152
conduct of class, 148–149
in Equitation, 247–248
history of, 139–140
overview, 143–144
technique and calculations, 144–145
training for, 150–152
Jumpin' Jak Flash+++// (horse), **104, 105, 106, 107**

Kale, Howard, Jr., 20
Kehilan, 10, 11–12
Kellogg, W. K., 15, 267

Al-Khamsa, 3–4, 10
Khemosabi++++ (horse), 90–91
King of the Wind (Henry), 14
Kowalski, Stasik, 17–18

LaCroix, Eugene, 19–20, 32, 57
LaCroix, Gene, 54, 57, 58
Ladies Side Saddle, 38, 237–241,
    238, **240**, **241**
La Gueriniere, Francois Robichon
    de, 37
lateral aids, 128
lead changes, 189, 193
Lert, Peter, 110
lineage, 10
Lipizzaner stallions, 118
longeing, 218, 218n
longe whips, 109
lope, 81
Louis XV, King of France, 14
Lowe, Jim, 41, 44, 50, 52

magazines, 266–267
Mahooney, Michelle, **141**, 142,
    145, 149–150
manes
    braiding, **113**, 113–115, **115**
    cutting, 114
    grooming tips, 259–260, 262
    pulling, 114, 114n
maneuvers, reining, 182–190
manners, 38
mares, 5–7, 227
MA Windsong (horse), **220**
Medallion Stallion Futurity,
    269–270
Mendelsohn, Jane, 146, 147
Mentor Network, 267
Michigan State University, 267

midthbah, 8
Mohammed (prophet), 3, 6
Morris, Desmond, 173
Mounted Native Costume, 38,
    234–237, **236**
movement, 62–63. *See also* gaits
MSU Magic J+// (horse),
    133, **134**
Müller, Erich, 19
Muniqi, 10, 11, 12
musical freestyle, 122, 122n
Myler brand bits, 112

names, interpretation of, 23–25
national championships, 31, 94,
    167, 168–171, 193, 249
National Reining Horse
    Association (NRHA),
    155, 272
Nazi Germans, 17–19
NDL Pericles+// (horse), **69**,
    75–76
neck of horse, 7–8
nosebands, 111, 138
NW Beaudacious+ (horse), **84**

Obstacle Driving, 232
O'Hara, John, 177–178, 183,
    185–189, 191, 193
oil, baby, 261
OKW Entrigue (horse), **125**
Oliveira, Nuno, 117, 118
outline, 82

pads, shoe, 52
paintings of Arabians, 8, **211**
Park, 37, 46–47, 48
Patton, George S., 19
pedigree, 10–13, **22**

performance, 38–42
piaffe, 132, 133, **134**
pirouettes, 131, 132
Pleasure Carriage Driving,
  230–231
pleasure classes. *See also* Western
  Pleasure
  Country English Pleasure,
    44–45, 47, 48, 49
  English Pleasure, 45–46, 48–49
  Hunter Pleasure, 59–67, **61**, **69**,
    75–76
  overview, 37
Pleasure Driving, 228, 229
Polish Arabians, 16–20
the pose ("stand up"), **211**, 212,
  215, 215–218, 223, 225
Potts, Gordon, 35, 82, 85, 86–87,
  258
Potts, Kim, 214, 217–221, **220**,
  223, 224
Potts, Wendy, 40, 41, 63, **69**,
  75, **238**
premium lists, 254–256, 257
presence, 38
Prine-Carr, Patience, **125**, 238,
  239, 241
Prix St. George, 131
prize lists, 254–256, 257
proverbs, Arabian, 77
pulling the mane, 114, 115n
purchasing horses, 266–268
Pyramid Society, 15–16, 31

quality, 38, 103

Raffles (horse), 15
Ramzes (horse), 140
Raswan, Carl, 11, 11n

Raswan (horse), 11n
Red Tape (horse), **47**
Rees, Lucy, 195
regional championship shows,
  30–31
reining
  associations for, 155, 190,
    271, 272
  class defined, 94n
  competition patterns, 174,
    176, 177
  conduct of the class, 175–176
  freestyles, 193
  horses for, 177–179
  maneuvers, 182–190
  overview, 173–175
  penalty charts for, 179–182
  shoeing for, 190
  show advice, 191
  training at home, 192–193
Reining Seat, 245–246,
  249, 249n
reins, romal, 87, 87n, 245
Richardson, Cynthia, 30
riders, 124, 242, 256. *See also*
  clothing requirements; *specific*
  riding classes
Robertson, Lorne, **167**,
  168–171
rollbacks, 190, 193
romal reins, 87, 87n, 245
Roosevelt, Theodore, 16
Roper, Lou, 157, 159, **160**, 162
rundowns and run-arounds,
  183–184
Russell, Katie, **61**
Russian Arabians, 20
Russian Revolution, 17, 20
al-Ruwayi, Hasan bin-Salah, 93

saddle horns, 207

saddles
    dressage, 137
    English Show Hack, 74
    Hunter Pleasure, 66
    hunters and jumpers, 152
    Hunt Seat, 55, 74
    Ladies Side Saddle, 237, **240**,
        241, 241–242
    Saddle Seat "cutback," 55
    Sport Horse Under Saddle, 112
    Western Pleasure, 90
    Working Western, 156

Saddle Seat
    categories of, 44–49
    clothing and tack, 55–57
    conformation, 49–50
    in Equitation, 244–245, 249
    gaits, 50–52
    riding, 53–55
    temperament, 52–53

Safire Star+// (horse), **61**

sale horses, 266–268

Schmidt, Carl, 11, 11n

schooling shows, 29

score sheets
    dressage, 122–124
    reining, 175–176
    reining penalty charts, 179–182
    Sport Horse In-Hand classes,
        98, **99**
    trail, 163–165

scotching, 184

Scottsdale Arabian Horse Show,
    31–34, **32**, **33**

Seglawi, 10, 11, 12

Selby, Roger, 15

shadebelly coats, **125**, 137

Shakespeare, William, 139

Shields, Bitsy, 102, 107, 110

shoeing, 52, 190, 205

Show Hack (Sport Horse),
    111–112. *See also* English
    Show Hack

"Showing Your Sport Horse
    In-Hand" (video), 108

showmanship, 209

shows
    associations promoting, 29,
        271–272
    classes (disciplines), 34–35 (*see
        also specific classes*)
    entry forms and documents,
        256–258
    fees, 255, 257
    history and evolution,
        28–29
    organizational pyramid of,
        29–34
    overview, 253
    premium lists for, 254–256, 257
    preparation for, 253–254,
        258–259
    procedures at, 262–264
    stress, advice on, 264–266

Side Saddle, Ladies, 38, 237–242,
    238, **240**, **241**

size of horse, 9, 50, 62, 179

SJ Mikhail+++// (horse),
    79–80, **80**

Skowronek (horse), 15

Slater, Pat, 27

sliding stops, 183, 184

slot, 165

Smith, Linell, 17

snaffle bits, 88, 89, 183n

Solomon, King, 3

Spanish Arabians, 20–21

Spanish Riding School of
  Vienna, 118
specialty classes
  costuming, 38, 235–237,
    239–240
  driving, 227–234, **229**
  Equitation, 242–250, **246**
  Ladies Side Saddle, 38,
    237–242, **238**, **240**, **241**
  Mounted Native Costume, 38,
    234–237, **236**
  overview, 227
  Youth Halter Showmanship,
    250–251
spins, 185–187, 192–193
split, 111
Sport Horse classes, 93–95, 97,
    111–112. *See also* Sport Horse
    In-Hand
Sport Horse In-Hand
  arena for, 98
  conformation, 100–102, 107
  general impressions, 103
  grooming and appointments,
    110–111
  judging, overview, 98–100
  movement, 102–103
  training at home, 108–110
  training the triangle, 103–107
Sport Horse National
    Championship Show, 31, 94
Sport Horse Show Hack, 111–112
Sport Horse Under Saddle,
    111–112
spurs, 137
stable livery, 231
stallions, renowned, 16
"stand up" (the pose), **211**, 212,
    215, 215–218, 223, 225

Staraba Rocket (Star) (horse),
    xiii–xiv
Starsearch SMA (horse), **146**, **147**
"The Stealing of the Mare" (Zeyd),
    1–2
stops, 184–185, 192
stress, 264–266
stretchy circle, 123, 127
stride counts, 132
strong trot, 51
studbooks, 24–25
stud farms, 15–16, 17–18
submission, 124
suitability, 39
sweat gear for horses, 219
sweepstakes, 268–269
Syrian halters, 224

tack. *See also specific classes for
    requirements*
  bits (*see* bits)
  bridles (*see* bridles)
  chains, 111, 224–225
  condition of, 111
  for driving, 229
  hackamores, 87–90, 183n
  halters, 111, 224, 251
  nosebands, 111, 138
  reins, 87, 87n, 245
  saddles (*see* saddles)
  Sport Horse *vs.* English Show
    Hack, 113
tail female line, 25
tails
  braiding, 67, 110, 115–116, **116**
  characteristics of, 8–9
  dressage, 115
  grooming tips, 259–260, 262
  hunter, 115

Tankersley, Bazy, 15, 178, 253
temperament, 52–53, 62, 70,
  78–80
Thoroughbreds, 14, 140
trail
  conduct of the class, 162–163
  course patterns and tests,
    157–161, **158**, **160**, **167**,
    168–171
  home preparation, 165–166
  horses for, 161–162
  scoring and penalties, 163–165
  show advice, 166
trailers, shoe, 190
trainers, 257, 257n
transitions, 188
trot, 51, 71–72
Trowbridge, Mary
  arena strategy, 40
  photograph with Red Tape, **47**
  Saddle Seat, 45, 46–47, 52, 53
  stress, advice on, 264–265
turning on the fence, **199**,
  199–200, 202

Under Saddle (Sport Horse),
  111–112
United States Army, 12
United States Dressage Federation,
  108, 272
United States Equestrian
  Federation (USEF) Rule
  Book
  on appointments for Saddle Seat,
    55–57
  clothing and tack, 66–67
  on dressage training levels, 126,
    127, 128, 129, 130, 131–133
  Equitation and, 249–250

Halter pose, 217
Sport Horse In-Hand
  judging, 99n
tack for Halter, 224
United States Equestrian
  Team, 174
United States National
  Championship Show, 31

vaqueros, 88
Vento, Russ, 258, 265
Veragua, Don Cristabal Colon,
  Duque de, 21

Wadduda 30, 6
WAHO (World Arabian Horse
  Organization), 21
walk, 51, 71, 81
walk-in, 183
walkovers, 161
war mares, 5–7
Washington, George, 14
Wentworth, Judith Anne Dorthea
  Blunt-Lytton, Baroness of,
  11, 15
Western Horsemanship, 249
Western Pleasure
  champions, 77, 78–80,
    90–91
  conformation, 77–78
  gaits, 80–81
  judging criteria, 82–85
  outline, 82
  overview, 77
  presentation, 87, 90
  temperament, 78–80
  training for, 85–87
Western Seat, 245–246,
  249, 249n

whips
  length restrictions, 111, 112,
    137, 225
  training use of, 108, 109, 110
  usage restrictions, 225
A Winter's Tale (Helprin), 59
*Witez II (horse), 17–18
W.K. Kellogg Arabian Horse
    Center, 267
WL Intruder+// (horse), **141**
Working Carriage, 230
Working Cow Horse
  advice to amateurs, 205–207
  cattle for, 195, 197–198,
    204–205, 205–206
  judging and scoring,
    201–203
  overview, 195–197
  pattern, riding the, 197–201
Working Hunters, 140–143, **141**,
    147–148

Working Western, 153–156. *See
    also* reining; trail; Working
    Cow Horse
World Arabian Horse Organization
    (WAHO), 21
World War I and II, 17
Wrigley, Greta, 129, 133,
    136–137, 265

Xenophon, 43, 118

Yazid (poet), 6
youth classes, 31, 193, 249,
    250–251
Youth Halter Showmanship,
    250–251
Youth National Championship
    show, 31

Zamboni-Contretas, Jill, 76
Zeyd, Abu, 1–2